Perspectives on Structural Realism

Perspectives on Structural Realism

Edited by

Andrew K. Hanami

With a Foreword by Stephen M. Walt

palgrave
macmillan

PERSPECTIVES ON STRUCTURAL REALISM

First published 2003 by
PALGRAVE MACMILLAN™
175 Fifth Avenue, New York, N.Y. 10010 and
Houndmills, Basingstoke, Hampshire, England RG21 6XS.
Companies and representatives throughout the world

PALGRAVE MACMILLAN is the global academic imprint of the Palgrave Macmillan division of St. Martin's Press, LLC and of Palgrave Macmillan Ltd. Macmillan® is a registered trademark in the United States, United Kingdom and other countries. Palgrave is a registered trademark in the European Union and other countries.

ISBN 0–312–29555–3 hardback

Library of Congress Cataloging-in-Publication Data
Perspectives on structural realism/Andrew K. Hanami, editor; with a foreword by Stephen M. Walt.
p. cm.
Includes bibliographical references and index.
ISBN 0–312–29555–3
1. International relations—Political aspects. 2, International relations—Psychological aspects. I. Hanami, Andrew K.

JZ1253.P47 2003
327.1'01—dc21 2003051724

A catalogue record for this book is available from the British Library.

Design by Newgen Imaging Systems (P) Ltd., Chennai, India.

First edition: November, 2003
10 9 8 7 6 5 4 3 2 1

Printed in the United States of America.

To
Kenneth N. Waltz
Scholar, Teacher, Friend

Contents

Acknowledgments

First and foremost, I wish to thank Kenneth N. Waltz for his kindness, leadership and counsel, as well as his wife Huddie who always welcomed me into their home where I learned so much about their grace, generosity and insight. I wish to also thank Ray Wolfinger whose encouragement kept me going through all moments of this project.

Special thanks to David Pervin whose sustained determination drove the book to fruition. For her earlier editing work, I also wish to acknowledge the efforts of Karen Ruth Adams. Jennifer Laughlin, Robert Liu, Jennifer Hiwa and Valerie served as research assistants on this project, and I owe them a debt of gratitude.

I wish also to thank my peerless teachers, colleagues and students from Berkeley, the School of International Studies in Stockton, and San Francisco State University for offering inspiration and stimulating ideas that have lasted through the years, including Jyoti Das Gupta, A. James Gregor, Robert Scalapino, Chalmers Johnson, Peter Sperlich, Richard N. Rosecrance, Cort Smith, Brian Klunk, Jerry Hewitt, Longina Jakubowska, Len Humphreys, Michael Hatch, Joseph Julian, DeVere Pentony, Aguibou Yansane and Sanjoy Banerjee.

Finally, I would like to thank the authors themselves who took the time to write or submit a chapter for this volume, and a number of others who unfortunately could not be included, for their contributions. All errors of fact and interpretation remain mine.

Foreword

Kenneth N. Waltz is the preeminent international relations theorist of the postwar era. His work has been read and pondered by several generations of scholars, and even those who ultimately disagree with his arguments must confront his ideas and come to terms with them.

Three features of his work explain his unique standing in our field. First, in a field where it is difficult to write a single important work, Waltz has made at least four seminal contributions. His first book, *Man, the State and War*, organized several centuries of writing about the causes of war into three distinct "images," creating an enduring typology and providing penetrating evaluations of these different perspectives. One also finds in this work the seeds of what would become the central preoccupation of Waltz' later work; namely, the impact of the *structure* of the international system on the behavior of states. His second book, *Foreign Policy and Democratic Politics*, provided an elegant and powerful analysis of how that *domestic* structures affect the way democratic leaders conduct foreign policy. His third book, *Theory of International Politics*, has probably been the most influential work in the field since its publication in 1979. Scholars of every theoretical persuasion have taken this work as their principal point of departure (or their principal target) for over two decades, and it remains a landmark in the field even today. Lastly, Waltz' famous 1981 monograph, *The Spread of Nuclear Weapons: More May Be Better*, offered a powerful challenge to the conventional wisdom about nuclear proliferation and remains a focal point in this important policy area.

A second feature of Waltz' scholarship is its remarkable staying power. *Man, the State and War* is 42 years old; *Theory of International Politics* was published over two decades ago; and his monograph on proliferation is nearly as venerable. Yet each of these works remains a staple in the field: read, reread and debated by students and scholars alike. In an enterprise where fads are endemic and where most works fade into obscurity within a year, the durability of Waltz' insights and the importance of his arguments are remarkable. As Thomas Schelling once remarked of Waltz, "it takes him a long time to write, because everything he does is read for a long time" (quoted in Robert Jervis, "The Contributions of President Kenneth N. Waltz," *PS: Political Science and Politics* (Fall 1987): 857).

Third, Waltz' own career is a model of sustained productivity and quality control. Not only has Waltz written several genuinely seminal works, but he has produced outstanding scholarship in each of the past *five* decades. In the 1950s, it was *Man, the State, and War*. In the 1960s, it was *Foreign Policy and Democratic Politics* and his controversial essay on "The Stability of a Bipolar World." In the 1970s, his works included the important essay "The Myth of National Interdependence," and in 1979, *Theory of International Politics*. In the 1980s, he published "The Spread of Nuclear Weapons" along with several provocative essays on different aspects of U.S. defense policy. But he did not stop there. Waltz has continued to produce work of very high quality throughout the 1990s and remains a vital force in the field today. His essay "Nuclear Myths and Political Realities" received the Heinz Eulau Prize of the American Political Science Association in 1990 (awarded annually for the best article published in the *American Political Science Review*), and his recent writings on the emerging international system have made important contributions as well. Just last year, Waltz' spirited defense of realism was the lead article in the Summer 2000 issue of *International Security*, and a typically trenchant critique of recent writings on "globalization" graced the Spring 2000 issue of *The National Interest*.

This is a record of achievement that all might envy but few will approach. Among political scientists, perhaps only Samuel P. Huntingdon of Harvard University and Robert Dahl of Yale have amassed a similar record of scholarly distinction and achievement. It is hardly surprising, therefore, that Waltz has received a number of professional accolades, serving as President of the American Political Science Association in 1988 and receiving the James Madison Prize of the American Political Science Association in 1999. This award, given biannually to the political scientist whose work has made a "lasting contribution" to the discipline, is eloquent testimony to his standing in our field.

This volume, which features essays by a number of Waltz' students, is an honor of a different sort. It is our testament to the "lasting contribution" that Waltz has made to those of us who had the good fortune to study with him. Although Waltz' primary contribution to the study of politics is his own scholarship, his influence also extends to the many students he has taught and inspired at Columbia, Swarthmore, Brandeis and Berkeley. In addition to the contributors to this book, the ranks of Waltz' students include James Fearon, Shai Feldman, Joseph Joffe, Christopher Layne and William Rose, to name but a few. There are also countless undergraduates at Columbia, Swarthmore, Brandeis and Berkeley who have received the benefits of Waltz' teaching.

What was Ken like as a teacher? Although all of his students remember specific bits of advice, Ken taught primarily by example. Both in the classroom and in his office, Ken spent relatively little time *telling* us what to do. Instead, he concentrated on showing us, by his own powers of analysis and his own conduct, exactly *how* to do it. Each of his students undoubtedly learned different lessons from their interactions with Ken, but I suspect most of us would agree that the following features of his teaching were especially significant.

The first lesson was the importance of asking a big question. Much of contemporary political science examines issues of trivial importance, as a brief perusal of any APSA convention program will reveal. By contrast, Waltz' research agenda never lacked ambition, whatever one ultimately thinks of his conclusions. *Man, the State and War* organizes, synthesizes and critiques nearly four centuries of writing on the causes of war, and *Theory of International Politics* offers a general theory that explains the conduct of self-regarding actors in any anarchic realm. The essays on proliferation and nuclear strategy explain how mankind should deal with issues that could affect the fate of entire societies. Other writings investigate the impact of economic interdependence, the nature of the post–Cold War international system or the continued relevance of realism in the face of recent empirical developments and theoretical challenges. By asking big questions and offering powerful answers, Waltz ensured that his scholarship would be of central importance to our collective endeavor. Although it was daunting to ponder that Ken's own dissertation was an instant classic, his example reminded us that scholars should aim high.

Second, Ken taught his students to be fearless in challenging the prevailing orthodoxy. This trait is partly due to his position as a "realist"—a body of thought that has never been all that popular in liberal America—but also due to his basic independence of mind. Thus, when most scholars—including the other eminent postwar realist, Hans Morgenthau—were extolling the virtues of multipolarity, Waltz was arguing that *bipolarity* was in fact a more stable structure. When most academics were still silent about Vietnam, Waltz was an early critic (and like Morgenthau, for essentially realist reasons). When "interdependence" became the buzzword *du jour* in the early 1970s, Waltz was there to challenge both the empirical claim that interdependence was high and the theoretical claim that it would inevitably foster peace and cooperation. Waltz was also a persistent critic of the defense excesses of the Reagan administration in the 1980s, in part because he recognized the weaknesses of the Soviet Union far earlier than most others did.

This independence of mind was not due to simple contrarianism—Ken does not court controversy merely for its own sake. Rather, Ken's ability to spot what others were missing flowed directly from his theoretical vision. Because realists understand that power is central to politics, Ken could see that the stakes in Vietnam were not worth the resources the U.S. was pouring into that unfortunate country. Because realists know that states guard their autonomy jealously, he recognized that interdependence was often a source of conflict rather than an inducement to cooperate. Because he recognized the power of nuclear deterrence and the ways that structural forces help constrain even unreliable leaders, he could identify the weaknesses in much of the conventional wisdom on proliferation and argue that the measured spread of nuclear weaponry might not be as destabilizing as many others feared.

For his students, Ken's willingness to take positions outside the mainstream taught us to follow our thoughts wherever they led, even if the conclusions seemed at odds with the conventional "wisdom." Academics like to think of themselves as independent thinkers, but pressures to conform are in fact quite powerful. By refusing to "cut his convictions to fit this year's fashions," Waltz taught us to follow our thoughts wherever they led, even if it took us outside the mainstream and beyond the popular consensus.

Third, Ken also gave us the freedom to disagree with him. He conveyed his own views forcefully—especially in his own seminars—but when it was time for us to set out on our own, he did not insist that we follow the theoretical path he had set. Many scholars seem to think that advising is a synonym for "cloning" and refuse to let their students undertake work (or worse still, reach conclusions) that might challenge their own positions. To his credit and our benefit, Ken knew that young scholars cannot simply follow in their advisor's footsteps; sooner or later, they have to blaze a trail on their own. And while Ken's influence on his students is often easy to discern, it is also worth noting that many of his students have taken issue with his own work and with each other's work as well. Ken likes independent thinkers rather than sycophants, and he never tried to force us into his mold.

Last but of course not least, we all profited from Ken's high standards. Anyone familiar with Ken's critical talents can imagine what it was like to give him chapters of a dissertation, and it is fair to say that he expected as much from our work as he did from that of any established scholar. In my own case, I can still recite large chunks of a letter he wrote commenting on several draft chapters of my own dissertation, chapters that were clearly not ready for prime time. Ken began by declaring that he had read the first 25 pages with "increasing dismay." Pulling no punches, he then informed me what I should have already known: "They are terrible." And then the crucial question: "Ask yourself why this is so. Were you trying to write too fast, or did you just not know what you wanted to say?"

I cannot say I was grateful for these comments when I read them, but I have come to appreciate the wisdom of his response. Ken understood that second-rate work should have no place in our business, and he taught us to raise our standards by refusing to accept less. I do not know if all of his students had similar experiences, but I do know that mine was not unique.

Ken once wrote that "a theory is never finished," and our collective effort to understand the behavior of states and systems continues. The path to theory is endless, but understanding the world as it is remains an indispensable part of any serious attempt to build a better one. We remain grateful to Ken for showing us the way.

Stephen M. Walt

CHAPTER 1

Introduction

Andrew K. Hanami

This book demonstrates the continuing, as well as broadening, deepening and even proliferation of structural realist theory. While most of us apply, amend or extend neorealist theory, two of our authors find significant exceptions with some of the precepts of neorealism as developed or left unexamined by Kenneth N. Waltz, challenging future research. Professors Robert Powell and Stephen Van Evera show us how structure seems not to have dissuaded states from pursuing foreign policies that stem more from internal motives rather than external structural or systemic constraints. Nonetheless, having been influenced by neorealism, it is interesting to see how we have each attempted to articulate refinement and clarity in explaining both the theory and its application in ways and contexts not previously attempted.

Most of us try to grapple with the basic tenets of neorealist thought and attempt to sweep aside some of the unnecessary confusion that has become attached to it over the years. Balance of power is particularly singled out, as is the function of power, anarchy, self-help, security and how they continue to advance understanding and explain recent political events.

Attempting to add precision, Dr. Susan Martin focuses on balance of power analyses. She believes that much misunderstanding has come from a derived interpretation of neorealism as also a theory of domestic-oriented foreign policy theory. She identifies two traditions within the balance of power approach, systemic balances among states and any given state's behavior toward structure. Dr. Martin warns us not to confuse or combine the two. Balances of power between states, she tells us, are conditioned by anarchy and the desire of states to hold onto their relative ranking. State behavior in the context of structure, by contrast, is funded by the statesmen's selection of optimal foreign policy from their empirical observations—successes and failures of other states.

Dr. Martin contends that many leading scholars, including Vasquez, have blended the two and that has not helped to preserve theoretical clarity. She believes that we are better off understanding that while structure strongly influences balancing behavior of states, structure itself is only one variable that statesmen take into account when formulating their foreign policies. What is needed, instead, as Dr. Martin offers, is a new and simplified adjusted theory of balancing behavior that searches to identify a state's survival motive as a cause to counter an external threat. By her explicit definition, she attempts to organize the plethora of balance, bandwagoning alliance theory into more testable hypotheses. Her insightful treatment of a large debate concludes that neorealist theory is not inadequately explaining foreign policy behavior. Rather, it is the widespread and explicit mix of vague intimations made by some realist theorizing that has led to the perception that neorealism offers only convoluted, if contradictory edicts of international behavior. She returns us to a point from which fruitful research may continue across all fronts.

Professor Benny Miller introduces an innovative four-part typology, premised on realism, that explains the varied intensity of U.S. hegemonic use of force over a range of trouble spots around the globe. He argues that there is a "clear logic" to the degree of recent U.S. military intervention, which is based on costs and benefits that take into consideration regional "incentives and constraints," again illustrating the effects of structure. Professor Miller integrates classical realist theory with its emphasis on state interests with structural realism's constraint on state action to produce a model that renders U.S. military intervention from Bosnia to the Gulf War, and others, comprehensible. As the unipolar power, the U.S. tailors its response region-by-region, based on its degree of interest and the size of its likely opposition. Such a strategy does not endanger U.S. security. In countries still close to Russia, like Central Asia or the Caucasus, the U.S. will not intervene because the gains are problematic while sensitivities from the Kremlin remain a concern. This goes to the heart of balancing concerns, and illustrates how power and structure still shape U.S. policy toward a weakened but still nuclear-capable Russia. Professor Miller concludes that military intervention will occur only sparingly.

Blending structure and internal impulse, in the subfield of foreign policy studies, Professor Shibley Telhami says that neorealism has been generally neglected as an explanatory framework of state behavior. He specifies that the foreign policy choices of states can be delineated into two modes of general causation: opportunity and preferences. Neorealism, reminds Professor Telhami, is quite important in shaping a state's reaction to opportunity, but is relevant in shaping a state's preferences, as well. This is because a state's number one preference will always be self-preservation, echoing the centrality of security concerns. Though Hans J. Morgenthau believed that all states maximize power, Professor Telhami posits that neorealists since the time of Morgenthau merely believe that states actually maximize their opportunities to realize their foreign policy preferences. Here, Professor Telhami invokes the work of Fareed Zakaria, who says that states try to maximize their influence. Thus, structure is decisive here, because international structure, or the distribution of power across the system, delineates what states may do. In attempting to bridge the gap between structural opportunity and state preferences, Professor Telhami astutely suggests that variances in opportunity will determine the range of realizable preferences that any state can have at any given time, but that they are subject to change over time.

Professor Telhami concludes that material power is the unifying and prime explanatory premise of neorealism, and that states therefore seek to balance power among competing rival states. Sensitivity to changes in the international power structure is important to a leading state like the U.S., but as Professor Telhami points out, is even more important to smaller states in the Middle East, as the 1991 Gulf War has altered the foreign policy of all the Middle Eastern states since. Because of U.S. intervention and presence, the distribution of power within the region has changed, and with it the foreign policies of those states. Iraq, Egypt and most of the other important, conventionally armed Middle East states have declined as Israel and Saudi Arabia have risen. Power shifts are at the center of explanations for the changes in behavior. Professor Telhami's chapter is important because he features the role of structural power and further sharpens both the differences and common ground between neorealists and domestic-oriented sources of foreign policy.

Professor Barry R. Posen takes a novel view of realist theory and the security dilemma. In the post–Cold War era as various Eurasian regimes have broken down, Professor Posen tests realist theory, in a sense, by placing it back downward into its more pure Hobbsian state: that is, as Hobbes has stated, violence is endemic in a state of nature, thus the need for authority. With the collapse of formal governments around the Balkans, for example, Professor Posen sees a return to the state of nature. The situation here is a more extreme case of Telhami's Middle East decline. In the Balkans, long-held ethnic grievances break out, and each group must assess the war potential of each neighboring ethnic group, as though they were still nation-states. Power, security and anarchy are key to his explanations. Thus realist theory, applied generally to relations between states, now is applied to relations between ethnic groups within and between states. The security dilemma is reintroduced in this new context because as one ethnic group appears more capable and threatening, that is, they gain in power, the other must reciprocate, or face negative consequences. This introduces a zero-sum quality into the security equation and illustrates again the continuing importance of balance of power, even among post-state actors.

Professor Posen concludes that realist theory continues to have a powerful explanatory and predictive ability in understanding how shifting capabilities among rival ethnic or religious groups affect each of their calculations. He remarks that in a world absent of much superpower intervention, the world remains a self-help system, and ethnic groups realize they may not count on receiving much outside help. Only large commitments of outside troops could guarantee some peace among them, but outside states are not likely to extend such security guarantees for sustained periods of time. Diminished states or former states suffer the chaos from loss of power, the inability to balance at satisfying levels that provide sufficient self-help for their societies.

Focusing on a single large country, Professor Avery Goldstein demonstrates how structural realist theory can be applied in depth to explain and postdict Chinese foreign policy over five decades. While earlier Chalmers Johnson provided the China literature with a lucid way of seeing Chinese foreign policy behavior as always a blend of politics and personality, Professor Goldstein demonstrates that even the strong and often one-dimensional personality of Mao adapted to changing structural realities, as the Chinese leader learned the contours and dangers of the larger international structure. Here too, balance of power calculations influenced a cult-led state leader's behavior.

Professor Goldstein posits that despite the huge complexity of China's domestic complexion, the real question is not "whether" neorealism explains China's foreign policy, but rather "how much." He describes China's grand strategy during the early phase of the Cold War as "distinctly realist," because Mao always identified the main enemy and allied with others, principally Stalin, to balance against the U.S. By the 1970s, China observed the Soviet military buildup on its northern border and initiated an entente with the U.S. to balance a growing Soviet challenge. Even after Mao's death, China manifested its realist instincts, by further downgrading its ideological tilt in favor of its limited partnership with the U.S.. Though there have been significant departures, the international structure has constrained and shaped China's foreign policy behavior despite its natural bandwagoning sentiments.

By the 1990s, China had even forged "strategic partnerships" with an economic theme that included doing business with Russia, Japan and the West. China sees this approach as building a relationship too costly, in the tradition of Richard Rosecrance, for other states to then act against China. This is particularly important, as the dominance of the U.S. is not all-directing. Though constrained by the structure of the system, in the post–Cold War era, China continues to seek policies not predictable by structural realism alone, because China seeks its own modernization, or self-help objectives, still possesses an insecure leadership and holds nuclear power. Professor Goldstein's chapter is invaluable because it is the only case study of a half-century's measure of the foreign policy behavior of an often called ideologically driven state in which, when carefully examined against structural realist theory, we find the elements of self-help, balance and power considerations often in command over ideology.

Using a quantitative approach, Professor Robert Powell takes the predictive utility of structural realism and puts it to a rigorous test. In applying game theory to predictions or explanatory correctness of structural realism, he finds that structural realism fails to explain why states bandwagon a majority of times, especially when the use of force prevails. Structural realist theory predicts, as he points out, that states will tend to "balance" the behavior of other states, but in fact his findings show that generally states have chosen to bandwagon or ally with another in order to preserve their security. Under game theory conditions, states in fact balanced only in a very "narrow range of circumstances." Professor Powell also finds that in contrast to structural realist theory, bipolar states are not a more stable system, in part, because the peaceful desires of states often result in conflict. But he concludes that neorealist theory, led by Waltz, has provided a significant, disciplining advance in the field of international politics by introducing the concept of structure and the expected behavior of states that see it. But he adds that ordinary language arguments ultimately fail to define structure and interaction, and that game theory represents the next step in advancement of theory because of its formal precision in identifying or distinguishing political structures.

Another exception, despite structural determinism, Professor Stephen Van Evera describes the many foolish things that states do in foreign policy. Following the work of Karl Deutsch, Professor Van Evera points out that states are prone toward miscalculation. He says this applies equally well to structure. As with the earlier "inside-out" explanations of Rosecrance,

Keohane, Nye and others, Professor Van Evera's analysis illuminates how internal factors of a state are responsible, in the main, for foreign policy actions, even when the consequences prove to be negative to state interests, and by implication, to a state's power status. Statesmen may pursue unrewarding paths, he points out, simply because as an organization, a state's internal structure discourages both the retainment and encouragement of innovative, risk-taking corrective measures of its most intelligent people.

Professor Van Evera says that bureaucracies reward repetitive, inner drives of its personnel, and that even in critical foreign policy, bureaucracies such as a state's intelligence or security apparatus, also fall prey to internal codes of behavior. The organizational thrust, as Martin Landau in his earlier work suggests, tells us that organizations filter incoming data and are chiefly preoccupied with organizational survival, and less so with the effects on the state overall, concentrating mainly on actions taken by a single bureau.

Political psychologists like Ole Holsti long explained that bureaucracies tend to collapse inward under crisis, which causes its personnel to search for fewer answers, and worse still, to stereotype, simplify and selectively pick what incoming data is to be digested. Professor Van Evera shows that such inward-looking leadership inadvertently leads to the advocacy of mistaken foreign policy despite the pressures or external influences of international structure. Thus in the short run at least, states could jeopardize their relative ranking in the international system by poorly conceived policies that end up not in self-help, but in self-hurt.

Dean Robert Gallucci offers a Washington realist's view of U.S. policy toward North Korea, and the potential spread of nuclear weapons. He cautions that offering North Korea positive economic incentives alone does not necessarily serve U.S. security interests. He points out that North Korea is interested in balancing regional powers by acquiring nuclear power, and by implication, how the structure of the international system both encourages and limits the behavior of small states. Gallucci believes that ultimately the North Korean regime is more interested in pursuing its security objectives than in economic growth.

In chapter 10, I examine the intention and some of the tenets of the inside-out theory, a dominant theme of the past three decades, as formulated by Richard Rosecrance, Robert Keohane and others, evaluating it against structural realism. I attempt to point out new ways of seeing state behavior within a systemic context, and offer a new formulation on how to understand the behavior of states toward one another, and at differing levels. I call this interconnectivity, which focuses on the degree to which states are connected, or as Kenneth Jowitt has stated, "disconnected" from the main grid of international power. Rather than simply relying on the question of whether states are interdependent, dependent or independent, I argue that such terms are too demanding of state relations, and opt for a more neutral conception to explain international relations.

Some states may be tightly interconnected, as with the U.S. and Japan, while most others are only somewhat connected across a few issues for finite periods of time. Others are considerably less connected. This has significant connotations for their foreign policy behaviors. Tightly connected states are both more cooperative and combative, at least in some ways, while unconnected states need not be as wary of each other. This means that states not on the radar screen of a major competitor may have greater freedom to maneuver through the international system, if they are capable and so inclined. This also includes non-state or near-state actors like Osama bin Laden whose actions on September 11 galvanized the White House's attention and led to the demise of his al Qaida organization in Afghanistan. Degrees of interconnectivity describes the general relations of states in a more descriptively accurate way than do the older terms, which after several decades, and under unipolarity, no longer fully explain the relations of states.

CHAPTER 2

Neorealism and Game Theory

Robert Powell

Neorealism, which has dominated much of international relations theory for the last two decades, is fundamentally a theory about the strategic interaction of a small number of units in an anarchically ordered realm. Noncooperative game theory, which has revolutionized economics and exerted ever-more influence in political science over the last two decades, is fundamentally an analytical tool for modeling the strategic interaction of a small number of actors in anarchic (as well as other) realms.[1] This essay examines the relation between neorealism and game theory and suggests that formalization is a natural next step in the development of what might be called *grand theory* in international relations, which is the attempt to understand international politics or at least its important aspects by examining the strategic logic of a sparely defined system based on a Hobbesian state of nature.

This examination begins by juxtaposing two articles. Kenneth Waltz wrote the first, "Realist Thought and Neorealist Theory," for a volume in honor of William T. R. Fox. In that essay, Waltz draws a parallel between the transformation of economic thinking into economic theory and the transformation of realist thinking about international politics into neorealist theory. But Waltz only partially develops this parallel. He does not consider a critical aspect that defines modern economics and differentiates it from international relations theory. Modern economics relies extensively on mathematical models to discipline ordinary-language arguments and insights. This reliance is the subject of the second paper, "The Fall and Rise of Development Economics," which Paul Krugman penned for a volume honoring and responding to Albert Hirschman.

The juxtaposition of these two papers poses a question: What would we see if we push Waltz' parallel further by looking at neorealism and international relations theory from a formal and, especially, game-theoretic perspective? This, of course, is a very broad question, and only one facet will be considered here.[2] What do we make of the concept of structure, which Waltz (1990b, 30) holds to be neorealism's most important contribution, when we view it from a game-theoretic vantage point?

The next section juxtaposes the Waltz and Krugman essays. It elaborates some of the advantages and disadvantages of using formal models, and it discusses some of the consequences of imposing the discipline of formal models on ordinary-language arguments. The subsequent section then offers a narrow critique of neorealism that focuses on the particular way that Waltz defined structure and some of the theoretical conclusions that follow from it. As will be seen, recent empirical and game-theoretic work casts doubt on these specific conclusions. The third section offers a broader appraisal of neorealism by locating its emphasis on structure in the intellectual development of international relations theory since the end of World War II. When viewed from this wider perspective, neorealism's concern with the disjunction between the units' individual properties and the outcomes of their interaction and the specific effort in *Theory of International Politics* to define the structure of the system as something distinct from the units in that system, mark a fundamental advance in international relations theory. Finally, the last section suggests that this advance naturally points toward a more game-theoretic approach to international relations theory or, at least, to a more game-theoretic approach to what might be called *grand* international relations theory.

Bounding Domains and Disciplining Arguments

Waltz (1990b) summarizes neorealism's contribution to the study of international politics and contrasts neorealism with traditional realism by sketching a parallel between the development of economic theory and of neorealism. The key to moving beyond the accumulation of ever-more disjoint economic observations and findings, Waltz believes, was an invention "that would permit economic phenomena to be seen as distinct processes, that would permit an economy to be viewed as a realm of affairs marked off from social and political life" (1990b, 23). That invention was a theory that simultaneously bounded the problem by focusing on some things and not others and that provided a conceptual picture of how the things in this bounded domain were causally related to one another. The first to achieve this were the Physiocrats.[3]

Similarly, the key to moving beyond classical realism's deep but often disjointed insights about international politics was to solve

> the problem of distinguishing factors internal to international political systems from those that are external... By depicting an international-political system as a whole, with structure and unit levels at once distinct and connected, neorealism establishes the autonomy of international politics and thus makes theory possible. (Waltz 1990b, 29)

Neorealism, in other words, bounds the problem by including some things and excluding others and by explaining how the things it does include are related to each other. Waltz' formulation, in particular, focuses on a system populated by units that "seek to ensure their survival" (1979, 91) and whose structure is defined by the ordering principle of anarchy and by the distribution of capabilities among the units (1979, 79–101).

Waltz uses the parallel between economic theory and neorealism to elucidate the differences between realist thinking and neorealist theory and to emphasize the importance of theory. But the analogy goes further. Neorealism and microeconomics are or at least can be seen to be the same kind of theory: both presume purposive units—be they states or firms; both make assumptions about the unit's goals or motivations—be it survival or profit maximization; and both make assumptions about the environment in which these units interact. These theories then try to explain what the outcomes of this interaction will be and how changes in the units' goals or in the environmental incentives would affect these outcomes.

The parallel between economic theory and neorealism, however, breaks down at a critical point. Modern economics uses mathematical models to express its theoretical ideas about the way things in the bounded domain of economics are related to one another. By contrast, neorealism—along with most other theories in international relations—generally employs ordinary-language arguments. What might we expect to see if we push Waltz' analogy harder by trying to look at neorealism from a formal perspective?

Paul Krugman (1994) provides some important insights in his stimulating account of the role of formal models in what he calls the fall and rise of development economics.[4] But before turning to his analysis, a brief discussion of the nature of formal models and of the modeling enterprise is in order.[5] Although models may be very simple and highly stylized, they are generally inspired by an empirical problem. A model, whether mathematical or not, is a constrained, best effort to capture what the modeler believes to be the essence of a complex empirical phenomenon or at least an important aspect of it. A good model provides at least a partial picture of a causal mechanism.

Two kinds of constraints limit a model. The first is practicality. A model is a tool and a tool must be simple enough to be used. A model that is too complicated to be used is of little value. The second constraint is the modeler's current understanding or intuition about the problem at hand. When constructing a model, the modeler tries to build into it what she believes to be the essential cause or causes, in order to see if they actually can explain part of the outcome.

A model helps us discipline our thinking about what we are trying to model, and this is the primary advantage of modeling. A mathematical model, in particular, "gives us a clear and precise language for communicating insights and notions...allows us to subject particular insights and intuitions to the test of logical consistency... [and] helps us to trace back from 'observations' to underlying assumptions; to see what assumptions are really at the heart of particular conclusions" (Kreps 1990, 6). Formalization provides a kind of accounting mechanism that permits us to think through some issues more carefully than ordinary-language arguments can. Accounting schemes make a firm's financial situation more transparent both to those inside the firm and those outside it. Formal models make arguments more transparent both to those making them and to those to whom the arguments are made.

Krugman's (1994) chronicle of the fall and rise of development economics is a discussion of the problem of method in the social sciences. It is a story about what happens when a new set of accounting standards—those of mathematical modeling in this case—are applied to a set of arguments that have developed according to a different set of standards. Krugman's analysis is full of insights relevant to neorealism and to international relations theory more generally, and his essay is well worth quoting at some length.[6] In Krugman's view, the crisis of high development theory in the late 1950s was neither empirical nor ideological: it was methodological. High development theorists were having a hard time expressing their ideas in the kind of tightly specified models that were becoming the unique language of discourse in economic analysis. They were faced with the choice of either adopting that increasingly dominant intellectual style or finding themselves pushed into the intellectual periphery. They did not make the transition, and as a result high development theory was by and large purged from economics, even development economics.

Hirschman's *Strategy* (1958) appeared at a critical point in this methodological crisis. It is a rich book, full of stimulating ideas. Its most important message at the time, however, was a rejection of the drive toward rigor. In effect, Hirschman said that both the theorist and the practical policy maker could and should ignore the pressures to produce buttoned-down, mathematically consistent analyses and adopt instead a sort of muscular pragmatism in grappling with the problem of development. Along with some others, notably Gunnar Myrdal, Hirschman did not wait for intellectual exile: he proudly gathered up his followers and led them into the wilderness himself. Unfortunately, they perished there.

The irony is, we can now see that high development theory made perfectly good sense after all. But in order to see that, we need to adopt exactly the intellectual attitude Hirschman rejected: a willingness to do violence to the richness and complexity of the real world in order to produce controlled, *silly* models that illustrate key concepts (1994, 40).

Krugman's account highlights two points that are especially important to a discussion of neorealism and game theory. First, one reason for applying a new set of standards to an existing set of arguments is to help us identify which of those arguments to accept and which arguments, while perhaps quite interesting and suggestive, cannot as yet be accepted.[7] Formal modeling, in particular, emphasizes the standards of transparency and internal consistency. We should expect, therefore, that when we begin to formalize neorealism (as well as any other theory that is based primarily on ordinary-language arguments), some arguments will be readily formalized and seen to meet this standard. Other arguments will fall short but can be made to do so with only minor amendments. Other arguments, which may very well seem to be saying something important about international politics, may be far beyond the pale of formalization at least at the outset. Finally, some arguments are likely to prove to be incorrect because the greater transparency of formalization will reveal internal inconsistencies.

The second point Krugman's essay emphasizes is related to the first. What we "know" is partly a function of the standards we use to evaluate arguments. Thus, when we apply a new set of standards to an existing set of arguments and discard some of the those arguments because they fail to satisfy those standards, there is a sense in which we "know" less than we did when we used the previous standards.

> Model building, especially in its early stages, involves the evolution of ignorance as well as knowledge; and someone with powerful intuition, with a deep sense of the complexities of reality, may well feel that from this point of view more is lost than is gained. (Krugman 1994, 50)

This evolution of ignorance is the source of the irony that Krugman observes in the rise of development economics. In retrospect, it is clear that increasing returns to scale was critical to high development theory. But economists were not well equipped to model increasing returns to scale in the 1950s and only began to do so in the mid-1970s.[8] Eventually, however, economists were able to capture this key insight in models that satisfied the accepted standards of formalization. And, at least in the view of those espousing these standards, the new arguments provided a better understanding of the key idea and a much more secure foundation for future work.

Of course, things did not have to turn out this way, which is the point of formalization. Economists eventually were able to model some of the key insights of development economics. But the goal of formalization is not simply to buttress old ideas with mathematical models—to put old wine in new bottles as it were. Among other things, formalization helps us separate those ideas that do have something important to tell us about the world from those that do not. Sometimes old wine turns out to be vinegar.

Pushing the parallel between economics and neorealism, it seems clear that when we begin to use game theory to model neorealism—as well as other theories of international relations—we should initially expect to find that we "know" less than we thought we did.[9] How much we will eventually be able to relearn remains to be seen.

Structure and Game Theory: A Narrow Critique

No concept is more important to neorealism, or at least Waltz' version of it, than the notion of structure. "The idea that international politics can be thought of as a system with a precisely defined structure is neorealism's fundamental departure from traditional realism" (Waltz 1990b, 30). Indeed, structure is so central to Waltz' theory and has played such a dominant role in international relations theory that neorealism is sometimes called structural realism. This section focuses on Waltz' specific formulation of structure and some of the conclusions claimed to follow from it.

Waltz' goal in defining structure was to provide a "positional picture" of the system (1986, 330). If structure could be defined in a theoretically useful manner, systems with similar structures would exhibit broadly similar behavior whether the units be "tribes, nations, oligopolistic firms, or street gangs" (1990b, 37). "Structure, if properly defined, is transposable" and does not depend on the nature of the underlying units (Waltz 1986, 330). Waltz' theory, therefore, is really a theory of politics and not just international relations.

With this goal in mind, Waltz characterized a political structure according to first, its ordering principle; second, the functional differentiation or non-differentiation of the units; and, third, the distribution of capabilities across the units (1979, 79–101). When applied to international political structures, only the last of these characteristics is relevant in Waltz' view. That is, international systems are anarchically ordered and the units are functionally non-differentiated. Only the distribution of capabilities varies, and then the only significant variation is whether the system is bipolar or multipolar.

This formulation has been controversial from the start. Many criticize Waltz' very spare definition of structure and want to call more factors structural. Nye (1988), for example, argues that military technology should be included in the definition of structure. Buzan, Jones and Little propose "a much more open and much more comprehensive definition of structure" (1993, 11).[10] Others have been critical of Waltz' characterization of the international system as anarchic and functionally non-differentiated (e.g. Ruggie 1986).

Waltz' general response to these criticisms is that adding more to structure might make it more descriptively accurate, but it would also rob the theory of its power (1990b, 30–32). By adopting a spare definition of structure, Waltz hopes his theory will "tell us a small number of big and important things" (1986, 329). Two of the most important are: (i) bipolar systems are more peaceful than of multipolar systems because the danger of miscalculation is less in a bipolar system (1979, 161–93, especially, 172); and (ii) balances of power tend to form in anarchic systems (1979, 121). The first of these claims is extraordinarily difficult to test empirically given the empirical record that we have, and recent game-theoretic work in international relations casts doubt on the second.

By convention, the modern states system begins in 1648 with the Treaty of Westphalia. The system was multipolar until 1945 and bipolar from 1945 until the collapse of the Soviet Union. The U.S. and the Soviet Union, of course, did not go to war during the latter era. But the significance of this is difficult to determine because of the confounding effects of nuclear weapons. As Waltz himself puts it, "Never since the Treaty of Westphalia . . . have great powers enjoyed a longer period of peace than we have known since the Second World War. One can scarcely believe that the presence of nuclear weapons does not greatly help to explain this happy condition" (1990a, 744). In a partial effort to overcome these confounding effects, Hopf (1991) studies Europe between 1495 and 1559. He finds no significant difference in stability between the multipolar era of 1495–1521 and the bipolar era of 1521–1559.[11] In sum, the existing empirical evidence that bipolar systems are significantly more peaceprone than multipolar systems is at best mixed.

Neorealism also argues that states tend to balance against power. Indeed, "balance-of-power politics prevail whenever two, *and only two*, requirements are met: that the order be anarchic and that it be populated by units wishing to survive" (1979, 121, emphasis added). As with so much of international relations theory, we do not have a large-scale, widely accepted, empirical test of this proposition. Nevertheless, the diplomatic historian Paul Schroeder believes, on the basis of his reading of European history, that bandwagoning is more prevalent than balancing (1994a,b). Scwheller (1994) also sees more bandwagoning than balancing. Indeed, even Walt observes that balances of power often "fail to form" before offering his balance-of-threat theory (1988, 279–82; 1987).[12]

Even though we do not know if balancing is empirically more or less prevalent than bandwagoning, we can still try to assess the theoretical argument that balancing prevails whenever the system is anarchic and the units wish to survive. If the deduction is correct, then we should generally find that states balance in game-theoretic models of systems that satisfy those two conditions. This, however, is certainly not the case in repeated games, which have been widely used to model various issues in international politics (see, e.g., Axelrod 1984; Keohane 1985; Oye 1986).

The folk theorem for repeated game shows that essentially any division of benefits is the outcome of some subgame-perfect equilibrium (Fudenberg and Tirole 1991, 151–60). The basic logic underlying these equilibria is that if one player were to deviate from the agreed division by taking more in the current period, then the other players would collectively punish the deviator for a sufficiently long period of time that the total cost of suffering the future punishment would outweigh the immediate gain of deviating. Thus, the fear of punishment deters the players from deviating. Moreover, the definition of subgame perfection ensures that these threats are credible in the sense that following through on the threats is in the threatener's own self-interest. These equilibria therefore are consistent with the assumption anarchy.

Note, however, that the basic mechanism underlying these equilibria—credibly threatening to impose future costs sufficient to outweigh immediate gains—are more reminiscent of the League of Nations and collective security than of balance-of-power politics. If one state deviates, the other states collectively punish it. But the actors in repeated games seek to survive insofar as they must do this in order to maximize their long-run payoffs. And, the environment is anarchic in that there is no central authority to enforce threats or promises. Repeated games, therefore, afford a formal counterexample to the claim that balances tend to form whenever the system is anarchic and the units wish to survive.

But how important is this counterexample? Repeated games, after all, provide a very poor model of the international system, especially when the use of force is at issue (Fearon 1998; Powell 1991). The absence of balancing in

Powell (1999) is more troubling and substantially undermines the claim that anarchy implies balancing.

Powell (1999) studies a two-stage game in which the distribution of power is explicitly linked to the distribution of power among three states, *A*, S_1, and S_2. In the first stage, a potential attacker *A* has to decide if it wants to attack either S_1 or S_2 separately, attack both of them simultaneously or attack neither of them. The game ends if *A* does not attack. If *A* attacks one of the other states, say S_1, then S_2 must choose among the three options of balancing against *A* by aligning with S_1, bandwagoning with *A* by joining in the attack or standing aside while *A* and S_1 fight.

In this simple formulation, the first stage can end in one of only two ways. Either two states are eliminated during the first stage and the game ends, or one of the states is eliminated in the first stage and the two surviving states move on to the second stage. If, for example, *A* attacks S_1 and S_2 balances against *A* by aligning with S_1, then either *A* prevails and the game ends, or the coalition of S_1 and S_2 eliminates *A* and those states move on to the second stage. If, alternatively, *A* attacks S_1 and S_2 aligns with *A*, then either S_2 prevails and the game ends, or the coalition of *A* and S_2 prevails and *A* and S_2 move on to the second stage. Similarly, if S_2 stands aside while *A* and S_1 fight, then S_2 and the victor of the conflict between *A* and S_1 go on to the second round.

The elimination of one of the states may affect the distributions of power and benefits between the two surviving states. Even if these two states were satisfied with each other at the outset of the game, the changes in the distributions of power and benefits wrought by the fighting in the first stage may leave one of the surviving states dissatisfied with the other. During the second stage, the two surviving states bargain about revising the territorial distribution that exists between them.

The outcome of this bargaining and the states' payoffs in the game depend on the distributions of power and benefits that exist at the beginning of the second stage. But these distributions depend on the initial distributions of power and benefits that existed among the three states at the outset of the game and on the alignment decisions that those states made during the first stage. Thus, the model relates states' alignment decisions directly to the distribution of power. And, solving the game shows that states are much more likely to wait or bandwagon than balance during the first stage. Indeed, states seem to balance only in a relatively narrow range of circumstances.

These formal results must be interpreted carefully. States balance less than they bandwagon in the anarchic environment formalized in the model. Notwithstanding this formal deduction, "real" states may actually balance more than they bandwagon although this is yet to be established empirically.[13] Even so, it is also clear that the argument that states seeking to survive tend to balance whenever the system is anarchic fails to hold when we require this argument to satisfy the standards of formal modeling. Unfortunately, we cannot as yet formally explain why states balance—if they actually do. We therefore "know" less than we thought we did about states' alignment decisions, and this illustrates Krugman's observation that "model building, especially in the early stages, involves the evolution of ignorance as well as knowledge" (1994, 50).

In sum, two of neorealism's clearest and most important claims about the effects of structure—that bipolar systems are more peaceprone and that anarchy implies balancing—do not fare very well in light of the historical record we have and the game-theoretic work in international relations. There is, however, a second, broader way of assessing neorealism's contribution, and this task is taken up in the next section.

Structure and Game Theory: A Broader View

This second way of seeing neorealism places emphasis on structure in the context of a set of theoretical concerns that can be traced back at least as far as the early 1950s and the aftermath of World War II. Seen in this way, neorealism's stress on structure grows out of but is also a significant advance on prior efforts to construct a theory of international politics. It is also an advance that leads naturally to a more game-theoretic approach, which uses models to help discipline our thinking about international relations.

In 1949, William Fox surveyed the interwar research in international relations and concluded that a "body of political theory dealing with a system characterized by an absence of central authority has yet to be developed" (1949, 79). Much progress toward such a theory would be made over the next 30 years, and two related issues would receive a great deal of attention. The first is that there is frequently a disjunction in international politics between the outcomes that states desire and the outcomes that actually result from the states' interaction. That is, the strategic arena in which the states find themselves and the incentives that that arena creates somehow intervene between desires and outcomes. War, for example, sometimes occurs even though none of the belligerents want it. The second concern refines the first. *Can we characterize the international system theoretically with a simple stylization and then explain how the postulated features of this environment lead to certain kinds of outcomes?* Can we, for example, show that anarchy in combination with some other stylized features of the international system generally leads to balancing or that an even distribution of power makes war less likely?

The idea that there may be a disjunction between desires and outcomes is implicit in some of the earliest post–World War II work.[14] In 1950, John Herz introduced the "security dilemma" as a prelude to his discussion of realism and idealism.[15] When states or, more generally, units exist in an anarchic setting in which there is no central authority over them, then they

> must be, and usually are, concerned about their security from being attacked... Striving to attain security from such attack, they are driven to acquire more and more power to escape the impact of the power of others. This, in turn, renders the others more insecure and compels them to prepare for the worst... , and the vicious circle of security and power accumulation is on. (1950, 157)

That is, anarchy *induces* even security seeking states to try to maximize their power, and this may leave them less secure, which is the opposite of what they intended.[16]

While there is a disjunction in the security dilemma between desired outcomes—greater security—and actual outcomes—less security—Herz does not emphasize this point. He seems to believe that the causal link from anarchy and security seeking to power maximization is rather transparent. Indeed, his brief account of the security dilemma serves as a way of distinguishing between realism and liberalism after which he surveys some of the "successive failures [of liberalism] in the face of the facts observed and acclaimed by Political Realism" (1950, 159).

Herbert Butterfield (1950) developed the idea of a security dilemma at about the same time as but independently of Herz.[17] Butterfield, however, does stress the disjunction between desired and actual outcomes, a disjunction that he sees as the "tragic element in human conflict" (1950, 154). His goal is to understand and elaborate the logic of this predicament whereas Herz essentially takes it for granted (Butterfield 1950, 148). Butterfield explains how "the greatest war in history could be produced... between two powers both of which were desperately anxious to avoid conflict of any sort" because each state "is desperately unsure of the intentions of the other party" (1950, 153). Once again desires are disjoint from outcomes.[18]

This disjunction is also present in some of the early postwar formulations of balance-of-power theory as well as still earlier ones.[19] Wolfers, for example, summarizes what he sees as the purest form of the realist conception of international politics. It is "based on the proposition that 'states seek to enhance their power' " (Wolfers 1951, 40). But even though "no state is interested in a mere balance of power, the efforts of all states to maximize power may lead to equilibrium" (Wolfers 1951, 41). That is, each state's attempts to maximize its power leads to a balance of power through something akin to a Smithian invisible hand. Desired ends are again divorced from realized outcomes.

Waltz' *Man, the State, and War* (1959) can be seen in part as a kind of culmination of this theme. By locating the causes of war in three images and then emphasizing the third, Waltz brought the importance of strategic interdependence and the general disjunction between desires and outcomes to the fore. As just noted, specific examples of this separation were more or less explicit in earlier work—that between the desire for security and its attainment in Herz (1950), that between the desire to avoid conflict and war in Butterfield (1950), that between the goal of maximizing one's power and the presence of a balance of power (Wolfers 1951) and of course in Rousseau's stag hunt that Waltz used to illustrate the third image. But Waltz' analysis of the third image and his contrasting it with first- and second-image explanations framed these specific examples more generally and thereby gave us a clearer sense of what the issue is. Indeed, Waltz stated the issue so clearly and forcefully that we still speak in terms of his three levels 40 years after the publication of *Man, the State, and War*. To understand international politics, we have to understand the strategic incentives that the international system creates as well as the desires of the states in the system.

But what precisely are these incentives and how do they specifically shape state behavior? Or, putting the question somewhat more theoretically, if an important part of our understanding of international politics is going to turn on comprehending the strategic interaction that divides desires from outcomes, can we construct a theory in which we stylize some of the critical features of the international system, derive the strategic incentives entailed in them, and then explicitly trace the effects that these incentives have on the outcomes of state interaction?

Waltz provided a typology of existing theories or arguments in *Man, the State, and War* but did not present a theory. For example, the defining feature of the third image was anarchy (1959, 159). But Waltz never traced an explicit path from anarchy to outcomes. Rather, anarchy served as a permissive cause: wars occur in anarchic systems because "there is nothing to prevent them" (Waltz 1959, 232).

Efforts to construct a theory of international politics by explicitly linking stylized features of the international system to the strategic incentives they create and subsequently to the behavior they induce can also be traced back to early post–World War II work. The work of Herz, Wolfers and Butterfield described here can be seen in part as early examples of these efforts. These scholars do link aspects of the international system to incentives and behavior. This, however, is generally not the central focus of their work—perhaps because they seem to believe that the strategic logic of their stylizations is obvious.

Herz (1950, 157), for example, explicates the logic of the security dilemma in a paragraph and devotes most of his attention to a critique of liberalism. Wolfers takes a few sentences to link anarchy and states' desire to maximize their power to the formation of a balances of power (1951, 40–41), and then he turns to a longer discussion of state interests. Even Butterfield (1950) seems to believe that the strategic logic of the Hobbesian predicament is relatively straightforward and that the primary difficulty lies in rising above the passions of the time in order to see the predicament.

Morton Kaplan, by contrast, focuses explicitly on trying to link stylized features of the international system to the outcomes of state behavior.[20] In *System and Process in International Politics*, he distinguishes between different international systems in terms of the rules that the states follow (1957, 21–53). For example, three of the six rules characterizing a balance-of-power system are: (i) "act to increase capabilities but negotiate rather than fight"; (ii) "fight rather than pass up an opportunity to increase capabilities"; and (iii) "stop fighting rather than eliminate an essential actor" (1957, 23). Kaplan then derives the outcomes we should expect to see in a system in which the actors follow the various sets of rules.

Kaplan, Burns and Quandt (1960) also explicitly try to relate stylized features of the international system to the behavior they induce. Indeed, these scholars model the international system as a rudimentary game.[21] Then they use this game to study the relation between stability and the number of states in the system. For example, is, "there some lower bound upon the number of nation states necessary for stability? An upper bound?" (Kaplan, Burns and Quandt 1960, 240).

These and other early efforts to construct theories of international politics did not get very far or have much of a long-run impact on the field of international relations. One reason for this may be that some of these theoretical efforts were not internally coherent. For example, shortly after Kaplan published *System and Process*, Riker (1962, 171–73) noted that these rules were inconsistent and therefore that it was impossible to follow all of them simultaneously.[22]

A second, related reason for the limited impact may have been that some of these early efforts lacked a clear sense of what a theory of international politics should look like. These early efforts, for instance, sometimes tended to confound what one would expect to be an assumption of a theory with what one would expect to be a conclusion. To wit, it is probably more natural to interpret Kaplan's rules as behaviors that are to be explained rather than as assumptions. What underlying set of state interests and environmental features jointly induce states to behave in these distinctive ways?

Unlike earlier efforts, *Theory of International Politics* has had a profound effect on the field of international relations. That book set the terms of reference for much of the field for almost two decades, something that is all the more remarkable in light of the fractured nature of the field. Just as *Man, the State, and War* succeeded earlier work on the distinction between desired ends and actual outcomes but marked a significant advance on that work, *Theory of International Politics* succeeded earlier attempts to construct a theory but also marked a significant advance.

This advance was made in two related steps. The first was to provide a much clearer understanding of the structure of a system. Previous efforts to construct theories of international politics used the terms "system" and "structure." But the meaning of these terms was often unclear. Indeed, "structure" was frequently conflated with the properties of the states or with the outcomes of the states' interaction. For example, Kaplan's rules (1957), as observed earlier, are probably best seen as being the outcomes induced by different underlying structures. Lacking a clear notion of structure and the causal directions associated with it, structure tended to become a catch-all of seemingly relevant causes and effects all mixed together. Waltz considered structure to be theoretically distinct from the units comprising the system. "Definitions of structure, must leave aside, or abstract from, the characteristics of units, their behavior, and their interactions" (1979, 79). Structure is what intervenes between what the units actually want and what they achieve. Structure may be seen as a set of constraints that define the strategic arena in which the units pursue their ends.

The second step built on this conceptualization of structure. Waltz went on to offer a particular and relatively clear description of the structure of an international system and then showed what one did with it. Namely, he tried to derive implications about the patterns of state interaction from the strategic incentives created by this structure, for example, anarchy implies a tendency to balance.[23] He also demonstrated a kind of comparative-statics analysis in which he traced the effects of varying the "parameters." In particular, he examined how changes in the distribution of power affected the stability of the system, for example, bipolar systems are more stable than multipolar systems.

As discussed in the previous section, some of these arguments appear to be incomplete and in need of modification when they are modeled formally.

But this misses the larger point. Advances must be judged relative to the state of the discipline that exists at the time. When seen in the broader context of the intellectual development of international relations theory, neorealism stands out as a dramatic advance. *Theory of International Politics* provided a much clearer vision of what a theory of international politics would look like and how one would use it. This advance is all the more striking because ordinary-language arguments are not well suited to defining and discussing structure, much less to analyzing the strategic interaction it induces.

Whither or Wither Grand Theory?

Game theory has transformed economics and reshaped some areas of political science in the last 20 years. Game theory provides an opportunity for neorealism and international relations theory more generally. But, it also poses a challenge just as mathematical modeling posed a challenge to high development theory in the late 1950s. The challenge arises because game theory provides a better language for pursuing the goals of structural realism, which are to understand the implications of political structures, in at least two related ways.

First, it is very difficult to use ordinary-language arguments to distinguish between structure and units and to see the importance of doing. Indeed, making this distinction and demonstrating its importance much more clearly than had previously been done is structural realism's major accomplishment. Game theory, by contrast, provides a much more precise and transparent means of discussing structure.

To illustrate this point briefly, consider two different notions of structure as "constraints," which are easy to see and distinguish in a game-theoretic model but much more difficult to see and distinguish in ordinary language. Figure 2.1(a) presents the game tree of a very simple coordination game, and Figure 2.1(b) depicts the corresponding strategic form.

In this game both actors prefer to coordinate by playing the same action, that is, each prefers (A, A) or (B, B) to (A, B) or (B, A). But actor I prefers to coordinate on (A, A), and actor II prefers to coordinate on (B, B). In this simple game, we might want to call the "structure of the strategic interaction" the fact that each player only has two choices and that they have to decide between these alternatives without knowing what the other actor has done. That is, the game tree in Figure 2.1(a) describes the structure in which the strategic interaction takes place. This notion of structure seems most in keeping with the idea that a game or "system is composed of a structure and of interacting units" (Waltz 1979, 79). A game tree does what Waltz says political structures do: it answers the question "What is it that intervenes between

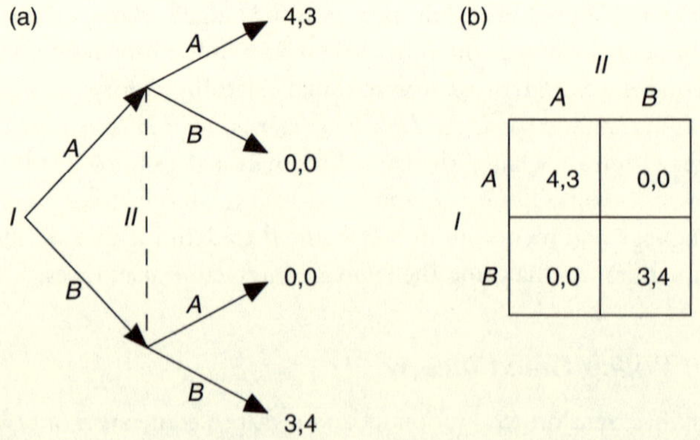

Figure 2.1 Two Notions of Structure: (a) the Game Tree of the Coordination Game; (b) the Strategic Form of the Coordination Game

interacting units and the results that their acts and interactions produce?" (Waltz 1979, 79). This notion of structure also implies that neither structure nor units are theoretically prior. Both are theoretical primitives.[24]

But now consider a second notion of constraint, which is related to the idea of an equilibrium. The game has two pure-strategy equilibria.[25] If both players expect the other to play *A*, then neither can gain by playing *B* instead. That is, neither player has any incentive to deviate from its own strategy of playing *A given that it expects the other player to play* A. Similarly, if both players expect the other to play *B*, neither can gain by playing *A* instead. No player has any incentive to deviate from its strategy of playing *B* given that it expects the other to play *B*. Thus, each actor's best course of action depends on what it expects the other actor to do. These conjectures thus constrain that actor; they act "as a selector" (Waltz 1979, 73). But note that this conceptualization of structure is very different from the notion of structure as the underlying game tree. Equilibria are endogenous or "generated by the interaction of the principle parts" (Waltz 1979, 72). Change the underlying tree or the actors' payoffs and the equilibria may change.[26]

Which is the better way to think about structure probably depends on the problem at hand and is not the point. The point is, rather, that it may be important to be able to distinguish between these two ideas and that game theory provides a much more transparent language for doing so. In the forementioned example, it is easy to see the difference between structure as underlying game tree and as an equilibrium of the game. It is much more difficult to do this with ordinary-language arguments.

The second way that game theory provides a better language is related to the first. Game theory does more than let us be clearer about what we mean by structure. It also helps us trace its effects more carefully. As anyone who has tried to explain the strategic logic of a simple prisoner's dilemma to someone else without actually writing down the game knows, it is extremely difficult to analyze even simple strategic interactions with ordinary-language arguments. As the last decade of formal work in international relations has shown, many widely accepted arguments do not go through when modeled. This, of course, could just mean that formal and ordinary-language arguments are frequently incommensurate. But this is not the case. Once we see why an argument does not work in a model, we often can see that the ordinary-language argument failed to take some factor into account and *that the argument would fail or be much less compelling even on its own terms if it had taken this factor into account.*

In sum, it is important to emphasize that formal analysis is not a substitute for good ideas and creative insights. Models cannot tell us *a priori* which avenues of inquiry will prove most fruitful. Models build on good ideas by helping us trace the implications of our ideas and only after much hard work help us assess the fruitfulness of a particular set of assumptions. But good ideas and deep insights are not a substitute for careful reasoning about what follows from them. These things are synergistic and we need both.

Neorealism grows out of a long tradition of what might be called *grand* theory in international relations, which is the attempt to understand international politics or at least important aspects of it by examining the strategic logic of a sparely defined system based on a Hobbesian state of nature. Game theory is the best tool we have for analyzing strategic interaction. It provides the clearest and most transparent language we have for examining the strategic interaction that lies at the heart of grand theory.[27] Only time will tell if international relations accepts what these tools have to offer—as well as the evolution of ignorance that comes with it—or if grand theory will go off into a wilderness of "-isms."

Notes

Department of Political Science, University of California—Berkeley, Berkeley, CA 94720-1950. I am grateful to Karen Adams, Andrew Hanami and Kenneth Waltz for their comments and criticisms of this paper.

1. See Kreps (1990) for a discussion of the game-theoretic revolution in economics.
2. Powell (1999) considers other aspects of this question.
3. Meek (1963) provides an overview of the physiocrats.

4. See Krugman (1995) for an elaboration of some of these issues.
5. Powell (1999) provides a more extended discussion of the modeling enterprise in the study of international politics and, especially, the relation between formal models and empirical observation. Myerson (1992) considers the potential contribution of game theory to the social sciences.
6. Indeed, Krugman borrows a central analogy from Craig Murphy, a specialist in international relations (Krugman 1995, 107).
7. Of course, an equally if not more important reason for looking at old ideas (and empirical regularities) in light of new standards is to come up with new ideas.
8. Krugman emphasizes that this limitation was only partly technical. It also reflected a blindspot caused by seeing the world through what had been modeled—perfectly competitive markets—and not what could be modeled.
9. Of course, some aspects of structural realism have already been modeled. See, e.g., Bueno de Mesquita and Lalman (1992), Fearon (1995), Morrow (1997), Niou and Ordeshook (1991, 1991), Powell (1999) and Smith (1998).
10. Also see Keohane (1986) and Keohane and Nye (1987).
11. Drawing on Levy (1983), Hopf measures stability or peacefulness in terms of the frequency, magnitude, duration and intensity of war.
12. For a discussion of balancing and neorealism, see Schweller (1997), Vasquez (1997), Walt (1997) and Waltz (1997).
13. As noted earlier, we do not have a large-scale, widely accepted, systematic empirical assessment of the proposition that states tend to balance rather than bandwagon.
14. And, of course, this notion can be found in still earlier works as will be seen later.
15. In a seminal paper, Jervis (1978) would later link the intensity of the security dilemma to the offense–defense balance and to the ability to distinguish offensive weapons from defensive ones. See Glaser (1997) for a review of the work on the security dilemma.
16. Strictly speaking, a state could strive for ever-more power but still not be trying to maximize its power. It might be trying to achieve increasing levels of power, which are asymptotically approaching some upper bound. But this interpretation of Herz seems somewhat tortured.
17. See Herz (1959, 234) for a comment on the relation between these two formulations.
18. Herz also underscored the idea that the states were solely motivated by security but did not highlight the importance of uncertainty about the other's intentions whereas Butterfield is somewhat less clear about motivations but much more explicit about the importance of uncertainty about intentions (Herz 1950, 157–59; Butterfield 1950, 153–54).
19. Knutsen (1997) traces the history of the concept of the balance of power.
20. He also provides an interesting early discussion of the use of game theory (1957, 169–244).
21. Because of the limitations of game theory that existed at the time, Kaplan, Burns and Quandt envisioned studying the game experimentally and not by formally characterizing the game's equilibrium. For a fully formal treatment of this issue,

which draws on recent innovation in game theory, see Niou and Ordeshook (1990, 1991).

22. Also see Weltman (1972).
23. Of course, these claims are also based on some underlying assumption about state motivation, which is usually what they seek, at minimum, to survive (Waltz 1979, 91).
24. See Wendt (1987) for an argument that neorealism takes units to be prior to the structure.
25. There is also mixed-strategy equilibrium.
26. If, e.g., player *I* can move before *II* and *II* knows what *I* did when deciding what to do, the unique equilibrium outcome of the game is for *I* to play *A* and for *II* to follow suit by playing *A*.
27. This, of course, is a relative statement, for the foundations of game theory as well as its predictive power are problematic. See Kreps (1990) for a discussion on some of the foundational issues and Kagel and Roth (1995) for experimental tests of some game-theoretic predictions about bargaining.

References

Axelrod, Robert. 1984. *The Evolution of Cooperation*. New York: Basic Books.

Bueno de Mesquita, Bruce and David Lalman. 1992. *Reason and War*. New Haven: Yale University Press.

Butterfield, Herbert. 1950. "The Tragic Element in Modern International Conflict," *Review of Politics* 12:147–64.

Buzan, Barry, Charles Jones and Richard Little. 1993. *The Logic of Anarchy*. New York: Columbia University Press.

Fearon, James. 1995. "Rationalist Explanations for War," *International Organization* 39:379–414.

——. 1998. "Bargaining, Enforcement, and International Cooperation," *International Organization* 52:269–306.

Fox, William. 1949. "Interwar International Relations Research," *World Politics* 2:67–79.

Fudenberg, Drew and Jean Tirole. 1991. *Game Theory*. Cambridge, MA: MIT Press.

Glaser, Charles. 1997. "The Security Dilemma Revisited," *World Politics* 50:171–210.

Herz, John. 1950. "Idealist Internationalism and the Security Dilemma," *World Politics* 2:157–80.

——. 1959. *International Politics in the Atomic Age*. New York: Columbia University Press.

Hirschman, Albert. 1958. *The Strategy of Economic Development*. New Haven: Yale University Press.

Hopf, Ted. 1991. "Polarity, the Offense-Defense Balance, and War," *American Political Science Review* 85:475–93.

Jervis, Robert. 1978. "Cooperation Under the Security Dilemma," *World Politics* 30:167–214.

Kagel, John and Alvin Roth. 1995. *The Handbook of Experimental Economics.* Princeton: Princeton University Press.

Kaplan, Morton. 1957. *System and Process in International Politics.* New York: John Wiley.

——, Arthur Lee Burns and Richard Quandt. 1960. "Theoretical Analysis of the 'Balance of Power,'" *Behavioral Science* 5:240–52.

Keohane, Robert. 1984. *After Hegemony.* Princeton: Princeton University Press.

——. 1986. "Theory of World Politics." In Robert Keohane, ed., *Neorealism and Its Critics.* New York: Columbia University Press.

—— and Joseph Nye. 1987. "Power and Interdependence Revisited," *International Organization* 41:725–43.

Knutsen, Torbjorn. 1997. *A History of International Relations Theory*, 2nd ed. New York: Manchester University Press.

Kreps, David. 1990. *Game Theory and Economic Modeling.* New York: Oxford University Press.

Krugman, Paul. 1994. "The Fall and Rise of Development Economics." In Lloyd Rodwin and Donald Schon, eds., *Rethinking the Development Experience.* Washington, DC: Brookings.

——. 1995. *Development, Geography, and Economic Theory.* Cambridge: MIT Press.

Levy, Jack. 1983. *War in the Modern Great Power System, 1495–1975.* Lexington, Kentucky: University of Kentucky Press.

Meek, Ronald. 1963. *The Economics of Physiocracy.* Cambridge, MA: Harvard University Press.

Meyerson, Roger. 1992. "On the Value of Game Theory in the Social Sciences," *Rationality and Society* 4:62–73.

Morrow, James. 1997. "When Do 'Relative Gains' Impede Cooperation?" *Journal of Conflict Resolution* 41:12–37.

Niou, Emerson and Peter Ordeshook. 1990. "Stability in Anarchic International Systems," *American Political Science Review* 84:1207–34.

—— and ——. 1991. "Realism versus Neoliberalism," *American Journal of Political Science* 35:481–511.

Nye, Joseph. 1988. "Neorealism and Neoliberalism," *World Politics* 40:235–51.

Oye, Kenneth. 1986. *Cooperation Under Anarchy.* Princeton: Princeton University Press.

Powell, Robert. 1991. "Absolute and Relative Gains in International Relations Theory," *American Political Science Review* 85:1303–20.

——. 1999. *Bargaining in the Shadow of Power.* Princeton: Princeton University Press.

Riker, William. 1962. *A Theory of Coalitions.* New Haven: Yale University Press.

Ruggie, John. 1986. "Continuity and Transformation in World Polity." In Robert Keohane, ed., *Neorealism and Its Critics.* New York: Columbia University Press.

Schroeder, Paul. 1984a. "Historical Reality versus Neorealist Thory," *International Security* 19:108–38.

——. 1984b. *The Transformation of European Politics, 1763–1848*. Oxford: Clarendon Press.

Scwheller, Randall. 1984. "Bandwagoning for Profit," *International Security* 19:72–107.

——. 1997. "New Realist Research on Alliances," *American Political Science Review* 91:927–31.

Smith, Alastair. 1998. "Extended Deterrence and Alliance Formation," *International Interactions* 24:151–79.

Vasquez, John. 1997. "The Realism Paradigm and Degenerative versus Progressive Research Programs," *American Political Science Review* 91:899–912.

Walt, Stephen. 1987. *The Origins of Alliances*. Ithaca: Cornell University Press.

——. 1988. "Testing Theories of Alliance Formation," *International Organization* 43:275–316.

——. 1997. "The Progressive Power of Realism," *American Political Science Review* 91:931–36.

Waltz, Kenneth. 1959. *Man, the State, and War*. New York: Columbia University Press.

——. 1979. *Theory of International Politics*. Reading, MA: Addison-Wesley.

——. 1986. "Reflections on Theory of International Politics." In Robert Keohane, ed., *Neorealism and Its Critics*. New York: Columbia University Press.

——. 1990a. "Nuclear Myths and Political Realities," *American Political Science Review* 84:731–45.

——. 1990b. "Realist Thought and Neorealist Theory," *Journal of International Affairs* 44:21–37.

——. 1997. "Evaluating Theories," *American Political Science Review* 91:913–18.

Weltman, John. 1972. "The Process of a Systemicist," *Journal of Politics* 34:592–611.

Wendt, Alexander. 1987. "The Agent-Structure Problem in International Relations Theory," *International Organization* 41:335–70.

Wolfers, Arnold. 1951. "The Pole of Power and the Pole of Indifference," *World Politics* 4:39–63.

CHAPTER 3

Integrated Realism and Hegemonic Military Intervention in Unipolarity

Benjamin Miller

Since the end of the Cold War, the U.S. has undertaken several military interventions abroad, fluctuating widely in scope from the massive intervention in the Gulf War through medium-scale intervention in Panama and Haiti to the limited and abruptly terminated engagement in Somalia. Similarly another regional crisis (Bosnia) was the occasion for great fluctuations of policy. The U.S. response to the crisis shifted from military disengagement in the first four years of the crisis to a considerable intervention on the ground in the last three years. It has also refrained from intervention on other occasions, notably in post-Soviet and African crises.

Is there a coherent logic behind these wide-ranging variations in post–Cold War U.S. intervention behavior? Numerous critics have argued that there is not, and that this erratic behavior reflects a lack of focus in U.S. foreign policy since the end of the Cold War and the collapse of the Soviet Union, the former archenemy.[1] For example, in a recent comprehensive treatment Gholz, Press and Sapolsky characterize U.S. behavior this way: "the U.S. intervenes often in the conflicts of others, but without a consistent rationale, without a clear sense of how to advance U.S. interests, and sometimes with unintended and expensive consequences" (1997, 5).[2]

In the following discussion I will challenge the conventional wisdom about the illogic and incoherence of recent U.S. military interventions. I will argue that in contrast to widespread opinion, there is a clear logic to post–Cold War interventions, even if it does not amount to a preconceived and purposive grand strategy. Indeed, the U.S. has followed, whether consciously or not, the logic of costs and benefits, namely different combinations of incentives and constraints in different regions. More specifically, the intensity of U.S. interests at stake and the intensity of the regional constraints on intervention (as reflected by the estimated costs of intervention, especially in terms of casualties) best account for the scope of U.S. military interventions in the post–Cold War era. My argument suggests that different types of regions are prone to specific levels of intervention or nonintervention because of the different combinations of U.S. interests and constraints in each region. Thus, this logic accounts for the variations in the scope of interventions and predicts different patterns of U.S. intervention in different regions. The realist explanation presented here integrates the classical realist focus on state interests with the structural realist emphasis on constraints on state action in order to provide a theoretical model of hegemonic military intervention in unipolarity. To illustrate this model, this study will outline briefly the variations in the scope of U.S. military engagement in all the major post–Cold War regional crises, notably the Persian Gulf (1990–1991, Fall 1994), Panama (1989), Somalia (1992–1994), Bosnia (since 1995), Kosovo (since 1999), Haiti (1994–1996) and also the cases of nonintervention in post-Soviet and African crises. The proposed explanation will demonstrate the continuing relevance of realism to major issues of post–Cold War U.S. foreign policy.

The first section will introduce the phenomenon explained in this chapter by differentiating among four degrees of hegemonic military intervention in regional crises. The second section will propose a theoretical explanation of variations in hegemonic military intervention based on the combined effects of incentives (or interests) and constraints (or costs) on the probability and level of its regional engagement. In the third section I apply this logic to account briefly for the variations in U.S. interventions in post–Cold War regional crises. In the concluding sections, I discuss the implications of this logic for future U.S. engagement in regional conflicts. This paper was originally written well before the September 11 attacks. The last section suggests briefly that the effects of September 11 on U.S. military involvement fits the logic of the model presented here.

The Phenomena to be Explained: A Typology of Hegemonic Military Interventions

I will distinguish among four degrees of hegemonic military involvement in regional crises according to the scope and the length of time of intervention, and the intensity of willingness to use force.[3] The two main indicators of the scope of intervention are the size of the manpower deployed and the firepower used (armor, artillery and airpower). Regional crises are seen in this chapter as situations of domestic, ethnic or inter-state turbulence in which there is a high likelihood that force will be used by the local parties. The four levels of intervention are as follows.

Massive intervention refers to a large-scale deployment of forces in reaction to a regional crisis, and a willingness to resort to them unless the great power's demands and objectives are met within a finite time period. The size of the intervening ground forces is in the range of hundreds of thousands of troops, in addition to a massive use of firepower. Massive intervention may be kept up for a considerable period of time, if necessary, to attain the Great Power's objectives.

Medium intervention indicates medium-scale involvement and a considerable willingness to use force and to maintain the deployment for a considerable period of time if necessary. The engaged troops number tens of thousands and they resort to maximum use of firepower to accomplish their mission.

Limited intervention refers to low-level military engagement on a temporary basis, with a limited willingness to use force. Several thousand soldiers are involved for a relatively short period of time; and they resort to only limited use of firepower.

Nonintervention indicates no military intervention, at most an occasional use of airpower, although diplomatic or economic involvement in the regional crisis is possible.

The question I will address in the following sections is what logic best explains such variations in the degree of foreign hegemonic military involvement under unipolarity.

The Explanatory Factors: The Combined Incentives and Constraints of the Hegemon vis-à-vis a Certain Region

The model presented here refers to a unipolar international system or a situation of Great Power hegemony. Indeed, as a result of the disintegration of the Soviet Union, a unipolar world has emerged since the late 1980s, at least for the short run, because of U.S. dominance in overall power resources, including a unique global power-projection capability.[4] The proposed model includes two major causal factors: the incentives and the constraints of the leading Great Power vis-à-vis a certain region. Leading realist explanations of state behavior and outcomes have not systematically taken into account the combined effects of both these factors. Thus, structural realism (or neorealism)[5] has underlined the constraining effects of the international distribution of capabilities on Great Power freedom of action, but it de-emphasized and failed to specify the role of different Great Power interests or incentives, and especially their variations under the same international system with regard to different regions.[6] Yet, it is reasonable to suggest that there are considerable differences in the intensity of the hegemon's interests at stake in different regions even in the same unipolar system.

Indeed, a structural realist analysis that focuses only on the international structure is by itself indeterminate with regard to the implications of unipolarity for hegemonic intervention. The main point is that due to the absence of rival powers, in a unipolar or a semi-unipolar system there are both low constraints and low incentives for hegemonic intervention in regional crises.

Low constraints should make intervention by the hegemon far more likely than in a bipolar or even a multipolar world where the presence of other Great Powers constrains the maneuvering room of all the Great Powers of the day. However, structural theory also leads us to expect low incentives for international engagement by the hegemon under unipolarity because the absence of other power poles means that there is no need for intense competition and costly balancing in different parts of the world. As a result, we may derive the expectation of fewer interventions by the hegemon than in other types of systems. Such an indeterminacy[7] should lead us to recognize the need for an addition of at least one major set of independent variables, namely, regionally derived incentives.

At the same time, some versions of classical realism, associated with the school of power politics, have focused on interests defined in terms of power (Morgenthau 1967, 430; 1978), but have paid less attention to the effects of constraints on Great Power action.[8] Although an identification of the level of Great Power interests involved in a regional crisis is very important, only a consideration of the combined effects of interests and constraints can generate more specific and determinate expectations about the level of Great Power military engagement in regional crises. Thus, the proposed "integrated realist" model combines the classical realist focus on state interests with the neorealist emphasis on constraints on state action. Yet, in contrast to structural realist analysis, these constraints are derived not from the international structure, but rather from the region in question, and may thus vary under the same international system. At the same time, my model draws on the neorealist view (and especially its dominant defensive version) of power as a means to preserve security rather than as an end for its own sake. This stands in contrast to the view of classical realism and of the aggressive version of neorealism that regards Great Powers as power maximizers.[9] The implication of the defensive neorealist view is that military force will be used only to defend important interests and that the level of military force employed in a given crisis will be in proportion to the regional opponent's capabilities. In other words, we should expect a high correlation between the use of force and the interests in question, and between the level of military force used and the expected resistance. Thus, the hegemon will not employ massive force to counter limited resistance. It will use such force only when faced with a considerable counterforce and will deploy a much lower level of forces when the rival is weaker. We should also expect a military intervention to take place when other less costly nonmilitary options have either been exhausted or when they can reasonably be expected not to accomplish the hegemon's goals.

To begin with constraints, even in a unipolar system, with an overall military hegemony on the global level, there might still be considerable differences in the intensity of the constraints posed by different regions on military intervention by the hegemon, and these constraints are reflected in the estimated costs of intervention during the decisionmaking process. The costs refer mostly to the estimated casualties of the intervening forces, which can be high or low depending on whether there are relatively powerful regional actors who may resist intervention and inflict high casualties on the intervening forces.

An important consideration in the estimation of the potential costs of intervention in regional crises refers to the distinction between the nature of the mission as peace enforcement or peacekeeping. In peace enforcement the intervention takes place before a cease-fire, let alone a peace agreement, is reached between the local parties. Thus, the intervening power has to impose a settlement on a reluctant party or parties. In contrast, peacekeeping takes place after a viable peace accord, or at least a cease-fire, takes hold and the external forces have to separate between the regional forces and to assist them in maintaining an agreement that they supposedly support and wish to implement. Thus, peacekeepers monitor or verify troop withdrawals, or supervise or provide security during an election. While in peace enforcement there is a willingness to deploy and use considerable force against those local parties who are seen as aggressive, peacekeeping depends on the consent of the regional actors and uses only minimal force for purposes of self-defense.[10] Accordingly, the estimated costs of peacekeeping are, in principle, much lower than of peace enforcement.

There is the possibility of a miscalculation of constraints and costs during the decisionmaking process, especially in the sense of underestimation.[11] The important point, however, is that the implications of an initial underestimation of costs, as we will see, are completely different depending on the level of hegemonic interests or incentives for intervention.

As for Great Power interests that provide the incentives for intervention, a critical distinction is between high-intrinsic, high-extrinsic and low interests.[12] High-intrinsic interests refer to the geostrategic importance of the region, the economic resources located there and the importance of the region for trade, investments and financial links with the hegemon.[13] In other words, control of such regions directly affects the world balance of power. High-extrinsic interests refer to the geographical proximity of the region in question to the hegemon or to its most important allies. Extrinsic interests are important but less vital than intrinsic interests because they do not directly affect the global balance of power. Low-interest regions are those without high-intrinsic or -extrinsic interests, that is, regions which lack key geostrategic or economic importance and that are also far away from the hegemon or its major allies. The concept of high-extrinsic interests thus provides an intermediate level of Great Power interests, and qualifies the extreme view of some structural realist "minimalists" that the U.S. has few important interests outside the industrialized regions of the developed world because most of the less developed areas do not affect the global balance of power[14]—a view that cannot account for a number of U.S. interventions that have taken place in regions not meeting the minimalists' criteria of intrinsic value. These unexplained interventions can be accounted for, at least partly, by the factor of geographical proximity to the Great Power or to its most vital allies, which makes even a region poor in resources more important than it would have been if located far away (see Desch 1993; Kagan 1999).[15]

In the aftermath of the Cold War, there have been growing calls for intervention on normative, moralistic, humanitarian or world order grounds for the purposes of the promotion of democracy,[16] defense of human rights[17] and containment of aggression against weaker parties. These principles obviously have a strong appeal in a pluralist democracy like the U.S. and may lead to significant diplomatic and economic moves such as sanctions, economic assistance or diplomatic promotion of regional settlements. Yet these values or "ideal" interests are by themselves unlikely to bring about sizable military interventions, because these principles have limited utility for compelling policymakers and the public to make the considerable investment involved in substantial military interventions.

Whereas material interests give rise to powerful domestic vested interests, the support of less tangible interests such as human rights concerns tends to be more diffuse. Thus, such causes are unlikely to generate enough domestic support for the extraction of the considerable resources from society needed for extended military intervention.[18] At the same time, norms or ideal interests can considerably reinforce, legitimize and help to sustain a realpolitik inclination to intervene when they are accompanied by major material interests or proximity to the Great Power or its major allies.

To sum up, for the purposes of the present model, the incentives (or interests) for intervention will be defined as high intrinsic (key resources), high extrinsic (proximity to the Great Power or to its major allies) or low; whereas the estimated constraints (or costs) will be defined as high or low. High and low costs will be defined primarily in terms of casualties, with high costs referring to hundreds or thousands of casualties and low costs designating casualties not exceeding dozens. Thus, six types of situations emerge according to a Great Power's combined incentives and constraints:

1 Situations of high-intrinsic interests and high constraints (i.e. high expected costs of intervention).
2 Situations of high-intrinsic interests and low costs.
3 Situations of high-extrinsic interests and low constraints.
4 Situations of high-extrinsic interests and high constraints.
5 Situations of low interests and low constraints.
6 Situations of low interests and high constraints.

Modeling the Causal Relations between Combinations of Hegemonic Interests and Costs in Different Regions and the Likelihood and Scope of Military Engagement

High Costs: High-Intrinsic Interests → Massive Intervention

Crises in regions with a combination of high-intrinsic interests and high constraints are likely to lead to massive hegemonic intervention. Crises in these regions that pose threats to major interests of the hegemon provide the incentives for a military involvement. At the same time, the large scale of the intervention is made necessary by the intensity of the expected regional constraints, to overcome which, the hegemon must resort to massive force. The importance of the interests at stake, in turn, provides the willingness to deploy such a large-scale force and to use it if the regional adversaries are not ready to accept the hegemon's demands. The significance of the interests at stake should also result in a relatively quick response by the hegemon to threats to its interests. The intervention is also likely to be sustained until the hegemon's objectives are met, even at the price of high levels of casualties.

Low Costs: High-Intrinsic Interests → Medium-Scale Intervention

The high-intrinsic interests of the hegemon in the region provide a willingness to deploy considerable forces in case of a crisis that seems to threaten the hegemon's interests. But to the extent that the expected resistance is low, there is no need to deploy more than medium-scale forces. Of all six situations, the combination of high-intrinsic interests and low constraints is the most conducive to mobilizing public support for the intervention, and in this situation a wide consensus is likely with regard to the intervention. Given the high-intrinsic interests of the hegemon in the region, the intervention will be sustained (and upgraded to massive) even if the costs rise unexpectedly and high levels of casualties are inflicted on the intervening forces.

Low Costs: High-Extrinsic Interests → Medium-Scale Intervention

Medium-scale interventions are also likely in regions where the hegemon has high-extrinsic interests and faces limited constraints. These have traditionally been Great Power spheres of influence: regions geographically proximate to the Great Power with militarily weak states. These areas are both relatively important and pose relatively low constraints for military interventions. Proximate states are relatively important because they can serve as a base for forces hostile to the Great Power, notably, rival Great Powers.[19] But even nonmilitary threats, such as illegal immigration, drug trafficking and terrorism, carry greater risks if their source is located nearby rather than far away. Especially unwelcome is the spread of instability near the Great Power's borders; and a Great Power will try to minimize the likelihood of such a spillover of chaos. Proximity also reduces the costs of military intervention and makes it easier than in more remote places. The low regional constraints make a massive intervention unnecessary, as a medium-scale engagement is sufficient to subdue threats to the hegemon's interests. Indeed, recurring interventions have taken place during the Cold War by both the U.S. and the Soviet Union in their respective spheres of influence (see Keal 1983).

Proximity may also lead to medium-scale interventions when the crisis takes place in an area proximate to the most important allies of the hegemon (and therefore it has extrinsic interests there) and the estimated costs of intervention are low. Even if these regions are not proximate to the hegemon itself, they are more important than other regions because they may have effects on the security, stability and well-being of the hegemon's most crucial allies, and thus have indirect effects on the intrinsic interests of the hegemon. The intervention in this case will be medium because of low expected costs that do not demand a massive intervention. If the costs of the intervention rise unexpectedly, the intervention is unlikely to be sustained beyond the level of a couple of hundreds of casualties at the very most.

High Costs: High-Extrinsic Interests → Nonintervention

Since the hegemon does not have intrinsic interests in such areas, high estimated costs of intervention there may result in nonintervention. This is especially the case in regions proximate not to the hegemon itself but to its allies. Because these regions are not close to the hegemon, the interests involved are somewhat lower than in the proximate spheres of influence. Moreover, these regions are faraway and the distance makes intervention there more expensive. As a result, when the estimated costs of intervention in extrinsically important areas are high, no intervention on the ground is to be expected apart, at most, from occasional limited use of airpower.

Low Costs: Low Interests → Limited Intervention or Nonintervention

In regions with low interests and expected low costs of intervention, a limited intervention is possible but not very likely. The anticipated low costs make it easier to decide on intervention, but the low importance of the region reduces the likelihood of such a decision. At any rate, the expected low costs together with the relatively small incentives for intervention lead us to expect at best a limited-scale intervention. Since low interests and low costs pull in opposite directions, a decision to get militarily involved in such regions is likely to be dependent on the values and beliefs of the decisionmakers that play an especially significant role in deciding on engagement. Thus, humanitarian considerations, as well as domestic politics and the media will play a greater-than-usual role in such situations. Yet, the weakness of the realpolitik logic for intervention means that such intervention, if it takes place, will tend to be relatively short-lived, especially in the event that the costs in casualties unexpectedly start to rise. In this case, the Great Power might cut its losses and run, even if the overall costs are still relatively low. This is because the low-intrinsic or -extrinsic importance of the region does not justify incurring even relatively limited costs.

High Costs: Low Interests → Nonintervention

Nonintervention is expected in regions where the intrinsic or extrinsic interests are low while the expected costs of intervention are high. The low interests provide few incentives for intervention, while the high costs make it extremely unlikely. Thus, a prompt and substantial intervention on the ground is unlikely to take place even if the issue is highlighted in the media and there are various calls for intervention from different groups due to humanitarian or world order concerns.

To sum up, the combined effects of the incentives and the constraints of a Great Power in a regional crisis allow to predict whether and how promptly it will undertake an intervention in the crisis; what will be the scope of the intervention; and how long it will be sustained if casualties rise beyond initial expectations. Thus, with regard to regions lacking in intrinsic importance (regions 3–6), the estimated costs make the difference in the decision whether to intervene or not. In other words, when estimated costs are high, only high-intrinsic interests will be considered important enough to bring about intervention (but then it will be massive to overcome the expected resistance). If the estimated costs are low, however, a limited intervention may take place on purely humanitarian grounds even when interests are low. Yet, if the actual costs of the intervention in terms of casualties exceed initial expectations, the degree of tolerance of casualties will be directly proportional to the level of the Great Power interests at stake in the regional crisis. In regions with intrinsic interests, high levels of casualties (in the range of thousands) are likely to be sustained. Under extrinsic interests, the intervention is likely to be discontinued after dozens, at the very most up to a couple of hundreds, of casualties. In regions with low interests, the tolerance for casualties will be extremely low, and thus even if a few soldiers get killed, it will be enough to induce decisionmakers to terminate the military intervention.

This analysis qualifies the recent far-reaching argument made by Luttwak (1994) that the extreme over-sensitivity of postindustrial societies to casualties means that the Great Powers are powerless to intervene anywhere. The major implication of this growing sensitivity to casualties is that Great Powers are much less inclined to intervene in unimportant places where they do not have significant interests even if the expected casualties are relatively low, as compared to the level of casualties that Great Powers were ready to sustain for insignificant interests in previous periods. Yet, as the model presented here suggests, once important interests are involved, Great Powers will be willing to sustain even relatively high levels of casualties, or at any rate, considerably higher levels than those in unimportant regions.[20]

Application of the Logic: American Military Intervention in Post–Cold War Regional Crises

This section will briefly examine the level of U.S. military engagement in the major post–Cold War crises in relation to the model, namely, to what extent the scope of the engagement was explained by the intensity of U.S. interests involved in the crises and the expected costs of intervention.

U.S. involvement in the various post–Cold War crises approximates the four degrees of military intervention mentioned earlier. The Gulf represents the massive type of involvement; in response to Iraq's invasion of Kuwait

230,000 troops were deployed in the Desert Shield Operation (from late August to early November 1990). In the Desert Storm campaign to liberate Kuwait, 540,000 U.S. soldiers were engaged.

Two examples of medium-scale engagement are the 1989 intervention in Panama and the 1994 deployment in the Gulf. Since the end of the Gulf War, the most threatening moves of Saddam Hussein took place in October 1994. In response to Iraqi military moves toward the Kuwaiti border, the U.S. had more than 21,000 troops "in theater" in the Persian Gulf, with another 42,000 scheduled for deployment there, building toward a target of around 63,000 and no less than 156,000 on standby.

Panama also approximates the medium-scale involvement. On the whole, there were 26,000 troops at the peak of the operation organized in five task forces. In fall 1994, an American intervention of a somewhat similar magnitude (about 20,000 troops) took place in Haiti. In this case, there was no need to resort to violence due to an agreement reached at the last minute with the military rulers of Haiti under a very credible threat of an imminent U.S. invasion.

In contrast, a limited type of intervention took place in Somalia starting in early December 1992. Although around 25,000 troops were deployed in Somalia by mid-January 1993, less than three months later U.S.-force levels had declined to half that amount. The declining U.S. commitment to Somalia was indicated by the Security Council decision to replace most of the American force by a 25,000-strong UN peacekeeping force in early May 1993. Only around 1,700 U.S. combat troops remained in Somalia. After the killing of 18 U.S. servicemen in early October 1993, President Clinton stated that the U.S. would increase its military presence in and around Somalia by over 5,000 troops, but only for a period of less than six months, at the end of which time the U.S. forces would disengage from Somalia. Indeed, by the end of March 1994 the U.S. disengagement was completed.

In Bosnia the nonintervention pattern has been the dominant one until fall 1995, U.S. diplomatic involvement in the dispute and its limited use of airpower notwithstanding. Only following the establishment of a cease-fire in Bosnia, the initialing of a peace agreement by the leaders of Serbia, Croatia and Bosnia in Dayton, Ohio in November 1995 and the signing of the agreement in Paris in the following month, did the Clinton administration decide to deploy 20,000 U.S. troops in Bosnia (as a part of a NATO peacekeeping force of up to 60,000 soldiers). This decision signaled a change in the level of the U.S. military intervention from nonintervention to medium involvement.

At the same time, the U.S. did not even consider military intervention in other regional crises, notably post-Soviet crises such as the war between

Armenia and Azerbaijan, and the internal fighting in Georgia, Moldova and Tajikistan, as well as the African crises in Rwanda and Liberia.

Massive Intervention

The Gulf (1990–1991): High-Intrinsic Interests and High Regional Constraints There is a widespread consensus among analysts that the Gulf region is a vital U.S. interest because it is oil-rich (25 percent of current global oil production) and has the largest known reserves (about 65 percent) of this vital commodity in the world.[21]

The size of the deployed forces was determined by the strength of the regional constraints, notably, the size of the Iraqi army—the fourth largest in the world at about 1 million troops, its modern equipment and battle experience following the eight-year war with Iran.[22] It is true that during the war it became clear that this estimation was at least partly a myth and in fact, the Iraqis were "outnumbered, outtrained, outled, outclassed, outplanned, and, above all, outmotivated" (Mueller 1994, 156; see also Klare 1995, ch. 2). Still, even critics of the war recognize that the U.S. and its allies "went into battle expecting the enemy to be numerous, dedicated, duplicitous, well-armed, and tenacious on the defense" (Mueller 1994, 156).[23] Even best-case scenarios expected heavy losses of American lives up to the range of thousands.[24] Thus, the U.S. had to deploy a massive force to counter such a seemingly tough adversary.

Medium-Level Interventions

The 1994 Gulf Deployment: High-Intrinsic Interests and Low Costs The considerable and prompt U.S. deployment in the Gulf under a different administration in October 1994 reinforces our confidence that the presence of high-intrinsic interests in the Middle East tends to generate substantial U.S. engagements once there are perceived threats to important U.S. interests in the region. A major difference between this deployment and the Gulf War was the obvious decline in the power of the Iraqi adversary following its crippling defeat in the war and the continuing debilitating effects of the sanctions enforced vis-à-vis the Baghdad regime ever since its invasion of Kuwait. Accordingly, there was no need to deploy the kind of massive forces brought to the region to counter the perceived powerful Iraqi army in 1990. Substantial medium-level forces seemed to be quite sufficient for the task of containing the Iraqi army four years later.

Panama (1989) and Haiti (1994): High-Extrinsic Interests and Low Costs in the Proximate Sphere of Influence The U.S. involvement in Panama is an example of a Great Power intervention in its sphere of influence. Indeed, the U.S. has been the traditional hegemon in Central America, particularly in Panama. The geographical proximity of this region to the U.S. brings about important interests, reinforced in the case of Panama by the Canal and by the military bases located there serving as the springboard for military-intelligence activity of the U.S. in Central America. The Canal has been important as a sea line of communication connecting the Caribbean Sea with the Pacific Ocean and thus, it meets Desch's criterion of an extrinsically valuable area.[25] The proximity of Central America to the U.S. also reduces the costs of intervention, which are at any rate relatively low due to the absence of powerful regional powers.

The U.S. has been traditionally interested in maintaining its dominance in Central America by seeking to promote stable pro-American regimes in the region, particularly in Panama (Scranton 1992, 359). The local strongman, Manuel Noriega, seemed to be useful in this regard during most of the 1980s and thus the U.S. maintained friendly relations with him. Yet, toward the late 1980s he increasingly came to be seen in American eyes as a burden rather than an asset. The Noriega regime was seen by the Bush administration as threatening U.S. interests by sponsoring drug trafficking, and harassing and endangering U.S. citizens and military personnel in the Panama Canal. But the underlying incentives were related to the fear of loss of control over a strategically located state in the U.S. backyard.[26]

At the same time, due to the limited size of the Panamanian military, the low expected resistance did not make it necessary for the U.S. to deploy more than medium-sized forces. The Panamanian Defense Forces, which included 6,000 soldiers (in addition to 12,300 in the police and paramilitary units) were organized and equipped only for internal security. Twelve thousand U.S. troops were permanently deployed in Panama and were the only fighting force in the country. Together with the deployment of an additional force of that size, the U.S. military was expected to prevail without much difficulty.

The medium-sized invasion of Haiti in the fall of 1994 under the Clinton administration, which came to power with less commitment to use force abroad than most previous U.S. administrations, shows that irrespective of the specific importance of Haiti itself for U.S. interests, which might be limited or controversial (and thus the substantial domestic opposition to the intervention), different American administrations are inclined to continue the tradition of intervention in the U.S. backyard even in the post–Cold War era. This is due to the combination of high-extrinsic interests in a proximate region and the expected low costs of intervention there. Although one of the important incentives for the Haiti intervention was related to the Clinton administration's policy of "enlargement" of the community of democratic nations, it is significant that military force has been applied for this purpose only in proximate and weak Haiti, thus reflecting the low costs of such intervention. Moreover, an additional major U.S. incentive for intervention in Haiti was to stem the flow of illegal refugees to the U.S.—an interest that is closely related to proximity.[27]

Both the Gulf and the Panama and Haiti interventions reflect relatively enduring US commitments to their respective regions, which are typical of regions with high-intrinsic or -extrinsic Great Power interests. The enduring U.S. commitment to ensure the free flow of oil from the Gulf region dates from the Cold War era. U.S. involvement with the Panama Canal and with Central America in general is well established since the nineteenth century (see Gaddis Smith 1994).

Limited Intervention

Somalia (1992–1994): Limited-Temporary Intervention Under Low Interests and Initially Perceived Low Costs During the Cold War, the superpowers showed a considerable interest in the Horn of Africa as part of their global competition for political influence, and even became involved in the Ogaden War in the late 1970s by supporting their respective clients. With the end of the Cold War, however, U.S. interest in the region has declined drastically since the Horn did not have much intrinsic or extrinsic importance.[28]

At the same time, the estimated costs of the intervention in Somalia were very low because Somalia had neither central government nor external allies, which could mobilize effective opposition to the outside intervention. In contrast to Bosnia (or Vietnam), the terrain is desert and thus unfavorable to guerrilla warfare. There was no regular army but rather a collection of armed gangs, which specialized in harming civilians. The leader of the largest militia force, Mohammed Idid, who initially opposed external intervention, changed his mind and offered to assist the American force, stating that the Americans had to stay a year in Somalia.[29]

The combination of relatively low U.S. interests in post–Cold War Africa and the expected weakness of the local forces in Somalia enabled humanitarian considerations as well as the media and the public sympathy for the Somalian suffering to exert a considerable influence on the administration. Also very important was Bush's interest in foreign policy and his desire that the U.S. should play a strong role. These factors, rather than geostrategic considerations, played the crucial role in the U.S. decision to intervene in war-torn Somalia and to provide relief to its starving population.[30] Indeed, the considerable room for maneuver allowed by the supposedly low-cost operation made it possible for the Clinton administration to upgrade the objectives of the U.S. involvement beyond humanitarian purposes to "nation building"[31] manifested by attempts to disarm the warlords and restore some sort of local order.

Yet, the absence of realpolitik incentives in Somalia has meant that neither of these types of objectives (humanitarian or nation building) could bring about the mobilization of considerable resources. Such incentives could produce only a limited-scale intervention as compared to both the Gulf and the Panama interventions. Indeed, the absence of important geopolitical or economic interests in Somalia has meant that once it became clear that the costs were underestimated, U.S. forces departed from Somalia in a short order. Thus, following the death of 18 U.S. servicemen in Mogadishu on October 3, 1993, the Clinton administration decided on October 7 to pull out the U.S. forces from Somalia within six months, although the total number of U.S. casualties in Somalia was very low as compared to the engagements in the Gulf and Panama. This is because the hegemonic willingness to suffer for unimportant places in the absence of a global competition is very low.

Partly due to the lessons of Somalia, the U.S. failed to intervene promptly in the crisis in Rwanda despite the staggering dimensions of the loss of life and dislocation there, compared to the crises in Somalia or Bosnia. In this case, the combination of low interests and low constraints, characteristic of the U.S. with regard to African crises, produced a nonintervention policy in the crisis, or at best, a slow reaction to it, which was too late to save the many people killed in the mass massacres. The U.S. similarly failed to intervene in the renewed Civil War in Liberia in 1996 beyond rescuing its citizens, and also in the recent civil wars in Central Africa (Zaire and Congo).

Noninterventions

Bosnia: From Military Nonintervention Under High-Extrinsic Interests and Perceived High Costs to Medium-Level Engagement as the Expected Costs Decrease For almost four years, the U.S. was, on the whole, uninvolved militarily in the war in former Yugoslavia. This policy essentially continued under both Bush and Clinton, despite Clinton's campaign rhetoric. The reason was a combination of low-intrinsic interests and expected high costs.[32] The relatively low value of U.S. tangible intrinsic interests in the Balkans has tended to overwhelm the less tangible ideal interests that were mentioned as justifying intervention. These world order interests included the protection of international norms and principles such as the containment of aggression, and the humanitarian/moral interests of the termination of ethnic cleansing and other human rights abuses.[33] Despite the significance of these world order interests and moral and humanitarian motivations with regard to the Yugoslav crisis, they were insufficient on their own to generate a costly military intervention in the absence of intrinsic material interests and in the face of major regional constraints.

Yet, it would be wrong to portray U.S. interests in Bosnia as low as, for example, in post–Soviet republics or Africa. Rather, U.S. interests in Bosnia should be conceived of as extrinsic because of Bosnia's proximity to the most crucial allies of the U.S.—the West Europeans. This proximity led to a widespread fear that the spread of instability in the Balkans would adversely affect European stability,[34] for example, that massive flows of refugees would reinforce the power of various xenophobic and extremist movements in Western Europe and thus have negative effects on European integration. In addition, the involvement of the West Europeans in Bosnia entangled the crisis with the future of the main U.S. alliance—NATO, and with the security commitment of the U.S. to the key region of Western Europe.[35]

Yet, these extrinsic interests were insufficient to generate a U.S. military intervention alongside its allies until fall 1995.[36] The reason for this consistent refusal to engage militarily on the ground was the high expected costs of intervention in terms of casualties due to severe regional constraints. Such high costs acted as a deterrent against intervention in a place where the U.S. has only extrinsic, rather than intrinsic, interests. The mountainous terrain made a possible intervention in former Yugoslavia a much more difficult and expensive proposition than the Gulf War. The harsh geography acts to neutralize the effectiveness of air power, thus forcing the need for higher levels of ground forces (David 1994, 10–11). The Yugoslav army was considered to be a modern European army that has been trained to fight the Soviet Army. It was expected that an American interventionary force would have to face at least a 90,000-strong Serb force, probably assisted by the Serbian air force (Mearsheimer and Pape 1993, 22; Barkey 1993, 49). Moreover, the Serbs proved themselves as courageous guerrilla fighters in World War II against Nazi forces and succeeded in tying down 44 German divisions.[37] All these constraints combined, led to the estimated need for a force of 200,000–500,000 in order to quell the situation in Bosnia[38] and to the expectation of very high casualties in case of such an intervention.

This calculation of high costs was derived from the conception of a military intervention in Bosnia as an aggressive peace-enforcement or "robust peace maintenance," that is, enforcing peace on reluctant local parties

(Ullman 1996, 19). But the nature of a prospective U.S. military intervention in Bosnia changed drastically in August–November 1995 from peace enforcement to the much less costly one of peacekeeping following the achievement of a cease-fire on October 12 and a peace agreement initialed in November 21 in Dayton, Ohio and signed in Paris on December 14 by the leaders of Serbia, Croatia and Bosnia.

Following these events, President Clinton decided to fulfill his pledge to help keep the peace after a cessation of hostilities and after a peace agreement between the local protagonists had already been reached. Thus, the U.S. has deployed 20,000 troops in the framework of a 60,000-strong NATO force with an initial commitment to stay in Bosnia for one year. Yet, in light of the changed situation in Bosnia, the mission of the force has become one of keeping the peace rather than of enforcing it, and accordingly, the expected costs have become much lower, even if some American casualties are expected. Moreover, because of the extrinsic importance of Bosnia, it seems probable that the U.S. will be able to sustain a somewhat higher level of casualties than was the case in the purely humanitarian mission in Somalia, even if the level of tolerance for casualties will be much lower than it was in the Gulf War.

Kosovo The more active U.S. engagement since 1995 helped to establish peace in Bosnia, even if it was an uneasy one, through the Dayton agreements. But the very partial nature of the U.S. hegemony, especially its reluctance to use ground troops, handicapped its ability to advance peace in the region and to contain the aggressive nationalism of "Greater Serbia," notably the ethnic cleansing against the Albanians in Kosovo.

Despite the great difficulties in establishing peace in Kosovo, the massive U.S.-led NATO air campaign in Spring 1999 succeeded in containing Serbia and thus increased the prospects of regional stability, if the Western powers continue to be engaged in the Balkans militarily, diplomatically and economically. One of the major constraints on the ability of the U.S. and NATO to compel Serbia to change its abusive policy toward the Albanian Kosovars and to give them autonomy, was the refusal of the U.S. to risk the lives of American soldiers and airmen. Thus the U.S. did not deploy ground troops and did not issue a credible threat of ground intervention. The pilots bombed from above 15,000 feet and the antitank Apache helicopters were not used despite their presumed effectiveness against the Serbian "ethnic cleansers" because they fly much closer to the ground. Such a risk-free policy obviously weakened the hegemon's ability to advance peace and to coerce its opponents. The reason for this policy is the absence of vital strategic or economic interests in the region while an intervention on the ground was expected to be costly. Yet, the proximity to Western Europe provided an incentive for military action against the threat that Serbia posed to the stability in the Balkans because of U.S. extrinsic interests there. Persistent inaction could pose a threat to the coherence and credibility of the most important American alliance—NATO, which made a major contribution to European peace and stability in the post–World War II era. Moreover, there has been a major decline in the constraints on U.S. ability to conduct large-scale and protracted military operations in the Balkans following the end of the Cold War and the collapse of the countervailing Soviet power. In the post-bipolar era, the U.S. enjoys a high degree of strategic freedom, which enabled it to bomb Serbia for 78 days and thus eventually to bring about its submission to some of the major demands of NATO, including the withdrawal of the Serbian military, a deployment of a considerable NATO-led peacekeeping force on the ground, a return of the Albanian refugees and the establishment of some kind of autonomy for Kosovo in the future.

Post-Soviet Crises: Noninvolvement Under Low Interests and High Costs In light of the strong U.S. reservations against military intervention in Bosnia, despite its proximity to Central Europe, it should not be surprising that the U.S. did not at all consider involvement in post-Soviet crises on the periphery of the former Soviet Union. The U.S. interests in Central Asia and in the Caucasus have been still lower than in Bosnia,[39] while the expected costs of intervention in such remote places could be high, including adverse effects on the relations with the regional hegemon—Russia, and its potential hostile reaction.

Thus, on the whole, both the post–Cold War U.S. interventions (Panama, the Gulf, Somalia, the fall 1994 Gulf deployment, Haiti and Bosnia since 1995) and noninterventions (Bosnia until 1995, and the post-Soviet and African crises such as Rwanda and Liberia) fit the cost–benefit logic highlighted in this essay.

Conclusions

The discussion here leads us to expect that in the post–Cold War world, the U.S. will use the tool of military intervention only selectively and sparingly. Because of the high sensitivity to casualties, the U.S. is expected to give preference to nonmilitary means such as economic sanctions and covert action. Only when these means are exhausted or when they do not seem to have much chance to be effective, the U.S. may resort to military action depending on the regionally derived incentives and constraints. More specifically, substantial (medium or massive) U.S. intervention may be expected only in regions in which the U.S. has clear-cut intrinsic or extrinsic interests. In contrast to the Cold War era, when almost all regions were considered important because of the zero-sum competition with the Soviets, and the related importance attributed to reputation and the credibility of commitments, in the post–Cold War period only few regions are considered to be worthy enough to incur the risks and costs associated with military interventions. The three most crucial regions, where threats to intrinsic (economic and strategic) U.S. interests may lead to a massive intervention are North East Asia, the Middle East and Western Europe, because control of these regions will have major effects on the world balance of power and the American economy. Whereas a crisis in Korea may bring about a massive American military engagement in the first region, and a crisis involving Iraq or Iran may bring about a similar intervention in the Middle East,[40] at the moment no such scenarios exist regarding Western Europe.

Medium-level interventions can take place also in regions where the U.S. has high-extrinsic interests, namely Central Europe and the Balkans—due to their proximity to Western Europe, and in Central America, the traditional U.S. sphere of influence—due to its proximity to the U.S. itself. In contrast, limited interventions may take place in unimportant regions, especially in Africa, but they will last only so long as the costs are very low. In the post-Soviet regions, no intervention is likely so long as the interests are low and the expected costs are high.

As a unipolar model would lead us to expect, the costs associated with U.S. foreign military intervention have declined with the Soviet demise. Yet, the Somali intervention shows that even in a place where an intervention is expected to be relatively inexpensive, the costs might well exceed initial expectations. When a somewhat similar phenomenon happened in Vietnam during the Cold War, the U.S. escalated its commitment. But in the post–Cold War era, as a complete contrast, when tangible interests are not engaged, the U.S. tends to withdraw quickly, as indeed it did following the killing of its soldiers in Mogadishu, even though the casualties were on a relatively small scale. At the same time, the mere prospects of considerable casualties in former Yugoslavia were sufficient to deter intervention there, despite the extrinsic U.S. interest deriving from the region's proximity to Western Europe. Only when the estimated costs had declined drastically after the conclusion of a local peace agreement, was the U.S. ready to commit a medium-level force to keep the peace in Bosnia. Thus, only in regions with high-intrinsic interests will the U.S. undertake intervention despite high expected costs.

September 11 and U.S. Military Intervention

With the disappearance of the Soviet threat in the post–Cold War era, U.S. incentives to intervene militarily overseas decreased because of the declining threats to U.S. national interests. In a unipolar world, in which the U.S. was the sole superpower separated by two vast oceans from the other Great Powers and the key areas of international conflicts, the public felt secure from international dangers, invulnerable to external attacks and complacent about foreign crises. It seemed like conflicts in faraway countries were not going to affect U.S. security and economy in a major way. The low stakes in regional conflicts resulted in unwillingness to tolerate casualities and thus to intervene on the ground in remote places. Thus the Clinton administration withdrew from Somalia following the death of 18 U.S. soldiers in Mogadishu in October 1993, believing that the low stakes there could not justify even such a relatively low level of casualties. In the post-1991 Balkans, both the senior Bush and the Clinton administrations were reluctant to intervene out of fear of U.S. casualties, which would be disproportionate to the non-vital U.S. interests in that part of the world. The coercive interventions that eventually took place there—in Bosnia in 1995 and in Kosovo in 1999—were pursued through airpower. Only when peace was established was the U.S. willing to deploy troops on the ground as part of a peacekeeping force.

This high sensitivity to ground intervention and to high casualties changed dramatically on September 11 because of the drastically rising stakes and the growing threats to national security. By resorting to "asymmetric warfare"—the use of nonconventional violent means to offset their overall huge conventional military inferiority—the terrorists were able to inflict major harm on the U.S. not only by killing thousands of innocent people but also by harming the economy and by creating a sense of insecurity and vulnerability among the American public.

The rise in the stakes has led to a drastic change in the willingness by the U.S. leadership and public to intervene militarily abroad for a protracted period—including potentially on the ground—and the closely related willingness to tolerate potential casualties.[41] This rising willingness shows at the very least that there was no basic domestic/cultural transformation in Western societies against military engagement abroad as was suggested by some analysts (i.e. Luttwak 1994). Rather, the attitude toward intervention depends on the balance between the stakes (based on the threats to U.S. national interests and security) and the costs involved in the specific case of military engagement. The greater the stakes, the greater will be the willingness to tolerate costs, including casualties. Thus, in the aftermath of September 11, internal constraints on intervention were reduced. Moreover, there is a major expansion in the geographical scope of U.S. intervention to a whole new region—Central Asia—where U.S. military intervention by airpower, and especially on the ground, was considered unthinkable until September 11. The low stakes were not perceived then, to justify the expected high costs of intervention in landlocked countries proximate to Russia and China.

The stakes in Afghanistan increased drastically following September 11 because of the close association between the terrorist network blamed for the attacks—al Qaeda—and the Taliban regime in Afghanistan, which harbored Osama Bin Laden and his associates. As a result, on October 7 the U.S. began an extended air campaign in Afghanistan—a country well known for its inhospitability to foreign military intervention—and deployed troops into Uzbekistan, which is supposedly under Russia's sphere of influence. The U.S. and this former Soviet republic signed an agreement that would give the U.S. military flexibility in operating from bases there in return for U.S. assurances to protect Uzbikistan's security.[42] Following the start of the air campaign, the U.S. deployed special forces in Northern Afghanistan to help the coordination of the U.S. bombing and to advise the military operations of the anti-Taliban Northern Alliance. Later, 1,400 marines and other forces were deployed to a base near Kandahar in Southern Afghanistan to coordinate the bombing and the attacks against the remaining Taliban and the al Qaeda strongholds.[43]

The number of U.S. troops deployed on the ground is still limited, but thus far there has been no need for more troops due to the effectiveness of the combination of airpower, the anti-Taliban Afghan opposition and the U.S. commandos. Still, the ground deployments into the dangerous terrain and battle zones in faraway Central Asia, in addition to the use of airpower and major naval deployments in the Arabian Sea, show a greater willingness to risk U.S. casualties than was the case in the 1990s. This is because the September 11 attacks raised the national security stakes involved in the war against terrorism, especially the battle against the al Qaeda network, which showed willingness and capacity to harm the U.S.. The location of al Qaeda's headquarters and training camps in Afghanistan closely linked the fate of this country with U.S. national security and thus the new willingness to intervene there, including militarily on the ground, is a drastic reversal of the U.S. disengagement from this region following the Soviet withdrawal from Afghanistan in 1989. At the same time, one might expect that in potential interventions with lesser national security stakes, like humanitarian interventions, the willingness to tolerate casualties will be much lower.

Notes

1. As a prominent analyst has observed, following the end of the Cold War, the United States has lost more than an enemy; it has lost the guide to its policy (Maynes 1990, 5; cited in Haass 1997, 3).
2. Cf. Joffe (1995, 94), Posen and Ross (1996–1997, 49).
3. My focus is on overt foreign military intervention, and more precisely, on different levels of troop deployment by one state in the sovereign territory of another state, in situations in which there is a certain likelihood that this deployment will be resisted and force will have to be used by the intervening power.
4. For the argument about the emergence of a unipolar world in the aftermath of the Soviet decline, see Krauthammer (1990–1991), and esp. Wohlforth (2000). For a more refined argument about American leadership in the 1990s, see Nye (1990). For skepticism by balance of power theorists about the endurance of a unipolar world, see Layne (1993), and Waltz (1993). For an analysis of the future of American power with the end of the Cold War, see Friedberg (1994). See also the debate between Huntington (1993) and Jervis (1993). For additional useful discussions of U.S. hegemony, see Eliot Cohen (1996), Haass (1997) and Mastanduno (1997).
5. The key structural realist work is Waltz (1979). For critiques, see Keohane (1986) and Buzan, Jones and Little (1993).
6. On the tendency of structural realist analysis to overlook variations in state interests as an independent factor, see Schweller (1993, 1994, 1996).
7. For balanced assessments of the indeterminacy of structural analysis for explaining certain outcomes, see Christensen and Snyder (1990), Snyder (1991), Van Evera (1990, 1991), Buzan (1991, ch. 4), and Haggard (1991). See also Miller (1995, ch. 4).
8. The fundamental assumption of the power politics approach is the quest of states for maximization of power. Thus, the classical realists, such as Morgenthau, saw power both as an end and as a means (see Waltz 1990, pp. 34–36). Great Powers, in particular, were viewed as frequently seeking to achieve hegemony (Spykman 1942; see also Gilpin 1981, 86, 92).
9. On the differences between aggressive and defensive realism and for citations, see Snyder (1991, 11–12), Brown, Lynn-Jones and Miller (1995), Frankel (1996a,b), and Miller (1996). Although there are strong connections between neorealism and defensive realism on the one hand and between classical and aggressive realism on the other, some recent neorealist works follow the tradition of classical/aggressive realism with regard to the core assumption of power maximization rather than of security preservation. This group includes Mearsheimer (1990, 1994/1995), Zakaria (1992, 1998), Huntington (1993) and Schweller (1994, 1996).
10. For a related distinction, see Haass (1994, 57–60).
11. For an analysis of assessment errors made by intervening states, see Kupchan (1992, 255–59).

12. In making this distinction I partly draw on Desch (1993, esp. p. 10).
13. See Papayoanou (1997), who especially emphasizes the importance of Great Power economic interests (trade and financial links) in a region.
14. See Van Evera (June 1990, 1992) and Walt (Summer 1989). For a critique, see David (Summer 1989; 1992–1993). For a useful overview of this debate and for his own middle-of-the-road view, see Desch (Summer 1989; Winter 1992, 1993, ch. 1; 1996). For updated post–Cold War overviews of this debate, see Posen and Ross (1996–1997) and Haass (1997).
15. On the strategic importance of proximity, see Spykman (1942, 165, 393–94, 448), cited in Desch (1993, 10, and Boulding 1962, 245–47). See also Kupchan (1992, 248). In the Cold War era, there was another factor that led to U.S. interventions in regions lacking intrinsic importance (notably Vietnam): reputational considerations and the credibility of commitment to defend vital interests elsewhere, stemming from the global superpower competition. Such considerations are much less likely to lead to intervention in unipolar eras, because reputational concerns become less important in a noncompetitive setting.
16. See Diamond (Summer 1992), Muravchik (1992), Halperin (Summer 1993) and Smith (November–December 1994).
17. See Stedman (1992/1993).
18. See Papayoanou (1997) and also Donnelly (1995).
19. See Desch (1993).
20. Drawing on the work of Mueller on the Vietnam War and of Freedman on the Falklands War, Freedman and Karsh suggest that the critical variable affecting public support of a war is not the costs of war in itself but whether the leadership has reasonable and attainable political objectives worth these costs (1993, p. 285).
21. Freedman and Karsh (1993, 180). See also Lieber (1995, 64).
22. Woodward (1991, 186); Toffler and Toffler (1993, 81–82); Klare (1995, 41–44).
23. On the expectations in the U.S. defense establishment that the Iraqis would put up a "tough fight," see Mueller (1994, p. 55), and Woodward (1991, pp. 216–17, 360).
24. See Mueller (1994, p. 55); Freedman and Karsh (1993, pp. 285–86). See also Klare (1995, ch. 2).
25. On the importance of lines of communication between areas proximate to the homeland and intrinsically important areas, see Desch (1993).
26. Scranton argues that the United States decided to intervene in Panama in order to maintain its hegemonic position in the region, particularly in Panama itself (1992, p. 359).
27. Clinton explained that he considered the use of military force in Haiti because of its geographical proximity to the United States and because of the refugee problem (*The New York Times* (hereafter, *NYT*) May 20, 1994, p. A1).
28. On the limited American interests in Somalia, see Wolfowitz (1994, p. 32).
29. "Troops for a tragedy," *Newsweek*, December 14, 1992, p. 13.
30. See Haass (1994, p. 44).

31. On the distinction between humanitarian and nation-building interventions, see Haass (1994, pp. 61–63).
32. Both the Bush and the Clinton administrations have shared the view about the low-intrinsic U.S. interests in former Yugoslavia. The former senior director for Europe and Eurasia on the Bush administration's National Security Council has suggested that the "American strategic interest in the integrity of Yugoslavia, per se, ended with the collapse of the Soviet threat to Europe" (Gompert, 1994, p. 33). In a memo to U.S. ambassadors on March 7, 1993, Secretary of State Christopher argued that the United States should push for peace in Bosnia lest the whole region explode, while stating that Bosnia itself was of no vital interest to the United States (The *NYT*, June 16, 1993, p. A13 cited in David 1994, p. 8, n. 27).
33. See Halverson (1994).
34. See Gati (1992, p. 76), Larrabee (1992, pp. 45–46) and David (1994, p. 12).
35. On this point, see President Clinton's address in *International Herald Tribune*, November 29, 1995, p. 6; the citation of Assistant Secretary of State Holbrooke in Mastanduno (1997, p. 69, n. 66; and Ullman 1996, pp. 31–34).
36. For elaboration of this point, see Miller and Kagan (1997).
37. On the limitations of this analogy, see Freedman (1994–1995, p. 62).
38. Mearsheimer and Pape (1993, p. 23); Dewar (1993, p. 33).
39. The importance of the Caspian basin might increase in the future due to the expected growing exploitation of the vast oil deposits located there.
40. Thus, the U.S. military buildup in the Gulf in Fall 1997 (and later also in winter 1998) in order to force Iraq to let UN (including American) inspectors back in to continue their search for nonconventional weapons in Iraq. These buildups did not need to exceed the medium level, however, because of the greatly weakened Iraqi military capability since its defeat in the Gulf War.
41. As shown by polls reported in *NYT*, September 16, 2001, pp. A1, 4; *NYT*, September 25, 2001, pp. A1, B6. Indeed, in a military analysis following the nighttime assault of the U.S. Army in Afghanistan on October 19, Michael R. Gordon regards it as demonstrating willingness to risk U.S. casualties. He suggests that in contrast to past conflicts, "the public seems to have shed its expectations of a casualty-free operation" (*NYT*, October 20, 2001, pp. A1, B2).
42. *NYT*, October 13, 2001, pp. A1, B2.
43. Michael R. Gordon, "Shifting Fronts, Rising Danger: The Afghanistan War Evolves." *NYT*, December 9, 2001, pp. A1 and B3.

Bibliography

Barkey, Brett (1993). "Bosnia: A Question of Intervention," *Strategic Review*, vol. 21, no. 4, pp. 48–49.

Boulding, Kenneth (1962). *Conflict and Defense: A General Theory* (New York: Harper, 1962).

Brown, Michael E., Sean Lynn-Jones and Steven Miller, eds. (1995). *The Perils of Anarchy: Contemporary Realism and International Security* (Cambridge: MIT Press).

Buzan, Barry (1991). *People, States & Fear: An Agenda for International Security Studies in the Post-Cold War Era* (Boulder, Colorado: Lynne Rienner, 2nd ed).

Buzan, Berry, Charles Jones and Richard Little (1993). *The Logic of Anarchy: Neorealism to Structural Realism* (New York: Columbia University Press).

Christensen, Thomas and Jack Snyder (Spring 1990). "Chain Gangs and Passed Bucks: Predicting Alliance Patterns in Multipolarity," *International Organization*, vol. 44, pp. 137–68.

Cohen, Eliot (1996). "Military Power and International Order: Is Force Finished?" In C. Crocker and Fen Hampson, eds., with Pamela Aall, *Managing Global Chaos* (Washington, D.C.: United States Institute of Peace).

David, Charles-Philippe (1994). "Procrastinating into the New World Order: American Policy Towards the Yugoslav Crisis" (Washington, D.C.: ISA).

David, Steven R. (Summer 1989). "Why the Third World Matters," *International Security*, vol. 14, pp. 50–85.

——(1992–1993). "Why the Third World still Matters," *International Security*, vol. 17, pp. 127–59.

Desch, Michael (Summer 1989). "The Keys that Lock Up the World," *International Security*, vol. 14, no. 1.

——(Winter, 1992). "Bases for the Future: US Military Interests in the Post-Cold War Third World," *Security Studies*, vol. 2, no. 2, pp. 201–24.

——(1993). *When the Third World Matters: Latin America and United States Grand Strategy* (Baltimore: The John Hopkins University Press).

——(Spring 1996). "Why Realists Disagree about the Third World (and Why They Shouldn't)," *Security Studies*, vol. 5, no. 3, pp. 358–84.

Dewar, Michael (February 1993). "Intervention in Bosnia—the Case Against.'" *The World Today*, vol. 49, no. 2, pp. 32–34.

Diamond, Larry (Summer 1992). "Promoting Democracy," *Foreign Policy*, no. 87, pp. 25–46.

Donnelly, Jack (1995). "State Sovereignty and International Intervention: The Case of Human Rights." In Gene M. Lyons and Michael Mastanduno, eds., *Beyond Westphalia? State Sovereignty and International Intervention* (Baltimore: The Jones Hopkins University Press, 1995), pp. 115–46.

Frankel, Benjamin (Spring 1996a). "Restating the Realist Case: An Introduction," *Security Studies*, vol. 5, no. 3.

——, ed. (Spring 1996b). "Realism: Restatement and Renewal," *Special Issue of Security Studies*, vol. 5, no. 3.

Freedman, Lawrence (Winter 1994–1995). "Why the West Failed," *Foreign Policy*, no. 97, pp. 53–69.

Freedman, Lawrence and Efraim Karsh (1993). *The Gulf Conflict 1990–91: Diplomacy and War in the New World Order* (Princeton: Princeton University Press).

Friedberg, Aaron (1994). "The End of the Cold War and the Future of American Power." In Geir Lundestad, ed., *The Fall of Great Powers: Peace, Stability, and Legitimacy* (Oxford: Oxford University Press).

Gati, Charles (Fall 1992). "From Sarajevo to Sarajevo," *Foreign Affairs*, vol. 71, no. 4.

Gholz, Eugene, Daryl G. Press and Harvey M. Sapolsky (Spring 1997). "Come Home, America: The Strategy of Restraint in the Face of Temptation," *International Security*, vol. 21, no. 4, pp. 5–48.

Gilpin, Robert (1981). *War & Change in World Politics* (Cambridge: Cambridge University Press).

Gompert, David (July/August 1994). "How to Defeat Serbia," *Foreign Affairs*, vol. 73, no. 4.

Haass, Richard N. (1994). *Intervention: The Use of American Military Force in the Post-Cold War World* (Washington: The Carnegie Endowment).

——(1997). *The Reluctant Sheriff: The United States after the Cold War* (New York: Council on Foreign Relations).

Haggard, Stephan (1991). "Structuralism and Its Critics: Recent Progress in International Relations Theory." In E. Adler and B. Crawford, eds., *Progress in Postwar International Relations* (New York: Columbia University Press).

Halperin, Morton (Summer 1993). "Guaranteeing Democracy," *Foreign Policy*, no. 93, pp. 105–22.

Halverson, Thomas (1994), "Disengagement by Stealth." In Lawrence Freedman, ed., *Military Intervention in European Conflicts* (Oxford: Blackwell).

Huntington, Samuel (January–February 1991). "America's Changing Strategic Interests," *Survival*, vol. XXXIII, no. 1, pp. 3–17.

——(Spring 1993). "Why International Primacy Matters," *International Security*, vol. 17, no. 4, pp. 68–83.

Jervis, Robert (Spring 1993). "International Primacy: Is the Game Worth the Candle?" *International Security*, vol. 17, no. 4, pp. 52–67.

Joffe, Josef (Spring 1995). " 'Bismarck' or 'Britain'? Toward an American Grand Strategy after Bipolarity," *International Security*, vol. 19, no. 4, pp. 94–117.

Johnson, Robert (Winter 1985–1986). "Exaggerating America's Stakes in Third World Conflicts," *International Security*, vol. 10, no. 3, pp. 32–68.

Kagan, Korina (1999). "Theory of Great Power Spheres-of-Influence." Ph. D. Dissertation, The Hebrew University of Jerusalem.

Kanter, Arnold and Linton F. Brooks, eds. (1994). *U.S. Intervention Policy for the Post-Cold War World: New Challenges and New Responses* (New York: Norton).

Keal, Paul (1983). *Unspoken Rules and Superpower Dominance* (London: Macmillan Press).

Keohane, Robert, ed. (1986). *Neorealism and Its Critics* (New York: Columbia University Press).

Klare, Michael (1995). *Rogue States and Nuclear Outlaws: America's Search for a New Foreign Policy* (New York: Hill and Wang).

Krasner, Stephen D. (1978). *Defending the National Interest* (Princeton: Princeton University Press).

Krauthammer, Charles (1990/1991). "The Unipolar Moment," *Foreign Affairs: America and the World*, vol. 70, pp. 23–33.

Kupchan, Charles (1992). "Getting In: The Initial Stage of Military Intervention." In A. Levite, B. Jentleson and L. Berman, eds., *Foreign Military Intervention: The Dynamics of Protracted Conflict* (New York: Columbia University Press).

Larrabee, Stephen (Summer 1992). "Instability and Change in the Balkans," *Survival*, vol. 34, no. 2.

Layne, Christopher (Spring 1993). "The Unipolar Illusion: Why New Great Powers will Rise," *International Security*, vol. 17, no. 4, pp. 5–51.

Lieber, Robert (1995). "The American Role in a Regional Security Regime." In Efraim Inbar, *Regional Security Regimes: Israel and Its Neighbors* (Albany, N.Y.: State University of New York Press).

——, ed. (1997). *Eagle Adrift: American Foreign Policy at the End of the Century* (New York: Longman).

Luttwak, Edward (July–August 1994). "Where are the Great Powers?" *Foreign Affairs*, vol. 73, no. 4.

Lynn-Jones, Sean M. and Steven E. Miller, eds. (1992). *America's Strategy in a Changing World—An International Security Reader* (Cambridge: MIT Press).

—— (1993). *The Cold War and After: Prospects for Peace—An International Security Reader* (Cambridge: MIT Press).

Mastanduno, Michael, "Preserving the Unipolar Moment: Realist Theories and U.S. Grand Strategy after the Cold War," *International Security*, vol. 21, no. 4 (Spring 1997), pp. 49–88.

Maynes, Charles C. (Spring 1990). "America without the Cold War," *Foreign Policy*, no. 78.

—— (Spring 1995). "Relearning Intervention," *Foreign Policy*, no. 98.

Mearsheimer, John (Summer 1990) "Back to the Future: Instability in Europe After the Cold War," *International Security* 15, no. 1: 5–56.

—— (Winter 1994–1995) "The False Promise of International Institutions," *International Security*, vol. 19, no. 3.

Mearsheimer, John and Robert Pape (June 14, 1993). "The Answer—A Partition Plan for Bosnia," *The New Republic*, pp. 22–8.

Miller, Benjamin (Summer 1994). "Polarity, Nuclear Weapons, and Major War," *Security Studies*, vol. 3, no. 4.

—— (1995). *When Opponents Cooperate: Great Power Conflict and Collaboration in World Politics* (Ann Arbor: The University of Michigan Press).

—— (Spring 1996). "Competing Realist Perspectives on Great Power Crisis Behavior," *Security Studies*, vol. 5, no. 3.

—— and Korina Kagan (March 1997). "The Great Powers and Regional Conflicts: Eastern Europe and the Balkans from the Post-Napoleonic era to the Post-Cold War Era," *International Studies Quarterly*, vol. 41, no. 1.

Morgenthau, Hans J. (April 1967). "To Intervene or Not to Intervene," *Foreign Affairs*, vol. 45.

—— (1978). *Politics Among Nations* (New York: Knopf, 5th ed.).

Mueller, John (1994). *Policy and Opinion in the Gulf War* (Chicago: Chicago University Press).

Muravchik, Joshua (1992). *Exporting Democracy* (Washington, D.C.: Enterprise).

Nye, Joseph (1990). *Bound to Lead* (New York: Basic Books).

Papayoanou, Paul (1997). "Great Powers and Regional Orders: Possibilities and Prospects after the Cold War." In David Lake and Patrick Morgan, eds., *Regional Orders: Building Security in a New World* (University Park, Pennsylvania: The Pennsylvania State University Press).

Posen, Barry R. and Andrew L. Ross (Winter 1996–1997). "Competing Visions for U.S. Grand Strategy," *International Security*, vol. 21, no. 3, pp. 5–53.

Richard H. Ullman, 1996. "The Wars in Yugoslavia and the International System after the Cold War" In Richard H. Ullman, ed., *The World and Yugoslavia's Wars* (New York: Council on Foreign Relations).

Schweller, Randall (March 1993). "Tripolarity and the Second World War," *International Studies Quarterly*, vol. 37, no. 1.

——(Summer 1994). "Bandwagoning for Profit: Bringing the Revisionist State Back In," *International Security*, vol. 19, no. 1.

——(Spring 1996). "Neorealism's Status-Quo Bias," *Security Studies*, vol. 5, no. 3.

Scranton, Margaret (1992). "Panama." In Peter Schraerder, ed., *Intervention into the 1990s: US Foreign Policy in the Third World* (Boulder: Lynne Rienner, 2nd ed.).

Smith, Gaddis (1994). *The Last Years of the Monroe Doctrine* (New York: Hill and Wang).

Smith, Tony (November/December 1994). "In Defense of Intervention," *Foreign Affairs*, vol. 73, no. 6, pp. 34–46.

Snyder, Jack (1991). *Myths of Empire: Domestic Politics and International Ambition* (Ithaca: Cornell University Press).

Spykman, N. (1942). *America's Strategy in World Politics* (New York: Harcourt, Brace & Co).

Stedman, Stephen (1992/1993). "The New Interventionists," *Foreign Affairs*, America and the World, vol. 72, no. 1.

Tucker, Robert W. and David C. Hendrickson (1992). *The Imperial Temptation: The New World Order and America's Purpose* (New York: Council on Foreign Relations Press).

Toffler, Alvin and Heidi Toffler (1993). *War and Anti-War* (Boston: Little Brown, Hebrew translation).

Van Evera, Stephen (June 1990). "Why Europe Matters, Why the Third World Doesn't: American Grand Strategy after the Cold War," *Journal of Strategic Studies*, vol. 13, no. 2.

——(Winter 1990–1991). "Primed for Peace: Europe after the Cold War," *International Security*, vol. 15, no. 3.

——(1992). "The United States and the Third World: When to Intervene?" In Kenneth Oye, Robert Lieber and Donald Rothchild, eds., *Eagle in a New World: American Grand Strategy in the Post-Cold War Era* (New York: HarperCollins).

Walt, Stephen (Summer 1989). "The Case for Finite Containment: Analyzing US Grand Strategy," *International Security*, vol. 14, no. 1.

Waltz, Kenneth (1979). *Theory of International Politics* (Reading, Mass.: Addison-Wesley Publishing Company).

——(Spring/Summer 1990). "Realist Thought and Neorealist Theory," *Journal of International Affairs*, vol. 44, no. 1.

——(Fall 1993). "The Emerging Structure of International Politics," *International Security*, vol. 18, no. 2, pp. 44–79.

Wohlforth, William C. (2000). "The Stability of a Unipolar World." In *America's Strategic Choices*, ed. Michael E. Brown, Owen R. Cote, Jr., Sean Lynn-Jones and Steven Miller, eds. (Cambridge: MIT), pp. 273–309.

Wolfowitz, Paul (1994). "Clinton's First Year," *Foreign Affairs,* vol. 73, no. 1, pp. 28–43.

Woodward, Bob (1991). *The Commanders* (New York: Star).

Zakaria, Fareed (Summer 1992). "Realism and Domestic Politics: A Review Essay," *International Security,* vol. 17, no. 1, pp. 177–98.

——(1998). *From Wealth to Power: The Unusual Origins of America's World Role* (Princeton: Princeton University Press).

CHAPTER 4

From Balance of Power to Balancing Behavior: The Long and Winding Road

Susan B. Martin

The relation between structural realist theory and the study of foreign policy has long been problematic and controversial. Kenneth Waltz has clearly argued that structural realism is a theory of international outcomes, not a theory of foreign policy, and that indeed it cannot be a theory of foreign policy. At the same time, Waltz clearly thinks that structural realism can help us to understand state behavior, and when exploring the economic and military effects of structural causes in *Theory of International Politics*, he uses the behavior of particular states as illustrations.[1]

The tension between structural realism and the study of foreign policy is particularly evident in work within the balance of power tradition. Balance of power analyses comprise a chaotic tradition that has always included what might be labeled "systemic" and "foreign policy" approaches. Recent work has largely been inspired by the systemic, neorealist balance of power theory presented by Waltz, and has attempted to use neorealism as a basis for explaining the balancing behavior of states. This work has been widely criticized, portrayed as a degenerating research design, as historically inaccurate, and as made irrelevant by the end of the Cold War.[2]

This chapter defends balance of power theory against those who call for its abandonment while at the same time recognizing that there are problems with current work. I trace the current problems with balance of power analyses to confusion about how to use systemic theory as a basis for explanations of foreign policy. In particular, I argue that the scope of systemic balance of power theory has been overestimated, and that attempts to use systemic balance of power theory as a basis for studies of state behavior are problematic because they fail to analyze exactly what it means for a state to balance.

The first section of this chapter briefly reviews the literature on balance of power and examines the problems encountered when one moves from systemic balance of power theory to the balancing behavior of states. I argue that a more complete definition of balancing behavior, rooted in systemic balance of power theory, is both possible and necessary. This is the aim of the next two sections. The first examines systemic balance of power theory in more depth and clarifies what it is about international politics that systemic balance of power theory does and does not capture. The following section then develops a definition of balancing behavior. In conclusion, I present a simple model of balancing behavior based upon this definition, and argue that this model will allow us to explore the utility of neorealist versus other explanations of state balancing behavior.

The Balance of Power Tradition

Within the tradition of balance of power theory one can identify two main strands: the first is systemic balance of power theory, which is concerned with the reoccurrence of rough balances of power within the international system, while the second focuses on balance of power theory as a guide to, or explanation of, state behavior. The former is evident in Thucydides's description of how changes in the distribution of power led to war between Athens and Sparta, in Ludwig Dehio's discussion of the role of flanking powers in preventing the emergence of a hegemon in Europe, and in the thought of Jean Jacques Rousseau.[3] In these discussions, the focus is not on explaining the behavior of a particular state, but on explaining how changes in the distribution of power within an anarchic international system shape the constraints, opportunities and incentives facing states. It is this strand of balance of power theory that is distilled and clarified in the systemic balance of power theory presented by Waltz.[4]

The second strand of the balance of power tradition focuses not on systemic constraints and international outcomes but on the behavior of states. This strand focuses on issues of foreign policy, examining whether states try to create balances of power as well as what determines when states "balance" or "bandwagon." As Inis Claude explains, this strand "treats balance of power as a policy of states or as a principle capable of inspiring the policy of states."[5] Arnold Wolfers's essay on balance of power is one example. In his discussion of four approaches to the balance of power, Wolfers dismisses the "automatic" or systemic notion of a balance of power as not suited to his purposes, which concern policy, not outcomes. The important question for him is "whether nations under certain circumstances do or should, as a matter of expediency, make power equilibrium rather than power superiority the target of their effort."[6]

Edward Gulick's work on the balance of power is another example of this strand. He sets himself two tasks in *Europe's Classic Balance of Power*: first, to derive general propositions about the balance of power from the thought of the theorists and practitioners of the period he is examining, and second, to trace the effects of those propositions on the foreign policy of states.[7] Paul Schroeder also examines how statesmen understand international politics and how that understanding influences their behavior, although he reaches quite different conclusions about balance of power theory in his work *The Transformation of European Politics*.[8] While Gulick argues in *Europe's Classic Balance of Power* that the period following the end of the Napoleonic Wars represents the "classic" balance of power, for Schroeder this was a period in which international politics was transformed from competitive balance of power politics to the politics of concert and political equilibrium. Thus both Schroeder and Gulick are interested in how ideas shape international politics, although they reach very different conclusions about the influence of balance of power ideas on the actions of government leaders and the states they lead.[9]

In recent work, the line between the two strands—the one focusing on systemic outcomes and the other on the behavior of states—has been blurred by scholars who attempt to use the systemic balance of power theory associated with neorealism as a basis for work that focuses on the behavior of states.[10] This work, as well as the critical reaction to it, has given rise to a great deal of confusion about balance of power theory.[11] Much if not all of this confusion is a result of two problems. First, there is a basic misunderstanding of the utility of systemic balance of power theory. Systemic theory actually has a very narrow scope, because it is limited to an explanation of international outcomes. Second, because the scope of systemic theory is misunderstood, analysts move from systemic balance of power theory to the study of state behavior without recognizing the implications of the change in the level of analysis. When one moves beyond the systemic level to an explanation of foreign policy, the explanatory framework has to be adapted. This is not a new insight: J. David Singer argues in his 1961 article on levels of analysis that when one moves from one level of analysis to another, an "act of translation" is required.[12]

The rest of this chapter is devoted to an analysis of these two problems. The next section examines the utility of systemic theory; in doing so, I identify the source of confusion about the scope of systemic theory. In the next section, I undertake Singer's act of translation in an effort to produce a useful definition of balancing. Thus, the next two sections will move us from systemic balance of power theory to a definition of balancing behavior.

Systemic Balance of Power Theory

According to systemic balance of power theory, the formation of balances of power follows more or less directly from the anarchic nature of the international system. A systemic characteristic—anarchy—leads to a systemic outcome—the recurrent formation of rough balances of power. The theory states that any time two or more states that wish to survive, exist in an anarchic system, rough balances of power form.[13]

In this sense, systemic balance of power theory argues that anarchy is an underlying cause of the formation of balances of power, just as anarchy is understood to be an underlying or permissive cause of war.[14] But just as a purely systemic explanation of war cannot explain how or why a particular war occurs, a purely systemic explanation of the formation of balances of power cannot explain how or when a particular balance of power forms. Systemic balance of power theory tells us that rough balances of power tend to recur and that any power advantage gained by one state over others will be temporary. The long-term maintenance of a significant disequilibrium of power would contradict the theory, although the precise meaning of the terms "long-term" and "significant" are not clear.[15]

In this way, systemic balance of power theory's argument about the recurrence of balances of power parallels the argument that Waltz makes about the recurrence of war in *Man, the State, and War*. But the understanding of the international system presented in *Theory of International Politics* is more developed than that which is presented in *Man, the State, and War*, and that development has given rise to some confusion about the kind of claims that systemic theory makes.

In *Theory of International Politics*, Waltz argues that the system is composed of a structure and of units, and that two characteristics of the structure—anarchy and polarity—have two kinds of effects. The first effect of structure is as an intervening variable. Structure intervenes between the actions and intentions of states and the outcomes that result. This effect of structure means that there is a disconnect between what states intend and the outcomes that are produced. Thus Waltz argues that balances of power form even if states pursue hegemony; the effect of structure also means that two defense-minded states may nonetheless find themselves at war because the defensive preparations of each are seen as a threat by the other.[16] It is because of this effect of structure that the intentions of international actors cannot be inferred from outcomes; it also means that complete explanations of international outcomes require at least some systemic component.

The second effect of structure is on the constraints and opportunities that states face. The structure of the international system has this second effect because states, or rather those who act for them, are seen as sentient beings who aim to understand their environment and calculate the best way to act within it.[17] It is this understanding of structure that leads to the concepts of emulation and selection. In calculating how best to pursue their ends, states are expected to take note of the success and failures of other states, and to imitate those who succeed. States who fail to do this, or who do this less well than others, may be "selected out" by competitive forces.[18]

One example of this kind of effect is the contention that anarchy encourages states to care about relative gains.[19] A second example follows from the introduction of polarity as a characteristic of structure.[20] Changes in polarity (more specifically, from bipolarity to multipolarity or vice versa) modify both the constraints and opportunities available to states and the outcomes that are likely to result, without, however, changing the basic effects that follow from anarchy. Thus, in both bipolar and multipolar systems, rough balances of power are expected to form. But the opportunities and incentives that states face in bipolar and multipolar systems are different: in multipolar systems, states can ally with other Great Powers to counter a threat, while in bipolarity each Great Power has to rely on internal balancing to counter the other. Waltz argues that the greater reliability and preciseness of internal balances means that balances of power will form with greater efficiency in bipolar systems.[21]

Thus the nature of the international system affects international politics in two ways. The first argument, which parallels the argument made in *Man, the State, and War*, is that the anarchic nature of the international system serves as an intervening variable and is a necessary part of any explanation of systemic outcomes. The second argument focuses on how the structure of the system affects the constraints and incentives that states face.

It is this second kind of implication that has led to much of the confusion about the kinds of claims that systemic theory can make.[22] Because structure affects the behavior of states, systemic balance of power theory is often taken as a theory of balancing behavior. Waltz is often interpreted as saying that neorealist systemic theory can provide predictions or explanations of particular state actions. This argument has been forcefully made by Colin Elman. His belief that systemic theory can make such predictions lies behind his argument for the possibility of a neorealist, systemic theory of foreign policy, and he argues that Waltz does use his theory to make these sorts of predictions in *Theory of International Politics.*[23] John Vasquez, Stephan Haggard, and others agree; all take Waltz' comments on how structure influences the constraints and opportunities faced by states, and interpret them as determinate foreign policy predictions. This is perhaps most evident in Vasquez: he takes Waltz' discussion of "balance of power theory" and interprets it as a "balancing theory," blurring the distinction between behavior and outcomes that is central to systemic theory. The "fundamental law" of international politics for Waltz is the repeated creation of rough balances of power—a law concerning outcomes. Vasquez interprets it as a law that states will always "balance."[24]

Although structure does affect behavior, it does not determine it.[25] Emulation and selection do not produce uniform state behavior, and systemic effects do not always, or even usually, dominate other sources of state behavior. The incentives and opportunities the system offers for balancing behavior are only one potential source of a state's behavior.[26] Systemic theories cannot not explain behavior per se, but they can help to account for patterns of behavior that occur despite changes in the identities and the motives of the actors.[27]

This is the fundamental reason why systemic neorealist theory is not, and cannot be, a theory of foreign policy, despite Colin Elman's assertion to the contrary.[28] A theory that includes only systemic variables cannot generate determinate foreign policy predictions under most circumstances. Waltz explains, "An international-political [i.e. systemic] theory can explain states' behavior only when external pressures dominate the internal disposition of states, which seldom happens. When they do not, a theory of international politics needs help."[29] Thus, when applying neorealism to the study of foreign policy, it is necessary to move beyond the systemic level of analysis.[30]

Balancing Behavior

The previous section argues that systemic theory is limited to explaining systemic outcomes. This means that when using a systemic theory as the basis for an explanation of state behavior, adjustments have to be made. Singer refers to these adjustments as "an act of translation": when moving from the systemic to the state level, for example, it is necessary to analyze what variables at the state level, what sort of state actions or policies, correspond to the relevant variable at the systemic level.[31] The central insight of systemic international relations theory—that international outcomes are not reducible to the individual actions or intentions of states—is itself a reason why this act of translation has to take place.[32] If an international outcome that we are interested in cannot be reduced to specific actions taken by states, then when taking propositions or ideas about the causes of outcomes at the systemic level and applying them to state behavior, we have to think carefully about what sorts of things at the state level of analysis correspond to particular international outcomes. We have to translate the variables we are interested in at one level into the corresponding variables at other levels. This act of translation has not been adequately performed by most of the analysts who use neorealism as a basis for their studies of state behavior.

The problems this lack of translation creates are two-fold. First, the propositions that can be generated from systemic theory about state behavior are stated in terms of generalities, in terms of what states "tend" to do or what the systemic incentives encourage them to do. Propositions about what states tend to do cannot be translated into propositions about what states "do"; that states "tend" to balance does not suggest that all states will balance at all times.[33] Nor does a tendency for states to balance mean that states will balance promptly and efficiently. No determinate proposition about what states "do" can be generated from the systemic level, because state behavior is a function of causes at all three levels of analysis.[34] This means that explanations of what states "do" that draw on the systemic level have to recognize the multiple causes of state behavior, and if they want to focus on systemic causes, they have to examine the way systemic causes interact with causes at other levels and theorize about the conditions under which those systemic causes will dominate.[35] This is necessary not only for international relations scholars interested in the balancing behavior of states, but also for all theorists who base their work on systemic theory.

The general nature of the propositions that can be generated from systemic theory can also be seen in the work of offensive and defensive realists. Both claim neorealism as the foundation for their theories, yet they make divergent assumptions about the motivation of states. Defensive realists assume that states are primary motivated by survival, while offensive realists assume that that states are power hungry.[36] It is this ability of neorealism to serve as the basis for opposite claims that lead critics to charge that it is essentially unfalsifiable and a degenerating research program.[37]

However, the problem is not with neorealism per se but with how neorealist propositions at the systemic level have been translated into propositions at the unit level. Neorealism itself portrays states as neither exclusively offensive nor as exclusively defensive. It simply assumes that states "are unitary actors who, at a minimum, seek their own preservation and, at a maximum, drive for universal domination."[38] This assumption suffices for explanations of systemic outcomes, but to explain state behavior, more specific assumptions are necessary. The question for proponents of offensive or defensive realism is not which provides the correct interpretation of neorealism, but which school's auxiliary assumptions about state motivations lead to the most compelling explanations of state behavior.

I suspect that this is not an either/or question, but that each assumption will help us to understand the behavior of states in different situations.[39] In other words, the question is not whether all state behavior is best explained by the assumptions made by offensive or defensive realists, but under what circumstances behavior is best explained by the auxiliary assumptions contained in each school's application of neorealism.[40]

A second problem created by the failure to translate concepts taken from the systemic level is also evident in studies of balancing behavior, and that is the lack of discussion of what it means for states to "balance." Work on balance of power theory has taken the systemic propositions that "balances reoccur" and that "states tend to balance" and proceeded to examine whether or not states "balance," with little or no analysis of what sorts of state behavior should fall under that rubric. At the systemic level, "balancing" is any action that leads to the formation of a rough balance of power. At the extreme, this includes actions taken by states that seek hegemony, for according to neorealist theory, systemic effects are such that even if every state in the system aims for a preponderance of power, a rough balance of power will form.[41]

Analysts of the balancing behavior of states tend to focus on alliances, but that is inadequate, for two reasons: first, there are other ways to balance, so that by focusing on alliances we exclude some instances of balancing behavior. Not only does the focus on alliances exclude the many possibilities for internal balancing, but it also ignores other forms of external balancing.[42] For example, Levy argues in a review of Paul Schroeder's work that external balancing techniques include "the creation of buffer states, territorial partitions, compensations, indemnities, other forms of intervention in the affairs of weaker states, and preventive war."[43]

Second, just as balancing incorporates a lot more than alliances, alliances too often include more than balancing. Alliances form for many reasons, some of which may have nothing to do with the existence of an external threat to state security. For example, Deborah Welch Larson argues that states sometimes join alliances for status and prestige, Schroeder argues that alliances can serve management and control as well as defensive purposes, and Randall Schweller develops the possibility that alliances offer opportunities for profit.[44] Not all of these motives for alliance formation are necessarily incompatible with balancing behavior, but neither are they necessarily compatible. This means that if we equate "alliances" with "balancing," we will include some non-balancing behavior. We need a clear definition of "balancing" in order to sort out whether a particular alliance is an example of balancing behavior.

The lack of a clear understanding of what constitutes "balancing" also explains why there has been little investigation of "internal balancing."[45] The general assertion that states acquire arms in response to external threats is widely accepted, but once we examine specific decisions to acquire particular armaments, it becomes necessary to deal with other possible motives for acquiring arms—the interests of defense industries and the armed services, for example. These competing explanations become even more difficult to handle if one includes other, more indirect ways of increasing a country's power as examples of internal balancing.[46]

The lack of a clear definition of balancing behavior, and perhaps even more importantly, of a clear understanding of what is *not* balancing behavior, inhibits the development of work in the field. It leads to the criticisms that work on balance of power theory is *ad hoc* as well as to the idea that balance of power theorists constantly draw on the indeterminacy and generality of systemic theory to explain away any and all challenges.[47]

I have indicated that performing Singer's "act of translation" will help to avoid these problems. In order to demonstrate this, the rest of this chapter will focus on the translation of the systemic concept of balance of power as an outcome to a concept of balancing that will be useful in explanations of state behavior.

Systemic balance of power theory tells us that anarchy leads to the formation of balances of power through the competitive international politics that it engenders. Anarchy constrains each state to rely on itself whenever possible for its survival, and to use any and every means at its disposal for that goal. As states compete for the relative power necessary for security, a rough balance of power forms.

Three adjustments have to be made in order to move from this structural understanding of "balance of power" as an outcome to an understanding of "balancing" as a state strategy. The first is that the focus of the inquiry shifts from international outcomes to the motivations behind state behavior. As noted earlier, it is not possible to determine if a rough balance of power forms and, if it has, argue that states were balancing, because the effect of structure as an intervening variable means that we cannot infer intentions from the outcome. The only way to identify a balancing strategy is to look at the intentions or motivations behind a state's actions. The importance of examining motivations and intentions is reinforced by the observation that states may pursue the same policy for different reasons.

Second, the move from the systemic level also requires that we narrow the motivations that are associated with balancing behavior. Systemic balance of power theory tells us that balances result from the interaction of units who wish to survive in an anarchic environment. This suggests that the motivation underlying balancing behavior is survival. However, this is a not a useful possibility for studies of foreign policy, because not all behavior motivated by survival can be considered as balancing. After all, the opposite of balancing has been defined as bandwagoning, and bandwagoning is seen as a strategy that smaller states may have to pursue in order to survive.[48] At the heart of what we mean by balancing is the notion of opposing the most powerful or threatening state.[49] I therefore propose that the motivation underlying balancing be identified as the desire to counter a threat.

Third, it is necessary to expand the definition of threat to include sources of threat other than power. At the systemic level, neorealism equates "power" with "threat," because anarchy means that unbalanced power is in and of itself a threat. But when one moves beyond the systemic level, other possible sources of threat appear. For example, Stephen Walt argues that threat is a function of geographic proximity, offensive capabilities, and perceived intentions, not power imbalances alone.[50] I agree with Walt that when examining balancing behavior, we need to examine threat perception. However, it is important that our definition of balancing behavior leaves open what factors—whether an imbalance of power, geographic proximity, ideology, or something else—will lead to the perception of a threat by states.[51]

On the basis of these adjustments made necessary by the change in the level of analysis, I argue that "balancing" can best be understood as actions taken by a state to counter an external threat.[52] Defining balancing in this way has three advantages. First, it puts the question of motivation at the center of the analysis. Second, it does not limit the study of balancing to the study of alliance formation, but allows an exploration of other possible responses to threat; it also facilitates an investigation of the conditions that influence a state's choice of response. Third, it distinguishes between external sources of threat and other sources. Each of these advantages is explained in more detail in the following.

The first advantage of this definition of balancing behavior is that it addresses the question of motivations directly. To determine if an alliance is an example of balancing behavior, for example, it is necessary to show that states joined the alliance in order to counter an external threat. Determining the motivations and intentions behind a policy is not always easy. One has to take into account possible attempts by policy makers to obfuscate and mislead, especially since an external security threat is often seen as a useful way to sell a policy preferred for other reasons. But the difficulty of the task does not mean that we should, or can, avoid it.

In his analysis of the fit between neorealist theory and history, Schroeder argues that by focusing on perceptions of threat, Stephen Walt's balance of threat theory "makes it virtually impossible to distinguish between 'balancing' and 'bandwagoning' or to determine the real motives of actors, since any 'bandwagoning' state is likely to claim that it is actually 'balancing' against a threatening enemy."[53] Schroeder emphasizes the difficulties involved in using perceptions and motivations to explain state actions, because policy makers often have an incentive to lie. But in his own analysis, Schroeder cannot seem to avoid using either threat perceptions or motivations as part of his explanation for the behavior of states. For example, in the same article Schroeder argues that "almost all German states and principalities saw this move [the proposed exchange of the Austrian Netherlands for Bavaria in 1785] as a threat to the German 'balance.' "[54] Of course, he does not simply assert this claim about threat perception; he provides both evidence and a logical explanation for why that exchange was seen as a threat, and he then demonstrates how that threat motivated the response of the German states and principalities.

As this example shows, the analysis of motivations is an integral part of foreign policy analysis, one that cannot be avoided.[55] Putting motivations and threat perception at the center of the definition of balancing decreases the likelihood that explanations of balancing behavior will be based on implicit assumptions about motivations and threats. In addition, a focus on motivations will push analysts to evaluate when policy makers' claims about threat are rhetorical and when they are actually a motivation for policy.

A second advantage to defining balancing as actions taken to counter a threat is that it allows us to distinguish more clearly between balancing and other possible responses to threat. For example, Schroeder argues that states may also hide from or transcend a threat.[56] This in turn facilitates an examination of the circumstances under which states choose to balance rather than bandwagon, hide, or transcend. The identification of the factors that influence how a state decides to respond to threat will help move us beyond sterile debates about whether or not states "balance" and will help to provide evidence for the comparative usefulness of competing explanations of state behavior.

The third advantage of this definition of balancing is that it distinguishes between external threats and other sources of threat, and allows the exploration of differences among different kinds of threat. First, it is important to distinguish between internal and external sources of threat. Some work on alliances and balancing behavior in general has found that internal threats to domestic regimes may be important motivations for alliances or other behavior that is often classified as balancing. For example, Larson argues that rulers or other subgroups in weak, illegitimate states may use alliances or other types of foreign policy to pursue their own, particular ends, and Haggard notes that many of the alliances that Walt examines in the Middle East were at least in part a response to threats to domestic legitimacy.[57] While this question of domestic versus international sources of states' foreign policy is an interesting one that bears on the usefulness of applications of neorealism to the behavior of states, it is not related directly to the question of states' balancing behavior. In other words, whether states balance in response to external threats is a different question from whether states can use alliances or other foreign policy tools to promote domestic ends, and the definition of balancing proposed here makes this distinction clear by limiting "balancing" to the response of states to external threats.[58]

Second, it may be important to distinguish between different kinds of *external* threats when studying balancing behavior. There is some suggestion in the literature that British sea power posed a different kind of hegemonic threat than that posed by continental military power, and that this difference meant that states responded differently to British hegemony than they did to attempts for hegemony on the Continent.[59] The characteristics of economic threats may also differ from the characteristics of military threats in ways that are significant for how states chose to balance.[60] Threats posed by states would also seem to differ in significant ways from the sort of collective international environment threats that have begun to attract attention.[61] Thus, an examination of different kinds of threats will reveal if, and if so how, the characteristics of the threat faced, shapes the response of states.

Conclusion

I have proposed that we define balancing as a state's attempt to counter an external threat. In order to classify an action taken by a state as balancing according to this definition, it is first necessary to demonstrate that the action taken was in response to a perceived threat, and then to argue that the action was taken in order to counter (instead of to appease, hide from, or bandwagon with) the threat. This suggests a very simple model of balancing behavior, one that includes both the process of threat perception and the action taken to respond to the threat.

Possible External Threats→Threat Perception→Response to Threat

The definition of balancing proposed here thus facilitates an examination of the different processes that systemic balance of power theory "black-boxes." By separating the question of threat perception from the question of how states respond to perceived threats, it allows us to isolate and compare hypotheses about the variables that are important at each stage.[62] Intentions may be more important than power imbalances as a source of threat perception, for example, but power (capabilities) may still be the primary determinant of how a state responds to a perceived threat.

While I based this definition on neorealist balance of power theory, the simple model it suggests allows us to investigate rival hypotheses about states' perceptions of, and reactions to, threat. Neorealism suggests that power imbalances are the most important source of threat and that relative capabilities determine how a state responds to threat.[63] But there are other possibilities. For example, in his work, Walt argues that geographic proximity, offensive power, and aggressive intentions along with power are important sources of threat.[64] And there are many alternative hypotheses about what determines how a state responds to threat. For instance, Schroeder's work challenges the notion that capabilities are the primary determinant of how a state responds to threat.[65] Powell argues that the "technology of coercion" or the extent to which military capabilities cumulate, as well as the relative willingness of the attacker to use force, are important determinants of how a state responds to threat.[66] Christensen and Snyder's analysis of chain ganging and buck passing reveals that technology, geography, and the perception of strategic incentives influence the way in which states respond to threat.[67] Kaufman suggests that ideology, domestic politics, and perceptions all affect a state's alignment decisions.[68] And Schweller finds that opportunities for profit and the "balance of interests" determines the alignment decisions of states.[69]

While the lack of a clear definition of balancing behavior has thus not impeded the development of rival hypotheses, it has impeded our ability to systematically evaluate and build upon these hypotheses. My hope is that the definition of balancing proposed here and the simple model of balancing behavior that follows from it will provide a framework for assessing the relation among different strands of work on balance of power. Armed with this definition of balancing behavior, fruitful research on the balancing behavior of states should be possible, and I therefore resist the calls of critics of neorealism to abandon balance of power theory as an unproductive enterprise.

I have argued that many of the problems with balance of power theory are problems with the uses that have been made of the theory and not with the theory itself. My defense of balance of power theory may strike some as strange, because it is based on the limited scope of systemic balance of power theory—its inability to do anything more than explain recurrent patterns of outcomes and to identify incentives and constraints facing states. But these same limitations are clear in Waltz' *Theory of International Politics*, and have been noted by other observers as well.[70]

These limitations of systemic balance of power theory should not be allowed to obscure its contribution. Systemic balance of power theory accounts for the recurrent formation of rough balances of power, and systemic theory generally helps to explain the disjuncture between intentions and outcomes that routinely characterizes international politics. It identifies the ways in which the structure of the international system shapes the incentives and opportunities facing states. But systemic theory by itself cannot explain particular outcomes nor provide an explanation for the behavior of states, and much difficult work remains to be done in applying that theory to the behavior of states.

The first step toward a neorealist explanation of balancing behavior has been taken here. I have provided a definition of balancing behavior that is consistent with systemic theory yet leads to a general model of balancing behavior that allows us to draw on factors at other levels of analysis. It remains for future work in this field, to apply this model of balancing behavior and to assess the relative explanatory power of factors included in neorealist versus other types of explanations.

Notes

1. Kenneth N. Waltz, *Theory of International Politics* (New York: Random House, 1979).
2. Recent work on, and challenges to, balance of power theory includes Thomas J. Christensen and Jack Snyder, "Chain Gangs and Passed Bucks: Predicting Alliance Patterns in Multipolarity," *International Organization* 44, no. 2 (Spring 1990), 137–68; Robert G. Kaufman, " 'To Balance or to Bandwagon?' Alignment

Decisions in 1930s Europe," *Security Studies* 1, no. 3 (Spring 1992), 417–47; Robert Jervis and Jack Snyder, eds., *Dominoes and Bandwagons* (New York: Oxford University Press, 1991); Eric J. Labs, "Do Weak States Bandwagon?" *Security Studies* 1, no. 3 (Spring 1992), 383–416; Emerson M. S. Niou, Peter C. Ordeshook and Gregory F. Rose, *The Balance of Power: Stability in International Systems* (Cambridge: Cambridge University Press, 1989); Paul W. Schroeder, "The Nineteenth Century System: Balance of Power or Political Equilibrium?" *Review of International Studies* 15 (1989), 135–53; Paul W. Schroeder, "Historical Reality versus Neo-Realist Theory," *International Security* 19, no. 1 (Summer 1994), 108–48; Paul W. Schroeder, *The Transformation of European Politics 1763–1848* (New York: Oxford University Press, [1994] 1996); Randall Schweller, "Bandwagoning for Profit: Bringing the Revisionist State Back In," *International Security* 19, no. 1 (Summer 1994), 72–107; John A. Vasquez, "The Realist Paradigm and Degenerative versus Progressive Research Programs: An Appraisal of Neotraditional Research on Waltz's Balancing Proposition," *American Political Science Review* 91, no. 4 (December 1997), 899–912; Stephen M. Walt, "Alliance Formation and the Balance of World Power," *International Security* 9, no. 4 (Spring 1985), 3–43; Stephen M. Walt, "Testing Theories of Alliance Formation: The Case of Southeast Asia," *International Organization* 42, no. 2 (Spring 1988), 275–316; Stephen M. Walt, *The Origins of Alliances* (Ithaca: Cornell University Press, 1987). The classic analysis of the meaning of balance of power is found in Ernst B. Haas, "The Balance of Power: Prescription, Concept, or Propaganda?" *World Politics* 5, no. 3 (July 1953), 442–77; see also Inis L. Claude Jr., *Power and International Relations* (New York: Random House, 1967).

3. See Thucydides, *The Peloponnesian War* trans. Richard Crawley, rev. T. E. Wick (New York: The Modern Library, 1982), [I 23], 14; Ludwig Dehio, *The Precarious Balance: Four Centuries of the European Power Struggle*, trans. Charles Fulman (New York: Basic Books, 1962); and the discussion of Rousseau in Edward Vose Gulick, *Europe's Classic Balance of Power* (New York: W.W. Norton and Company, 1955), ix, 84–85. See also Claude, *Power and International Relations*, 43–47, 93; Arnold Wolfers, "The Balance of Power in Theory and Practice" in *Discord and Collaboration: Essays on International Politics*, (Baltimore: The Johns Hopkins University Press, 1962), 117–31.
4. Waltz, *Theory of International Politics*.
5. Claude, *Power and International Relations* 18.
6. Wolfers, "The Balance of Power in Theory and Practice," 124. Morton Kaplan also argues that states explicitly try to create and maintain balances of power. Morton Kaplan, *System and Process in International Politics* (New York: John Wiley and Sons, 1957).
7. See, e.g., Gulick, *Europe's Classic Balance of Power*, viii, ix–x.
8. See also Paul W. Schroeder, "The Nineteenth Century System: Balance of Power or Political Equilibrium?" e.g. 136, 141, in which he traces changes in policy makers' and theorists' understanding of "balance of power" in the nineteenth century.

9. It is important to note that Schroeder's argument depends not just on the ideas of individual decision makers but on a kind of ideational "system," which he argues shapes international politics. Schroeder defines a "system" as the "understandings, assumptions, learned skills and responses, rules, norms, procedures, etc., which agents acquire and use in pursuing their individual divergent aims within the framework of a shared practice." Schroeder, *Transformation*, x.
10. Examples include Walt, *Origins*; Christensen and Snyder, "Chain Gangs"; Barry Posen, *The Sources of Military Doctrine* (Ithaca, NY: Cornell University Press, 1984).
11. See citations in note 1, especially Vasquez, "The Realist Paradigm," and the following responses to it: Kenneth N. Waltz, "Evaluating Theories," *American Political Science Review* 91, no. 4 (December 1997), 913–17; Thomas J. Christensen and Jack Snyder, "Progressive Research on Degenerate Alliances," *American Political Science Review* 91, no. 4 (December 1997), 919–22; Colin Elman and Miriam Fendius Elman, "Lakatos and Neorealism: A Rely to Vasquez," *American Political Science Review* 91, no. 4 (December 1997), 923–26; Randall L. Schweller, "New Realist Research on Alliances: Refining, not Refuting, Waltz's Balancing Proposition," *American Political Science Review* 91, no. 4 (December 1997), 927–30; and Stephen M. Walt, "The Progressive Power of Realism," *American Political Science Review* 91, no. 4 (December 1997), 931–35.
12. J. David Singer, "The Level-of-Analysis Problem in International Relations," *World Politics* XIV, no. 1 (October 1961), 77–92.
13. Waltz, *Theory of International Politics*, 118.
14. Kenneth N. Waltz, *Man, the State, and War* (New York: Columbia University Press, 1959).
15. The predictions made by systemic theory are indeterminate and can be difficult to falsify. See Waltz, *Theory of International Politics*, 124–25.
16. I am of course referring here to what is known as the "security dilemma." On the security dilemma see John Herz, "Idealist Internationalism and the Security Dilemma," *World Politics* II, no. 2 (January 1950), 157–80; and Robert Jervis, "Cooperation Under the Security Dilemma," *World Politics* 30, no. 3 (January 1978), 167–214.
17. Thus this understanding of structure belies those who argue that neorealism treats states as "billiard balls." States, or the units in the system, are not merely units subject to systemic forces beyond their control, but actively seek to understand and influence that environment, and their actions do affect, although they do not solely determine, outcomes.
18. See Waltz, *Theory of International Politics*, 73–77 and 127–28; Christensen and Snyder, "Chain Gangs," 140. Socialization results in states emulating the successful practices of other states, while the rigors of competition under anarchy selects out actors according to the consequences of their actions.
19. Waltz, *Theory of International Politics*, 105–06. The literature on relative gains is voluminous; a useful overview of the issues involved is provided by the debate

among Joseph M. Grieco, Robert Powell, and Duncan Snidal, "The Relative Gains Problem for International Cooperation," *American Political Science Review* 87, no. 3 (September 93), 729–43; see also Joseph M. Grieco, *Cooperation among Nations* (Ithaca, NY: Cornell University Press, 1990); Peter Liberman, "Trading with the Enemy: Security and Relative Economic Gains," *International Security* 21, no. 1 (Summer 96), 147–75; Robert Powell, "Absolute versus Relative Gains in International Relations Theory," *American Political Science Review* 85, no. 4 (December 1991), 1303–20; Robert Powell, "Guns, Butter and Anarchy," *American Political Science Review* 87, no. 1 (March 1993), 115–32; Robert Powell, *In the Shadow of Power: States and Strategies in International Politics* (Princeton, NJ: Princeton University Press, 1999), esp. 40–81; Duncan Snidal, "Relative Gains and the Pattern of International Cooperation," *American Political Science Review* 85, no. 3 (September 91), 701–26; Duncan Snidal, "International Cooperation among Relative Gains Maximizers," *International Studies Quarterly* 35, no. 4 (December 1991), 103–23.

20. See Stephan Haggard, "Structuralism and Its Critics," in *Progress in Postwar International Relations*, ed. Emmanuel Adler and Beverly Crawford (New York: Columbia University Press, 1991), 407; Christensen and Snyder, "Chain Gangs," 140–43.
21. Waltz, *Theory of International Politics*, 163–70.
22. This confusion helps to explain why the systemic concept of balance of power has not been translated into a concept useful for analyzing the behavior of states.
23. Colin Elman, "Why *Not* a Neorealist Theory of Foreign Policy?" *Security Studies* 6, no. 1 (Autumn 1996), 10.
24. Vasquez, "The Realist Paradigm," 903; see Waltz, *Theory of International Politics*, 117.
25. Thus Haggard overstates the effect of structure when he argues that according to neorealism, "once structural conditions are identified with sufficient precision, behavior can be predicted with little or no reference either to the internal politics and decision making processes of states or to the cognitive processes of individuals." Haggard, "Structuralism and its Critics," 406–07; see also 408. At most, structural theory can provide what Elman refers to as "predictions about 'consequences.' Such theories have dependent variables that describe the costs or benefits to a state or states of alternative courses of action." Elman, "Why *Not* A Neorealist Theory of Foreign Policy?," 13. For arguments that the predictions of this sort that neorealism provides do not hold up to empirical scrutiny, see Richard Rosecrance and Arthur A. Stein, eds., *The Domestic Bases of Grand Strategy* (Ithaca: Cornell University Press, 1993).
26. Kenneth N. Waltz, "International Politics is Not Foreign Policy," *Security Studies* 6, no. 1 (Autumn 1996), 54 and 55; Colin Elman, "A Response to Waltz," *Security Studies* 6, no. 1 (Autumn 1996), 56. In *Man the State and War*, Waltz clearly argues that when explaining a particular event—the occurrence of a particular war or in this case, the decision of a state to balance or not to balance against a threat, factors from all three levels of analysis are needed.

27. Waltz, *Theory of International Politics*, 122 and 117. Haggard does acknowledge this, but charges that Waltz admits this "only briefly" on page 72 of *Theory of International Politics*. Haggard, "Structuralism and Its Critics," 419. Elman's example of Waltz making a foreign policy prediction—that similarly stated states will act similarly, illustrated by the case of the United States and the Soviet Union—is an illustration of the similarities generated by structural constraints, not an explanation of specific behavior on the part of the United States and Soviet Union. Elman, "Why *Not* A Neorealist Theory of Foreign Policy?," 10. Waltz is not claiming that there are no differences in the behavior of the United States and the Soviet Union, only that structural theory helps us to understand why their general behavior is similar despite the differences in their internal characteristics. Waltz, *Theory of International Politics*, 72.
28. Waltz, *Theory of International Politics*; Elman, "Why *Not* A Neorealist Theory of Foreign Policy?" Waltz, "International Politics is Not Foreign Policy"; Elman, "A Response to Waltz."
29. Waltz, "International Politics is Not Foreign Policy," 55. Systemic theory does suggest that systemic factors will dominate in certain circumstances, and critics like Stephan Haggard and Elman are right that it is necessary to specify these circumstances more clearly. Haggard, "Structuralism and Its Critics," 417, 421; Elman, "Why *Not* A Neorealist Theory of Foreign Policy?," 30.
30. See Christensen and Snyder, "Chain Gangs," 138–39. Contra Elman, and as I will discuss in more detail later, this move beyond the systemic level does not necessarily entail the abandonment of neorealism. Elman, "Why *Not* A Neorealist Theory of Foreign Policy?" 38–39.
31. Singer, "The Level-of-Analysis Problem," 91.
32. Waltz, *Theory of International Politics*, e.g. 65.
33. Elman argues against this position in "Why *Not* A Neorealist Theory of Foreign Policy?" esp. 34–37; see also Waltz, "International Politics is Not Foreign Policy," 52–55; Elman, "A Response to Waltz," 56–59.
34. Christensen and Snyder, "Chain Gangs," 137–39; see also Haggard, "Structuralism and Its Critics," 407 and 410.
35. This also poses a problem for studies that evaluate systemic theory by examining its ability to explain particular outcomes or state behavior. In order to evaluate systemic theory's usefulness, it is necessary to examine its ability to account for recurrent systemic outcomes. Only particular *applications* of systemic theory, where systemic theory is adjusted and combined with variables from other levels of analysis, can be evaluated by an examination of explanations of state behavior or particular outcomes.
36. See, e.g., Eric J. Labs, "Beyond Victory: Offensive Realism and the Expansion of War Aims," *Security Studies* 6, no. 4 (Summer 1997), 1–49; Randall L. Schweller, "Neorealism's Status-Quo Bias: What Security Dilemma?" *Security Studies* 5, no. 3 (Spring 1996), 90–121.

37. Vasquez, "The Realist Paradigm," 902; see also Richard Ned Lebow, "The Long Peace, the End of the Cold War, and the Failure of Realism," *International Organization* 48, no. 2 (Spring 1994), 249–77.
38. Waltz, *Theory of International Politics*, 118.
39. Elman argues that neorealists need to choose between the offensive and defensive formulations. See Elman, "Why *Not* A Neorealist Theory of Foreign Policy?," 22–30 and footnote 65.
40. A similar argument can be made about whether states pursue relative or absolute gains. At different times and in different circumstances, states may in fact do both. The question is under what circumstances states are able to focus on absolute gains, and when they are constrained to purse relative gains.
41. Waltz, *Theory of International Politics*, 119.
42. On internal versus external balancing, see Waltz, *Theory of International Politics*, 168; see also Wolfers, "The Balance of Power in Theory and Practice," 127; Claude, *Power and International Relations*, 89. Note that Haggard argues that neorealism's prediction of internal balancing between the United States and the Soviet Union was "consistent with a wide-range of behaviors, from mutual postures of minimal deterrence to arms races and intense competition in the periphery." Haggard, "Structuralism and Its Critics," 408–09.
43. Jack S. Levy, "The Theoretical Foundations of Paul W. Schroeder's International System," *The International History Review* XVI, no. 4 (November 1994), 723; Schroeder, *Transformation*, 6–11. It is important to note that Schroeder would not necessarily classify these as balancing techniques; he argues, e.g., that while arrangements made in the Vienna settlement may have served balance of power purposes, they were not intended as such. Paul W. Schroeder, "The 19th Century International System: Changes in Structure," *World Politics* 39, no. 1 (October 1986), 17.
44. Deborah Welch Larson, "Bandwagon Images in American Foreign Policy: Myth or Reality?" in *Dominoes and Bandwagons*, ed. Robert Jervis and Jack Snyder (New York: Oxford University Press, 1991), 85–111; Paul W. Schroeder, "Alliances, 1815–1945: Weapons of Power and Tools of Management" in *Historical Dimensions of National Security*, ed. Klaus Knorr (Lawrence, KS: University Press of Kansas, 1976), esp. 255; Schweller, "Neorealism's Status-Quo Bias," 90–121. See also George Liska, *Nations in Alliance: The Limits of Interdependence* (Baltimore: The Johns Hopkins University Press, 1968), 26–41.
45. The work of João Resende-Santos is one exception. See João Resende-Santos, "Anarchy and the Emulation of Military Systems: Military Organization and Technology in South America, 1870–1930," *Security Studies* 5, no. 3 (Spring 1995), 190–245.
46. After all, power is widely recognized to encompass more than military strength, which implies that efforts to increase economic capability may also be a means of balancing. Cf. Wolfers, "The Balance of Power in Theory and Practice," 127.

47. In his article "The Realist Paradigm" Vasquez argues that the body of work applying Waltz' balance of power theory exhibits the symptoms of a degenerating research design, while Schroeder argues that balance of power arguments tend to explain "any outcome equally well." Schroeder, *Transformation*, 6; see also Schroeder, "Historical Reality," 124, 129–30.
48. See Walt, *Origins*, 173–75, 177–78; Waltz, "Evaluating Theories," 915.
49. For example, in his work on the alignment decisions of states, Robert Powell defines balancing as aligning with the weaker side of a conflict, while Walt defines balancing as "allying with others against the prevailing threat." Walt, *Origins*, 17. For Powell's definition of balancing, see *In the Shadow of Power*, 152–53.
50. Walt, *Origins*, e.g. 5. My definition of balancing differs from Walt's in that it does not limit balancing to the formation of alliances. Note that Waltz's main criticism of Walt revolves, not around Walt's use of the concept of "threat," but around the concept of "theory." Waltz explains that he sees " 'balance of threat' not as the name of a new theory but as part of a description of how makers of foreign policy think when making alliance decisions." Waltz, "Evaluating Theories," 916.
51. My argument that an explanation of a state's balancing behavior must include an analysis of the decision makers' intentions and threat perceptions is similar to arguments made by William Wohlforth; we both argue that realist explanations of foreign policy have to go beyond the systemic level. In his analysis of the end of the Cold War, Wohlforth argues that "for any balance of power theory to explain state behavior, it must specify the mechanism through which capabilities are translated into actions. That mechanism can only be the assessments of the people who act on behalf of states." William C. Wohlforth, "Realism and the End of the Cold War," *International Security* 19, no. 3 (Winter 1994–1995), 9; see also William C. Wohlforth, "The Perception of Power: Russia in the Pre-1914 Balance," *World Politics* 39, no. 3 (April 1987), 353–81.
52. Bandwagoning, the opposite of balancing, would then be defined as joining with the source of threat. Thus bandwagoning may include actions ranging from allying with the source of threat to supporting the policies or demands of the threatening state.
53. Schroeder, "Historical Reality," 119; Levy, "Theoretical Foundations," 726–27.
54. Schroeder, "Historical Reality," 118.
55. Singer, "The Level of Analysis Problem," 84–86.
56. Ignoring, or "hiding" from a threat, and "transcending" a threat through the creation of institutional arrangements or a formal agreement, are identified by Schroeder as ways that states can respond to threats. Schroeder, "Historical Reality," 117 and 128. At times he also seems to include specialization as a possible response to threat. Schroeder, "Historical Reality," 125 and 126; see also 128. Because specialization appears to be a response to the general threat posed by anarchy and not a response to a threat posed by a particular state, I have not included it as an alternative to balancing.

57. Larson, "Bandwagon Images," e.g. 89; Haggard, "Structuralism and Its Critics," 421–22.
58. It is important to note that domestic threats, when used as an indicator of weakness, are relevant to studies of balancing behavior when such weakness influences how a state responds to an external threat. This is the argument that weakness at home may translate into weakness abroad, undermining a state's ability to counter external threats. This line of argument is evident in Walt's discussion of Syria's policy in 1964 and at least partially in Larson's discussion of French policy in the 1930s. Walt, *Origins*, 87; Larson, "Bandwagon Images," 92 and 86.
59. See Schroeder, "The 19th Century International System: Changes in Structure," 16; Dehio, *The Precarious Balance*, 12, 108–09.
60. See, e.g., Susan Blair Martin, *Economic Threats, Balancing, and the Pattern of International Conflict and Cooperation*. Ph.D. Dissertation, Political Science Department, University of California Berkeley, Fall 1997.
61. See, e.g., Jessica Tuchman Mathews, "Redefining Security," *Foreign Affairs* 68, no. 2 (Spring 1989): 162–78.
62. Threat perception, though central to international relations, is understudied, and the work that has been done has not been well integrated into analyses of balancing behavior. While Walt's balance of threat theory opens up the possibility for a debate on what factors are the most important causes of threat perception, that challenge has been largely ignored. If work on the balancing behavior of states is to proceed, the challenge of investigating the factors that lead to threat perception will have to be met. My hope is that the definition of balancing behavior proposed here, by separating out more clearly the process of threat perception from the response to threat, will encourage more investigation into the factors that lead to threat perception. It should also facilitate investigation into whether different kinds of threats elicit different kinds of responses from states.
63. Elman conflates "neorealist" with "systemic" when he argues that the inclusion of variables from the domestic or individual level removes an analysis from the "neorealist" camp. Elman, "Why *Not* A Neorealist Theory of Foreign Policy?," 38–39. A model of balancing behavior that includes domestic or individual variables may still be "neorealist" if it incorporates a neorealist understanding of how the constraints of the international system shape the incentives and opportunities available to states. For example, in a neorealist model of balancing behavior, expectations about threat perception would be derived from neorealism's understanding of how anarchy constrains states to be concerned with relative gains and provides incentives for states to seek self-sufficiency.
64. Walt *Origins*, 22; Haggard, "Structuralism and Its Critics," 420–21; see also Walt, "Alliance Formation and the Balance of World Power"; Walt, "Testing Theories of Alliance Formation"; and Walt, "Alliance Formation in Southwest Asia: Balancing and Bandwagoning in Cold War Competition" in *Dominoes and Bandwagons*, ed. Robert Jervis and Jack Snyder (New York: Oxford University Press, 1991), 51–84. Although Elman argues that Walt's balance of threat approach is an example of an exhaustive structural theory, he notes "some critics

claim that Walt brings domestic variables in through the back door by including 'aggressive intentions' in the definition of threat." Elman, "Why *Not* a Neorealist Theory of Foreign Policy?," 33, footnote 82; see also Haggard, "Structuralism and Its Critics," 420–22.

65. Levy, "Theoretical Foundations," 726–27; Schroeder, "Historical Reality," 133. It is important to note that while many of Schroeder's insights can serve as the basis for hypotheses within the model of balancing presented earlier, his challenge to neorealism does extend beyond this model. His notions of "system" and "political equilibrium" suggest that international politics, at least in the nineteenth century, worked in a fundamentally different way than suggested by neorealism and the systemic theory, which serves as the basis for my model of balancing behavior. Schroeder presents a picture of states bound together in some sort of community; he argues that it was not the distribution of power but "political equilibrium" that mattered, and "subjectively political equilibrium meant the enjoyment of stability, peace, and guaranteed rights; freedom from threats and isolation; the recognition of one's legitimate interests, sphere of influence, and the right to a voice in general affairs; and especially for the great powers, assurance of equality in rank, status, and dignity, even if not in power." Schroeder, "The Nineteenth Century System: Balance of Power or Political Equilibrium," 144 and 143.
66. Powell, *In the Shadow of Power*, 149–96.
67. Christensen and Snyder, "Chain Gangs," 144. In response to Vasquez's critique of neorealist balance of power theory, Christensen and Snyder object to the classification of their article on "Chain Gangs" as a study of balancing behavior. Christensen and Snyder, "Progressive Research on Degenerate Alliances," 920. While it is true that they are exploring the "alliance maladies that complicate the balancing process," it is also true that when states chain gang they are overreacting to threat and balancing too tightly, while when they pass the buck they are failing to balance. So while the primary intention of Christensen and Snyder is not to study the conditions under which states balance, their argument has implications for such studies, and I therefore include technology, geography, and perception of strategic incentives as variables that may affect how states respond to threat.
68. Kaufman, "To Balance or Bandwagon?" Note that Kaufman explicitly calls for work that supplements "purely structural theories of alliances with variables from all three levels of analysis." Kaufman, "To Balance or Bandwagon?," 439.
69. Schweller, "Bandwagoning for Profit."
70. Haggard, "Structuralism and Its Critics," 49; Christensen and Snyder, "Chain Gangs," 137–38.

CHAPTER 5

The Security Dilemma and Ethnic Conflict

Barry R. Posen

The end of the Cold War has been accompanied by the emergence of nationalist, ethnic and religious conflict in Eurasia. However, the risks and intensity of these conflicts have varied from region to region: Ukrainians and Russians are still getting along relatively well; Serbs and Slovenians had a short, sharp clash; Serbs, Croats, and Bosnian Muslims have waged open warfare; and Armenians and Azeris seem destined to fight a slow-motion attrition war. The claim that newly released, age-old antipathies account for this violence, fails to explain the considerable variance in observable intergroup relations.

The purpose of this chapter is to apply a basic concept from the realist tradition of international relations theory, 'the security dilemma', to the special conditions that arise when proximate groups of people suddenly find themselves newly responsible for their own security. A group suddenly compelled to provide its own protection must ask the following questions about any neighbouring group; is it a threat? How much of a threat? Will the threat grow or diminish over time? Is there anything that must be done immediately? The answers to these questions strongly influence the chances for war.

This chapter assesses the factors that could produce an intense security dilemma when imperial order breaks down, thus producing an early resort to violence. The security dilemma is then employed to analyse two cases—the break-up of Yugoslavia and relations between Russia and Ukraine—to illustrate its utility. Finally, some actions are suggested to ameliorate the tendency towards violence.

Barry Posen. "The Security Dilemma and Ethnic Conflict." Survival. vol 35, no. 1, Spring 1993. pp. 27–47. Reprinted by permission of Oxford University Press.

The Security Dilemma

The collapse of imperial regimes can be profitably viewed as a problem of 'emerging anarchy'. The longest standing and most useful school of international relations theory—realism—explicitly addresses the consequences of anarchy—the absence of a sovereign—for political relations among states.[1] In areas such as the former Soviet Union or Yugoslavia, 'sovereigns' have disappeared. They leave in their wake a host of groups—ethnic, religious, cultural—of greater or lesser cohesion. These groups must pay attention to the first thing that states have historically addressed—the problem of security—even though many of these groups still lack many of the attributes of statehood.

Realist theory contends that the condition of anarchy makes security the first concern of states. It can be otherwise only if these political organizations do not care about their survival as independent entities. As long as some do care, there will be competition for the key to security—power. The competition will often continue to a point at which the competing entities have amassed more power than needed for security and, thus, consequently begin to threaten others. Those threatened will respond in turn.

Relative power is difficult to measure and is often subjectively appraised: what seems sufficient to one state's defence will seem, and will often be, offensive to its neighbours. Because neighbours wish to remain autonomous and secure, they will react by trying to strengthen their own positions. States can trigger these reactions even if they have no expansionist inclinations. This is the security dilemma: what one does to enhance one's own security causes reactions that, in the end, can make one less secure. Cooperation among states to mute these competitions can be difficult because someone else's 'cheating' may leave one in a militarily weakened position. All fear betrayal.

Often statesmen do not recognize that this problem exists: they do not empathize with their neighbours: they are unaware that their own actions can seem threatening. Often it does not matter if they know of this problem. The nature of their situation compels them to take the steps they do.

The security dilemma is particularly intense when two conditions hold. First, when offensive and defensive military forces are more or less identical, states cannot signal their defensive intent—that is, their limited objectives—by the kinds of military forces they choose to deploy. Any forces on hand are suitable for offensive campaigns. For example, many believe that armoured forces are the best means of defence against an attack by armoured forces. However, because armour has a great deal of offensive potential, states so outfitted cannot distinguish one another's intentions. They must assume the worst because the worst is possible.

A second condition arises from the effectiveness of the offense versus the defence. If offensive operations are more effective than defensive operations, states will choose the offensive if they wish to survive. This may encourage pre-emptive war in the event of a political crisis because the perceived superiority of the offensive creates incentives to strike first whenever war appears likely. In addition, in the situation in which offensive capability is strong, a modest superiority in numbers will appear to provide greatly increased prospects for military success. Thus, the offensive advantage can cause preventive war if a state achieves a military advantage, however fleeting.

The barriers to cooperation inherent in international politics provide clues to the problems that arise as central authority collapses in multiethnic empires. The security dilemma affects relations among these groups, just as it affects relations among states. Indeed, because these groups have the added problem of building new state structures from the wreckage of old empires, they are doubly vulnerable.

Here it is argued that the process of imperial collapse produces conditions that make offensive and defensive capabilities indistinguishable and make the offence superior to the defence. In addition, uneven progress in the formation of state structures will create windows of opportunity and vulnerability. These factors have a powerful influence on the prospects for conflict, regardless of the internal politics of the groups emerging from old empires. Analysts inclined to the view that most of the trouble lies elsewhere, either in the specific nature of group identities or in the short-term incentives for new leaders to 'play the nationalist card' to secure their power, need to understand the security dilemma and its consequences. Across the board, these strategic problems show that very little nationalist rabble-rousing or nationalistic combativeness is required to generate very dangerous situations.

The Indistinguishability of Offence and Defence

Newly independent groups must first determine whether neighbouring groups are a threat. They will examine one another's military capabilities to do so. Because the weaponry available to these groups will often be quite rudimentary, their offensive military capabilities will be as much a function of the quantity and commitment of the soldiers they can mobilize as the particular characteristics of the weapons they control. Thus, each group will have to assess the other's offensive military potential in terms of its cohesion and its past military record.

The nature of military technology and organization is usually taken to be the main factor affecting the distinguishability of offence and defence. Yet, clear distinctions between offensive and defensive capabilities are historically rare, and they are particularly difficult to make in the realm of land warfare. For example, the force structures of armed neutrals such as Finland, Sweden and Switzerland are often categorized as defensive. These countries rely more heavily on infantry, which is thought to have weak offensive potential, than on tanks and other mechanized weaponry, which are thought to have strong offensive potential. However, their weak offensive capabilities have also been a function of the massive military power of what used to be their most plausible adversary, the Soviet Union. Against states of similar size, similarly armed, all three countries would have considerable offensive capabilities—particularly if their infantries were extraordinarily motivated—as German and French infantry were at the outset of World War I as Chinese and North Vietnamese infantry were against the Americans and as Iran's infantry was against the Iraqis.

Ever since the French Revolution put the first politically motivated mass armies into the field, strong national identity has been understood by both scholars and practitioners to be a key ingredient of the combat power of armies.[2] A group identity helps the individual members cooperate to achieve their purposes. When humans can readily cooperate, the whole exceeds the sum of the parts, creating a unit stronger relative to those groups with a weaker identity. Thus, the 'groupness' of the ethnic, religious, cultural and linguistic collectives that emerge from collapsed empires gives each of them an inherent offensive military power.

The military capabilities available to newly independent groups will often be less sophisticated: infantry-based armies will be easy to organize, augmented by whatever heavier equipment is inherited or seized from the old regime. Their offensive potential will be stronger the more cohesive their sponsoring group appears to be. Particularly in the close quarters in which these groups often find themselves, the combination of infantry-based, or quasi-mechanized ground forces with strong group solidarity is likely to encourage groups to fear each other. Their capabilities will appear offensive.

The solidarity of the opposing group will strongly influence how each group assesses the magnitude of the military threat of the others. In general, however, it is quite difficult to perform such assessments. One expects these groups to be 'exclusive' and hence, defensive. Frenchmen generally do not want to turn Germans into Frenchmen, or the reverse. Nevertheless, the drive for security in one group can be so great that it produces near-genocidal behavior towards neighbouring groups. Because so much conflict has been identified with 'group' identity throughout history, those who emerge as the leaders of any group and who confront the task of self-defence for the first time will be sceptical that the strong group identity of others is benign.

What methods are available to the newly independent groups to assess the offensive implications of another's sense of identity?[3] The main mechanism that they will use is history: how did other groups behave the last time they were unconstrained? Is there a record of offensive military activity by the other? Unfortunately, the conditions under which this assessment occurs suggest that these groups are more likely to assume that their neighbours are dangerous than not.

The reason is that the historical reviews that new groups undertake rarely meet the scholarly standards that modern history and social science hold as norms (or at least as ideals) in the West. First, the recently departed multi-ethnic empires probably suppressed or manipulated the facts of previous rivalries to reinforce their own rule; the previous regimes in the Soviet Union and Yugoslavia lacked any systemic commitment to truth in historical scholarship. Second, the members of these various groups no doubt did not forget the record of their old rivalries; it was preserved in oral history. This history was undoubtedly magnified in the telling and was seldom subjected to critical appraisal. Third, because their history is mostly oral, each group has a difficult time divining another's view of the past. Fourth, as central authority begins to collapse and local politicians begin to struggle for power, they will begin to write down their versions of history in political speeches. Yet, because the purpose of speeches is domestic political mobilization, these stories are likely to be emotionally charged.

The result is a worst-case analysis. Unless proven otherwise, one group is likely to assume that another group's sense of identity, and the cohesion that it produces, is a danger. Proving it to be otherwise is likely to be very difficult. Because the cohesion of one's own group is an essential means of defence against the possible depredations of neighbours, efforts to reinforce cohesion are likely to be undertaken. Propagandists are put to work writing a politicized history of the group, and the mass media are directed to disseminate that history. The media may either willingly, or under compulsion, report unfolding events in terms that magnify the threat to the group. As neighboring groups observe this, they do the same.

In sum, the military capability of groups will often be dependent on their cohesion, rather than their meagre military assets. This cohesion is a threat in its own right because it can provide the emotional power for infantry armies to take the offensive. An historical record of large-scale armed clashes, much less wholesale mistreatment of unarmed civilians, however subjective, will further the tendency for groups to see other groups as threats. They will all simultaneously 'arm'—militarily and ideologically—against each other.

The Superiority of Offensive over Defensive Action

Two factors have generally been sees as affecting the superiority of offensive over defensive action—technology and geography. Technology is usually treated as a universal variable, which affects the military capabilities of all the states in a given competition. Geography is a situational variable, which makes offence particularly appealing to specific states for specific reasons. This is what matters most when empires collapse.

In the rare historical cases in which technology has clearly determined the offence–defence balance, such as World War I, soldiers and statesmen have often failed to appreciate its impact. Thus, technology need not be examined further, with one exception; nuclear weapons. If a group inherits a nuclear deterrent, and its neighbours do as well, 'groupness' is not likely to affect the security dilemma with as much intensity as would be the case in non-nuclear cases. Because group solidarity would not contribute to the ability of either side to mount a counterforce nuclear attack, nationalism is less important from a military standpoint in a nuclear relationship.

Political geography will frequently create an 'offence-dominant world' when empires collapse. Some groups will have greater offensive capabilities because they will effectively surround some or all of the other groups. These other groups may be forced to adopt offensive strategies to break the ring of encirclement. Islands of one group's population are often stranded in a sea of another. Where one territorially concentrated group has 'islands' of settlement of its members distributed across the nominal territory of another group (irredenta), the protection of these islands in the event of hostile action can seem extremely difficult. These islands may not be able to help one another; they may be subject to blockade and siege, and by virtue of their numbers relative to the surrounding population and because of topography, they may be militarily indefensible. Thus, the brethren of the stranded group may come to believe that only rapid offensive military action can save their irredenta from a horrible fate.[4]

The geographic factor is a variable, not a constant. Islands of population can be quite large, economically autonomous and militarily defensible. Alternatively, they can have large numbers of nearby brethren who form a powerful state, which could rescue them in the event of trouble. Potentially, hostile groups could have islands of another group's people within their states; these islands could serve as hostages. Alternatively, the brethren of the 'island' group could deploy nuclear weapons and thus punish the surrounding group if they misbehave. In short, it might be possible to defend irredenta without attacking or to deter would-be aggressors by threatening to retaliate in one way or another.

Isolated ethnic groups—ethnic islands—can produce incentives for preventive war. Theorists argue that perceived offensive advantages make preventive war more attractive: if one side has an advantage that will not be present later and if security can best be achieved by offensive military action in any case, then leaders will be inclined to attack during this 'window of opportunity'.[5] For example, if a surrounding population will ultimately be able to fend off relief attacks from the home territory of an island group's brethren, but is currently weak, then the brethren will be inclined to attack sooner rather than later.

In disputes among groups interspersed in the same territory, another kind of offensive advantage exists—a tactical offensive advantage. Often the goal of the disputants is to create ever-growing areas of homogeneous population for their brethren. Therefore, the other group's population must be induced to leave. The Serbs have introduced the term 'ethnic cleansing' to describe this objective, a term redolent with the horrors of 50 years earlier. The offence has tremendous tactical military advantages in operations such as these. Small military forces directed against unarmed or poorly armed civilians can generate tremendous terror. This has always been true, of course, but even simple modern weapons, such as machine guns and mortars, increase the havoc that small bands of fanatics can wreak against the defenceless. Consequently, small bands of each group have an incentive to attack the towns of the other in the hopes of driving the people away.[6] This is often quite successful, as the vast populations of war refugees in the world today attest.

The vulnerability of civilians makes it possible for small bands of fanatics to initiate conflict. Because they are small and fanatical, these bands are hard to control. (This allows the political leadership of the group to deny responsibility for the actions those bands take.) These activities produce disproportionate political results among the opposing group—magnifying initial fears by confirming them. The presence or absence of small gangs of fanatics is thus itself a key determinant of the ability of groups to avoid war as central political authority erodes. Although almost every society produces small numbers of people willing to engage in violence at any given moment, the rapid emergence of organized bands of particularly violent individuals is a sure sign of trouble.

The characteristic behaviour of international organizations, especially the United Nations (UN), reinforces the incentives for offensive action. Thus far, the UN has proven itself unable to anticipate conflict and provide the credible security guarantees that would mitigate the security dilemma. Once there is politically salient trouble in an area, the UN may try to intervene to 'keep the peace'. However, the conditions under which peacekeeping is attempted are favourable to the party that has had the most military success. As a general rule, the UN does not make peace: it negotiates cease-fires. Two parties in dispute generally agree to a cease-fire only because one is successful and is happy with its gains, while the other has lost, but fears even worse to come. Alternatively, the two sides have fought to a bloody stalemate and would like to rest. The UN thus protects, and to some extent legitimates, the military gains of the winning side, or gives both a respite to recover. This approach by the international community to intervention in ethnic conflict, helps create an incentive for offensive military operations.

Windows of Vulnerability and Opportunity

Where central authority has recently collapsed, the groups emerging from an old empire must calculate their power relative to each other at the time of collapse and make a guess about their relative power in the future. Such calculations must account for a variety of factors. Objectively, only one side can be better off. However, the complexity of these situations makes it possible for many competing groups to believe that their prospects in a war would be better earlier, rather than later. In addition, if the geographic situation creates incentives of the kind discussed earlier, the temptation to capitalize on these windows of opportunity may be great. These windows may also prove tempting to those who wish to expand for other reasons.

The relative rate of state formation strongly influences the incentives for preventive war. When central authority has collapsed or is collapsing, the groups emerging from the political rubble will try to form their own states. These groups must choose leaders, set up bureaucracies to collect taxes and provide services, organize police forces for internal security and organize military forces for external security. The material remnants of the old state (especially weaponry, foreign currency reserves, raw material stocks and industrial capabilities) will be unevenly distributed across the territories of the old empire. Some groups may have had a privileged position in the old system. Others will be less well placed.

The states formed by these groups will thus vary greatly in their strength. This will provide immediate military advantages to those who are farther along in the process of state formation. If those with greater advantages expect to remain in that position by virtue of their superior numbers, then they may see no window of opportunity. However, if they expect their advantage to wane or disappear, then they will have an incentive to solve outstanding issues while they are much stronger than the opposition.

This power differential may create incentives for preventive expropriation, which can generate a spiral of action and reaction. With military resources unevenly distributed and perhaps artificially scarce for some due to arms embargoes, cash shortages or constrained access to the outside world, small caches of armaments assume large importance. Any military depot will be a tempting target, especially for the poorly armed. Better armed groups also have a huge strong incentive to seize these weapons because this would increase their margin of superiority.

In addition, it matters whether or not the old regime imposed military conscription on all groups in society. Conscription makes arms theft quite easy because hijackers know what to look for and how to move it. Gains are highly cumulative because each side can quickly integrate whatever it steals into its existing forces. High cumulativity of conquered resources has often motivated states in the past to initiate preventive military actions.

Expectations about outside intervention will also affect preventive war calculations. Historically, this usually meant expectations about the intervention of allies on one sides or the other, and the value of such allies. Allies may be explicit or tacit. A group may expect itself or another to find friends abroad. It may calculate that the other group's natural allies are temporarily preoccupied, or a group may calculate that it or its adversary has many other adversaries who will attack in the event of conflict. The greater the number of potential allies for all groups, the more complex this calculation will be and the greater the chance for error. Thus, two opposing groups could both think that the expected behaviour of others makes them stronger in the short term.

A broader window-of-opportunity problem has been created by the large number of crises and conflicts that have been precipitated by the end of the Cold War. The electronic media provides free global strategic intelligence about these problems to anyone with the price of a short-wave radio, much less a satellite dish. Middle and great powers, and international organizations, are able to deal with only a small number of crises simultaneously. States that wish to initiate offensive military actions, but fear outside opposition, may move quickly if they learn that international organizations and great powers are preoccupied momentarily with other problems.

Croats and Serbs

Viewed through the lens of the security dilemma, the early stages of Yugoslavia's disintegration were strongly influenced by the following factors. First, the parties identified the re-emerging identities of the others as offensive threats. The last time these groups were free of constraint, during World War II, they slaughtered one another with abandon. In addition, the Yugoslav military system trained most men for war, and distributed infantry armament widely across the country. Second, the offensive appeared to have the advantage, particularly against Serbs 'marooned' in Croatian and Muslim territory. Third, the new republics were not equally powerful. Their power assets varied in terms of people and economic resources; access to the wealth and military assets of the previous regime; access to external allies; and possible outside enemies. Preventive war incentives were consequently high. Fourth, Small bands of fanatics soon appeared on the scene. Indeed, the political and military history of the region stressed the role of small, violent, committed groups; the resistance to the Turks; the Ustashe in the 1930s; and the Ustashe state and Serbian Chetniks during World War II.

Serbs and Croats both have a terrifying oral history of each other's behaviour. This history goes back hundreds of years, although the intense Croat–Serb conflict is only about 125 years old. The history of the region is quite warlike; the area was the frontier of the Habsburg and Turkish empires, and Croatia had been an integral part of the military apparatus of the Hapsburg empire. The imposition of harsh Hungarian rule in Croatia in 1868; the Hungarian divide-and-conquer strategy that pitted Croats and Serbs in Croatia against each other; the rise of the independent Serbian nation-state out of the Ottoman empire, formally recognized in Europe in 1878; and Serbian pretensions to speak for all south Slavs were the main origins of the Croat–Serb conflict. When Yugoslavia was formed after World War I, the Croats had a very different vision of the state than the Serbs. They hoped for a confederal system, while the Serbs planned to develop a centralized nation-state.[7] The Croats did not perceive themselves to be treated fairly under this arrangement, and this helped stimulate the development of a violent resistance movement, the Ustashe, which collaborated with the Fascist powers during the 1930s.

The Serbs had some reasons for assuming the worst about the existence of an independent Croatian state, given Croatian behaviour during World War II. Ustashe leadership was established in Croatia by Nazi Germany. The Serbs, both communist and non-communist, fought the Axis forces, including the Croats, and each other. (Some Croats also fought in Josef Tito's communist partisan movement against the Nazis.) Roughly a million people died in the fighting—some 5.9 per cent of Yugoslavia's pre-war population.[8] The Croats behaved with extraordinary brutality towards the Serbs, who suffered nearly 500,000 dead, more than twice as many dead as the Croats.[9] (Obviously, the Germans were responsible for many Serbian deaths as well.) Most of these were not killed in battle; they were civilians murdered in large-scale terrorist raids.

The Croats themselves suffered some 200,000 dead in World War II, which suggests that depredations were inflicted on many sides. (The non-communist, 'nationalist' Chetniks were among the most aggressive killers of Croats, which helps explain why the new Croatian republic is worried by the nationalist rhetoric of the new Serbian republic.) Having lived in a pre- and post-war Yugoslavia largely dominated by Serbs, the Croats had reason to suspect that the demise of the Yugoslavian Communist Party would be followed by a Serbian bid for hegemony. In 1971, the Croatian Communist Party had been purged of leaders who had favoured greater autonomy. In addition, the historical record of the Serbs during the past 200 years is one of regular efforts to establish an ever larger centralized Serbian national state on the Balkan Peninsula. Thus, Croats had sufficient reason to fear the Serbs.

Serbs in Croatia were scattered in a number of vulnerable islands; they could only be 'rescued' by offensive action from Serbia. Such a rescue, of course, would have been enormously complicated by an independent Bosnia, which in part explains the Serbian war there. In addition, Serbia could not count on maintaining absolute military superiority over the Croats forever; almost twice as many Serbs as Croats inhabit the territory of what was once Yugoslavia, but Croatia is slightly wealthier than Serbia.[10] Croatia also has some natural allies within former Yugoslavia, especially Bosnian Muslims, and seemed somewhat more adept at winning allies abroad. As Croatia adopted the trappings of statehood and achieved international recognition, its military power was expected to grow. From the Serbian point of view, Serbs in Croatia were insecure and expected to become more so as time went by.

From a military point of view, the Croats probably would have been better off postponing their secession until after they had made additional military preparations. However, their experience in 1971, more recent political developments and the military preparations of the Yugoslav army probably convinced them that the Serbs were about to strike and that the Croatian leadership would be rounded up and imprisoned or killed if they did not act quickly.

Each side not only had to assess the other's capabilities, but also its intentions, and there were plenty of signals of malign intent. Between 1987 and

1990, Slobodan Milosevic ended the administrative autonomy within Serbia that had been granted to Kosovo and Vojvodina in the 1974 constitution.[11] In August 1990, Serbs in the Dalmatia region of Croatia held a cultural autonomy referendum, which they defended with armed roadblocks against expected Croatian interference.[12] By October, the Yugoslav army began to impound all of the heavy weapons stored in Croatia for the use of the territorial defence forces, thus securing a vast military advantage over the nascent armed forces of the republic.[13] The Serbian window of opportunity, already large, grew larger. The Croats accelerated their own military preparations.

It is difficult to tell just how much interference the Croats planned, if any, in the referendum in Dalmatia. However, Croatia had stoked the fires of Serbian secessionism with a series of ominous rulings. In the spring of 1990, Serbs in Croatia were redefined as a minority, rather than a constituent nation, and were asked to take a loyalty oath. Serbian police were to be replaced with Croats, as were some local Serbian officials. No offer of cultural autonomy was made at the time. These Croatian policies undoubtedly intensified Serbian fears about the future and further tempted them to exploit their military superiority.

It appears that the Croats overestimated the reliability and influence of the Federal Republic of Germany as an ally due to some combination of World War II history, the widespread misperception created by the European media and by Western political leaders of Germany's near-superpower status, the presumed influence of the large Croatian émigré community in Germany and Germany's own diplomacy, which was quite favourable to Croatia even before its June 1991 declaration of independence.[14] This considerations may have encouraged Croatia to secede. Conversely, Serbian propaganda was quick to stress the German–Croatian connection and to speculate on future German ambitions in the Balkans.[15] Fair or not, this prospect would have had an impact on Serbia's preventive war calculus.

Russia and Ukraine

Through the lens of the security dilemma, several important factors in Russian–Ukrainian relations can be identified that suggest that the potential for conflict is not as great as for Yugoslavia. First, the propensity of Russians and Ukrainians to view one another's cohesion as an offensive military threat is slight. A principal stabilizing factor here is the presence of former Soviet nuclear forces in both Russia and Ukraine, which provides each republic with a powerful deterrent. Second, each side's perception of the other's 'identity' is comparatively benign. Third, settlement patterns create comparatively less pressure for offensive action. These three factors reduce the pressure for preventive war.[16]

The nuclear forces of the former Soviet Union—both those clearly under Commonwealth (effectively Russian) control and those with a more ambiguous status in Ukraine—have probably helped stabilize Russian–Ukrainian relations. This is because nuclear weapons make it dangerous for either to launch a campaign of violence against the other. Mutual deterrence prevails. In a clash of wills between two nuclear-armed states about attacks on minority populations, the state representing the interests of the victims would have more credibility; it would be the defender of the *status quo*. The potential military consequences of each side's 'groupness' is thus muted.

Most of the Soviet nuclear forces came under the control of the Russian Republic, thereby rendering large-scale anti-Russian violence in Ukraine very risky. The presence of large numbers of nuclear weapons on Ukrainian soil gives Ukraine a nuclear 'threat that leaves something to chance'. Although these weapons are believed to remain under the technical control of the Commonwealth (Russian) command structure, military action by Russians against Ukraine could precipitate a Ukrainian attempt to seize these weapons. Given the significant representation of Ukrainians in the Soviet officer and non-commissioned officer corps, it is quite likely that there are many Ukrainians who know a lot about nuclear weapons, making their seizure quite plausible. This would be a novel kind of nuclear crisis, but it would probably be enough of a crisis to produce the prudent behavior among nuclear powers that existed during the Cold War. An overt nationalist political campaign in Russia for action against Ukraine could also provoke Ukrainian seizure of these weapons.

Russian and Ukrainian histories of each other, as well as their past relations, are less terrifying than those found among groups within the former Yugoslavia. There is no record of large-scale Russian–Ukrainian military rivalry and no clear, salient incident of nationalist bloodletting. However, one dangerous historical episode could play a significant role in the development of an anti-Russian, Ukrainian history; the communist war on independent farmers and its concomitant famine in 1930–32 killed millions.[17] If Ukrainians begin to blame the famine on Russians, this would be quite dangerous politically. If, instead, the famine continues to be blamed on a Communist Party headed by a renegade Georgian psychopath, then this experience will cause less trouble. Ukrainian President Leonid Kravchuk, in his public utterances, tends to portray the Bolsheviks, not the Russians, as the culprit.[18]

That the famine has not played a large role in Ukrainian nationalist rhetoric is a good sign, but this event provides potential tinder. Russian nationalists should therefore be very careful how they portray future Russian–Ukrainian relations. If they project a subordinate status for Ukraine, then Ukrainian nationalists will have a strong incentive to portray the famine as a Russian crime in their effort to build cohesion to resist Russian domination. *Izvestia* reports that Sergei Baburin, leader of the Russian Unity bloc in the Russian parliament, informed the Ukrainain ambassador that 'either Ukraine reunites again with Russia or there will be war.'[19] Such statements will be heard and acted upon in Ukraine.

It is difficult for Ukrainian nationalists to argue convincingly that they were exploited by Russia.[20] Ukrainians seem to have achieved at least proportional representation in the Soviet governing and military apparatus.[21] They produced a share of Soviet gross national product (GNP) more than proportional to their share of population, and the kinds of goods they produced suggest that Ukraine enjoyed a fair share of industrial investment.[22] Ukrainian nationalists assert, however, that the Soviet Union extracted substantial economic resources from Ukraine—perhaps as much as half of Ukrainian GNP.[23]

Of greater importance, Ukrainian nationalists believe and many scholars agree that both the Russian empire and the later Soviet Union did everything possible to retard the growth of an independent Ukrainian identity and to Russify Ukraine. This experience led to the reassertion of Ukraine's cultural and political identity.[24] Alarmingly, *Rukh*, the main pro-independence party in Ukraine, has apparently drifted towards a more virulent nationalism, one that portrays Russia and Russians as the enemy.[25]

These worrisome signs must be put in context, however. In general, ethnic hatred has not played a great role in Ukrainian efforts to define their state. Initially, both of the large political parties in Ukraine tried to accommodate all groups in the country. There is no record of Ukrainian persecution of resident Russians. The Ukrainians and the Russians living in the eastern part of the country have had amicable relations for a great many years. A majority of Russians voted for Ukrainian independence. There are no reports of Ukrainian nationalist gangs operating against Russians.[26]

The history of relations between Russians and Ukrainians is thus conducive to peace. Neither has strong reasons to assume that the other's 'groupness' constitutes a strong offensive threat to its survival. That said, Russian–Ukrainian political history is conducive to Ukrainian mistrust, and the famine is a singular historical episode that could prove very problematic.

The security situation between the two republics is favourable from a stability standpoint. The 12 million Russians in the Ukraine (who constitute 21% of the population) are not settled in small vulnerable islands; many of the areas of settlement are proximate to each other and to the Russian border. Others are proximate to the Black Sea coast, which may help explain the intensity of the dispute over the ultimate disposition of the Black Sea Fleet. Large numbers of Russians are still to be found in the armed forces of the newly independent Ukraine, complicating any Ukrainian state action against resident Russians. The expulsion of Russians from the eastern Ukraine would thus be a tough job for the Ukrainians. Russia is also a nuclear power and thus in a position to make credible threats to protect the safety of its own. In addition, the proximity of many Ukrainian Russians to the border of the Russian Republic would facilitate a conventional rescue operation, should that prove necessary. The fact that Russia has at least three times the population, wealth and probable conventional combat power of Ukraine would favour such a rescue. In sum, Russia is not forced to take offensive conventional action to protect its nationals in Ukraine. Because Russians can probably protect their brethren in the Ukraine later, they have only limited incentives to solve the problem now.

To say that the Russians can protect their brethren, however, is not to say that military intervention in Ukraine would be cheap or safe. The Ukrainians inherited ample stocks of armaments from the Soviet Union; the Ukrainian presence in the Soviet military made fatuous any Russian thoughts of spiriting away this vast quantity of military equipment and guarantees that the Ukrainian military will know how to use the weaponry in its possession.[27] Efforts to coerce Ukraine would likely precipitate Ukrainian efforts to seize nuclear weapons now within its territory. Thus, although Russia clearly has the power to protect Ukrainian Russians in the event of oppression, lacking such a provocation, Russian nationalists would have great difficulty convincing their compatriots that Ukraine is ripe for the picking.

Finally, unlike Yugoslavia external factors reinforce restraint in Russian–Ukrainian relations. Because they are quite close to Western Europe and heavily armed, it is reasonable for Russians and Ukrainians to assume that conflict between the two republics would be condemned by outside powers. Each side has reason to fear being branded the aggressor in such a conflict because the U.S. and the Europeans lack any deep organic ties to either Russia or Ukraine. Thus, Western diplomacy should encourage even-handedness towards the two parties. Thus far, the West has shown a tendency to patronize the Ukrainians and dote on the Russians; this is a mistake. It would be better for both to believe that whoever was labelled the aggressor in a Russian–Ukrainian conflict could end up earning the enmity of the wealthiest and most powerful coalition of powers in the history of the world.

In sum, although there are some danger signs in Russian–Ukrainian relations, the security dilemma is not particularly intense in this case. To the extent that Western powers have an interest in peace between these two powers, efforts should be made to preserve this favourable state of affairs.

Comparison Summary

A brief review of these two cases highlights the factors that favoured war in Yugoslavia and that still favour peace in Russian–Ukrainian relations. This comparison also identifies some early warning indicators that should be monitored regarding Russia and Ukraine.

In Yugoslavia, Croats and Serbs found each other's identity a threat because of the primitive military capabilities they could field and the terrible record of their historical relationship. In the Russia–Ukraine case, nuclear weapons mute the conventional competition, making group cohesion less of a military asset. If Ukraine eliminates its nuclear arsenal, as it has pledged to do, it will increasingly come to rely on nationalism to strengthen an army that will only be able to stand against Russia through superior motivation. Eliminating Ukraine's nuclear arsenal will therefore make Russia stronger and Ukraine more nationalistic. This could prove dangerous.

In Yugoslavia, Serbs in Croatia were militarily vulnerable, and Serbs in Serbia had only one way to defend them—a speedy, powerful offensive. Russians in Ukraine are less geographically isolated and can be protected in several ways: Russians in Ukraine may be able to defend themselves by virtue of their numbers and their presence in the Ukrainian army; Russia itself could make nuclear threats; and the Russian army will probably maintain a marked quantitative superiority over Ukraine, which would facilitate a counter-offensive rescue operation, should one be needed. Systematic de-Russification of the Ukrainian armed forces, accompanied by a precipitate decline in Russia's military capabilities, would therefore be a sign of trouble in Russian–Ukrainian relations.

Although Ukrainians and Russians in the eastern Ukraine do live together, no violent bands have emerged and begun to engage in intercommunal terror. In Yugoslavia, such bands emerged early in the dissolution process. It may be that the Russian presence in the Ukrainian army has helped discourage such developments, or it may be that there are enough lawless places in the former Soviet Union to absorb those prone to violence. Aspiring Croatian and Serbian thugs had no other outlet for their violent inclinations. The appearance of small Russian or Ukrainian terrorist groups could have a powerful incendiary effect on relations between the two republics and would thus indicate trouble.

In Yugoslavia, the Serbs had many incentives for preventive war. They outnumbered the Croats by only two to one and enjoyed no economic advantage. The Croats were likely to find allies within the former Yugoslavia. They were also likely to find allies abroad. Serbia was less well placed. Serbia enjoyed privileged access to the spoils of Yugoslavia, so it was initially much more powerful militarily than Croatia. The combination of dependence on an offensive to protect brethren in Croatia, and a temporary but wide military advantage, proved to be too large a temptation to resist.

The Russians have few incentives for preventive war. With three times the human and material resources of Ukraine, it is unlikely that the balance of military power will soon shift against them, nor does it seem likely that Ukraine will be better than Russia at finding allies abroad. Ukrainian pledges to become a non-nuclear state make it attractive even for nationalist Russians to postpone aggression until later; making war now would be a risky proposition. If Ukraine's economy recovers much more quickly than Russia's, or if Ukraine finds powerful allies abroad while Russia finds itself isolated, or if Russia begins to fear that endless border wars will tie down many of its forces in the future, Russians might begin to think more about preventive action against Ukraine.

Even if many of the factors that currently favour peace change, Russia's possession of nuclear weapons should continue to mute its incentives for defensively motivated, preventive conventional war. It should be noted, however, that nuclear powers have a tendency to solve security problems conventionally—when they could—during the Cold War.

Conclusion

Three main conclusions follow from the preceding analysis. First, the security dilemma and realist international relations theory more generally have considerable ability to explain and predict the probability and intensity of military conflict among groups emerging from the wreckage of empires.

Second, the security dilemma suggests that the risks associated with these conflicts are quite high. Several of the causes of conflict and war highlighted by the security dilemma operate with considerable intensity among the groups emerging from empires. The kind of military power that these groups can initially develop and their competing versions of history will often produce mutual fear and competition. Settlement patterns, in conjunction with unequal and shifting power, will often produce incentives for preventive war. The cumulative effect of conquered resources will encourage preventive grabs of military equipment and other assets.

Finally, if outsiders wish to understand and perhaps reduce the odds of conflict, they must assess the local groups' strategic view of their situation. Which groups fear for their physical security and why? What military options are open to them? By making these groups feel less threatened and by reducing the salience of windows of opportunity, the odds of conflict may be reduced.

Because the international political system as a whole remains a self-help system, it will be difficult to act on such calculations. Outsiders rarely have major material or security interests at stake in regional disputes. It is difficult for international institutions to threaten credibly in advance to intervene, on humanitarian grounds, to protect groups that fear for the future. Vague humanitarian commitments will not make vulnerable groups feel safe and will probably not deter those who wish to repress them. In some cases, however, such commitments may be credible because the conflict has real security implications for powerful outside actors.

Groups drifting into conflict should be encouraged to discuss their individual histories of mutual relations. Competing versions of history should be reconciled if possible. Domestic policies that raise bitter memories of perceived past injustices or depredations should be examined. This exercise need not be managed by an international political institution; nongovernmental organizations could play a role. Discussions about regional history would be an intelligent use of the resources of many foundations. A few conferences will not, of course, easily undo generations of hateful, politicized history, bolstered by reams of more recent propaganda. The exercise would cost little and, therefore, should be tried.[28]

In some cases, outside powers could threaten not to act; this would discourage some kinds of aggressive behaviour. For example, outside powers could make clear that if a new state abuses a minority and then gets itself into a war with that minority and its allies, the abuser will find little sympathy abroad if it begins to lose. To accomplish this, however, outside powers must have a way of detecting mistreatment of minorities.

In other cases, it may be reasonable for outside powers to provide material resources, including armaments, to help groups protect themselves. However, this kind of hard-bitten policy is politically difficult for liberal democratic governments now dominating world politics to pursue, even on humanitarian grounds. In addition, it is an admittedly complicated game in its own right because it is difficult to determine the amount and type of military assistance needed to produce effective defensive forces, but not offensive capabilities. Nevertheless, considerable diplomatic leverage may be attained by the threat to supply armaments to one side or the other.

Non-proliferation policy also has a role to play. In some cases, nuclear weaponry may be an effective way of protecting the weak from the strong. Russia may behave with considerable restraint towards Ukraine as long as some nuclear weapons remain on Ukrainian territory, vulnerable to Ukrainian seizure. However, once the last weapon is gone, Russian nationalists may become much more assertive.

The future balance of power between Ukraine and Russia is less conducive to good relations than the current one, which is the reason Ukrainians have sought Western security guarantees as a *quid pro quo* for ratifying the Strategic Arms Reduction Talks (START) Treaty, for adhering to the Nuclear Non-Proliferation Treaty and for ridding themselves of nuclear weapons. Absent such guarantees and the measures needed to render them credible. Ukrainians can be expected to prolong the 'transition' phase to the non-nuclear status that they have promised.[29] It would be politically difficult for the U.S. to reverse the arms control initiatives already launched, but it is reasonable to stretch out their implementation. Recent suggestions to accelerate the denuclearization of Ukraine (and Belarus and Kazakhstan), therefore, have it exactly backwards.[30] The West should hold Ukraine to a steady, proportional withdrawal schedule over the longest period consistent with the prescribed outline of the START I agreement. Some of the benefits of nuclear deterrence could thus be secured during the coming difficult political and economic transition in Russia and Ukraine.

It will frequently prove impossible, however, to arrange military assets, external political commitments and political expectations so that all neighbouring groups are relatively secure and perceive themselves as such. War is then likely. These wars will confirm and intensify all the fears that led to their initiation. Their brutality will tempt outsiders to intervene, but peace efforts originating from the outside will be unsuccessful if they do not realistically address the fears that triggered the conflicts initially. In most cases, this will require a willingness to commit large numbers of troops and substantial amounts of military equipment to troubled areas for a long time.

Notes

I would like to thank Robert Art. John Mearsheimer, Steve Meyer, Harvey Sapolsky, Jack Snyder, and Steve Van Evera for comments. Daryl Press served ably as my research assistant. The 1992 annual summer conference of Harvard University's Olin Center for Strategic Studies provided the first opportunity to present these ideas. The Carnegie Corporation of New York funded release time.

1. The following realist literature is essential for those interested in the analysis of ethnic conflict: Kenneth Waltz. *Theory of International Politics* (Reading, MA: Addison Wesley, 1979), chapters 6 and 8; Robert Jervis, 'Cooperation Under the Security Dilemma', *World Politics*, no. 2 January 1978, pp. 167–213; Robert Jervis, *Perception and Misperception in International Politics* (Princeton, NJ: Princeton University Press, 1976), chapter 3; Thomas C. Schelling, *Arms and Influence* (New Haven, CT: Yale University Press, 1966, 1976), chapters 1 and 6.
2. See Carl Von Clausewitz, *On War* (Princeton, NJ: Princeton University Press, 1984), pp. 591–92; Robert Gilpin. 'The Richness of the Tradition of Political Realism', in Robert E. Keohane. *Neorealism and Its Critics* (New York: Columbia University Press, 1986) pp. 300–21, especially pp. 304–08.
3. This problem shades into an assessment of 'intentions,' another very difficult problem for states in international politics. This issue is treated as a capabilities problem because the emergence of anarchy forces leaders to focus on military potential, rather than on intentions. Under these conditions, every group will ask whether neighbouring groups have the cohesion, morale and martial spirit to take the offensive if their leaders call on them to do so.
4. It is plausible that the surrounding population will view irredenta in their midst as an offensive threat by the outside group. They may be perceived as a 'fifth column', that must be controlled, repressed or even expelled.
5. See Stephen Van Evera. 'The Cult of the Offensive and the Origins of the First World War'. *International Security*, vol. 9, no. 1. Summer 1984, pp. 58–107.
6. Why do they not go to the defence of their own, rather than attack the other? Here, it is hypothesized that such groups are scarce relative to the number of target towns and villages, so they cannot 'defend' their own with any great confidence.
7. James Gow, 'Deconstructing Yugoslavia', *Survival*, vol. 33, no. 4, July/August 1991, p. 292; J. B. Hoptner, *Yugoslavia in Crisis 1934–1941* (New York: Columbia University Press, 1962), pp. 1–9.
8. Ivo Banac, 'Political Change and National Diversity', *Daedalus*, vol. 119, no. 1, Winter 1990, pp. 145–50, estimates that 487,000 Serbs, 207,000 Croats, 86,000 Bosnian Muslims and 60,000 Jews died in Yugoslavia during the war.
9. Aleksa Djilas, *The Contested Country* (Cambridge, MA: Harvard University Press, 1991), pp. 103–28. See especially, chapter 4, 'The National State and Genocide: The Ustasha Movement, 1929–1945', especially pp. 120–27, which vividly describes large-scale Croatian murders of Serbs, as well as Jews and Gypsies: however, Djilas does not explain how 200,000 Croats also died.
10. See Sabrina Ramet, *Nationalism and Federalism in Yugoslavia 1962–1991* (Bloomington, IN: Indiana University Press, 2nd ed., 1992), appendix 2, p. 286.
11. Gow, op. cit. in note 6, p. 294. Vojvodina contains the only petroleum and gas in Yugoslavia proximate to Serbia, so this act probably had a strategic motive; see Central Intelligence Agency, *Atlas of Eastern Europe* (Washington, DC: US Government Printing Office, August 1990), p. 10.

12. International Institute for Strategic Studies, *Strategic Survey 1990–1991*, (London: Brassey's for the IISS, 1991), p. 167.
13. Gow, op. cit. in note 6, p. 299.
14. See John Newhouse, 'The diplomatic round', *The New Yorker*, 24 August 1992, especially p. 63. See also John Zametica, *The Yugoslav Conflict*, Adelphi Paper 270 (London: Brassey's for the IISS, 1992), pp. 63–65.
15. Ramet, op. cit. in note 10, p. 265.
16. Untangling the strategic from the purely nationalist aspects of the dispute about the Crimea is difficult. It is doubtful that Russian nationalists fear for the safety of Russians in Crimea because they are the clear majority there, and the Crimea is quite defensible. Russian nationalists want it because the conquest of the Crimea from the Turks is seen as a major Russian national achievement. It is likely that Ukrainians want to keep the Crimea because they fear that concessions on this point will lead to new Russian demands for territorial adjustments. Strategic elements are likely salient in both sides' calculus. Control of Crimea and the Black Sea Fleet would give Russia military dominance of the Ukraine's seaborne trade from Odessa.
17. Norman Stone, 'The Mark of History', *The National Interest*, vol. 27. Spring 1992, p. 37 gives a figure of eight million dead in the famine.
18. See interviews with Ukrainian President Leonid Kravchuk in *Le Figaro*, 23 January 1992 as quoted in Foreign Broadcast Information Service (hereafter FBIS), 27 January 1992 and in *Der Spiegel*, 3 February 1992, as quoted in FBIS, 2 April 1992.
19. Quoted in Roman Solchanyk, 'The Crimean imbroglio: Kiev and Moscow', *Radio Free Europe/Radio Library Research Report*, vol. 1, no. 40, 9 October 1992.
20. Abraham Brumberg, 'Not so free at last', *New York Review of Books*, 22 October 1992, p. 62, suggests that many Ukrainians believe that Moscow always views Ukraine as '... a colony to be exploited'.
21. Ukrainians made up roughly one-quarter of the Soviet officer corps and were also well represented in the Communist Party. See Brian Taylor, 'Red Army Blues: The Future of Military Power in the Former Soviet Union.' *Breakthroughs*, vol. 2, no. 1. Spring 1992, pp. 1–8; Adrian Karatnycky, 'The Ukrainian Factor'. *Foreign Affairs*, vol. 71, no. 3, Summer 1992, p. 107.
22. Ukraine had about 18% of Soviet population and is said to have produced, '33 percent of televisions, 25 percent of computation and automation equipment, 22 percent of tractors, 31 percent of harvesters'. See Karatnycky, op. cit. in note 20, pp. 96–97. Julian Cooper suggests that some 17.5% of defence workers in the USSR were to be found in the Ukraine in the mid-1980s, and some 13.7% of defence firms. See tables 5 and 7 in 'Reconversion industrielle', *La Décomposition de l'Armée Soviétique*, Dossier No. 45 (Paris: FEDN, April 1992), pp. 151, 153.
23. Valeriy Semivolos. 'An Army for Ukraine', *Vecherniye novosti*, 20 July 1991, p. 3 (as translated in *Commonwealth of Independent States, A Journal of Selected Press*

Translations, vol. 2, no. 2, Spring 1992, pp. 33–34). Semivolos suggests that 100 billion rubles out of a Ukrainian GNP of 218.5 bn. went to Moscow.

24. Brumberg, op. cit. in note 20, p. 60.
25. Ibid., pp. 59–60.
26. The appearance of self-styled Cossacks, however, is a cause for concern, but so far they have not revealed specific anti-Russian tendencies.
27. Taylor, op. cit. in note 21, p. 3, suggests there were 20 divisions based in Ukraine and 4,000 nuclear warheads. There were 28 air bases and 2–4 naval bases. Ostensibly, the ground- and air-launched tactical nuclear weapons are gone, leaving somewhat more than 1,200 strategic nuclear warheads associated with ballistic missiles and strategic bombers. The status of the Black Sea Fleet's nuclear weapons is unclear.
28. See Stephen Van Evera, *Managing the Eastern Crisis: Preventing War in the Former Soviet Empire* (Cambridge, MA: MIT Defense and Arms Control Studies Program, 6 January 1992), p. 12.
29. Security guarantees are an unlikely substitute for an independent Ukrainian deterrent. Recall the endless arguments about the credibility of the US nuclear guarantee to Germany, in which the United States stationed more than 300,000 troops and thousands of tactical nuclear warheads. The US guarantee to Germany was credible, but mainly due to the elaborate measures taken to make it so.
30. See Steven Miller, 'Western Diplomacy and the Soviet Nuclear Legacy', *Survival*, vol. 34, no. 3, Autumn 1992, pp. 21–22, especially footnote 57.

CHAPTER 6

An Essay on Neorealism and Foreign Policy

Shibley Telhami

As interest has risen in the study of foreign policy since the end of the Cold War, many scholars have grappled with the relevance of theories of international politics for examining the foreign policies or more appropriately, the external behavior of states. Realism, in all its variants, having been the dominant theory of world politics in the U.S. for half a century, has become a fashionable target of students of foreign policy. Even more so, many apparent adherents to the realist school have sought to differentiate themselves from other realists. One can thus find classical realism, neorealism, and even neoclassical realism, defensive and offensive realism, among others. The debates thus far have suffered from the shortcomings of earlier debates: a misconception of the relation between realism, especially neorealism, and foreign policy. Ultimately, these works constitute neither alternative theories of international politics, nor refinements of neorealism. Indeed, in many cases they present little conflict with neorealism.

Although Kenneth Waltz has been clear that his neorealist theory is not a theory of foreign policy, others continued to dispute him on this issue.[1] Some realists have certainly contributed to the impression that realism, if not neorealism, explains foreign policy by seemingly suggesting that internal factors mattered little in the conduct of foreign policy. In one of the earlier debates with the "radical left," Robert Tucker, for example, suggested that a socialist America would not behave significantly different from a capitalist

America.[2] As for Kenneth Waltz, however, his longest book was dedicated to second-image analysis, comparing British and American foreign policies.[3]

To say that neorealism is not, or does not provide a theory of foreign policy does not mean that it has no consequence for the study of foreign policy. To say that relative power alone, or the drive for self-preservation alone, does not shape the foreign policies of states is not to say that a theory of foreign policy can ignore these factors. Even as a theory of international politics, neorealism is by no means comprehensive. This, Kenneth Waltz intended even in his earlier work: "The third image described the framework of world politics, but without the first and second images there can be no knowledge of the forces that determine policy; the first and second images describe the forces in world politics, but without the third image it is impossible to assess their importance or predict their results."[4] Neorealism is therefore best conceived as a framework for further inquiry, not as the end of inquiry.

The question is thus this: how does neorealism inform the study of foreign policy, even if it does not provide a theory of foreign policy? I will begin by analyzing what might be inferred from structural realism about state behavior, and proceed to evaluate some of the recent attempts to restate, or complement, its assumptions and propositions.

Although structural realism is first and foremost a theory about outcomes of international interaction, one can infer some propositions about expected state behavior.[5] There are essentially two arenas of relevance: opportunity and preferences. Neorealism says much about opportunity, and some, although less, about state preferences.

The one explicit assumption that neorealism makes about states' preferences is that, above all, they seek self-preservation—an assumption that has little to do with "defense" or "offense." This is not to say that all states merely seek survival, or that some states are not offensive-minded. It is simply a minimalist assumption about the preferences of all states, no matter what else they seek to attain. This minimal assumption contrasts with Hans Morgenthau's assumption that all states are power maximizers, and Waltz argued that balances of power, as recurring outcomes of international relations, could be derived without assuming that all states seek to maximize material power. Although ultimately material power matters, it is not an end in itself, but is an instrument. As Zakaria notes, states seek to maximize influence, not power;[6] or to put it differently, states seek to maximize opportunities for implementing their preferences (whatever these may be). But for neorealism, material power remains the most effective measure, over time, of the degree of influence and opportunity that states have.

So what is the relation between power, state preferences, and state behavior? Although neorealism assumes only that all states seek self-preservation, it also assumes that states have other preferences, which may differ from one state to another. Otherwise, capabilities would be merely an instrument of self-preservation, which, once assured, would render relative gains useless. Since most neorealists (certainly Waltz) assume that nuclear deterrence (through a second-strike capability) gets as close as states are likely to get to security in an anarchic world, one would wonder if the Cold War was at all necessary for the U.S., which enjoyed nuclear deterrence for most of that period.

Here the answers come, by inference, not by assumption. For Waltz, "the distribution of capabilities" is a component of system structure.[7] Relative material power is conceived as the most important commodity of influence in an anarchic world. It is important for both self-preservation and for the degree of opportunity that states have in implementing their external preferences, beyond self-preservation.

What is the relation between increased opportunity and state preferences? From neorealist propositions one can only deduce that increased or decreased opportunity makes the attainment of states' preferences more or less possible. Across the system, and over time, one would expect exploitation of increased opportunity. Zakaria notes correctly, in addressing Jack Snyder's emphasis on interest-group politics in expansionary policy,[8] that success or failure of expansion policies is a function of relative international power. Overexpansion is correlated with relative power.[9] Tucker made a similar point much earlier arguing that "interests of states expand roughly with their power."[10] Furthermore, different distributions of capabilities alter the preferences of states, which Jervis described as "system effects."[11] But nowhere can one infer from neorealism that the preferences of states are affected in the same way by changes in relative power, or that states expand equally given the same opportunity. Nothing short of an internal examination of state preferences can reveal their motives. Zakaria himself ultimately concludes that state strength is a significant factor in accounting for the degree of actual expansion, given the opportunity, because "what matters is state power, not national power."[12]

How does such an approach provide an alternative, or a refinement to neorealism? In a review article of recent books on foreign policy, including Zakaria's book, Gideon Rose invents yet a new term, "Neoclassical Realism," to describe an alternative to neorealism. Rose notes correctly that "... Unfortunately there *is* no simple, straightforward classical realism. Rather, the term covers a host of authors who differ greatly from one another in assumptions, objectives, and methodologies."[13]

But Rose goes on to argue, not only that the four works he considers[14] provide "four theories of foreign policy" but that they are alternatives to "defensive" and "offensive" realism, which he acknowledges are theories of international relations but they "commonly address foreign policy behavior and it is this aspect of them that will be treated here" (p. 146). What makes these authors realists is that they argue that the scope and ambition of a country's foreign policy is driven first and foremost by its place in the international system; what makes them neoclassical is the belief that the impact of capabilities on foreign policy is "indirect and complex, because systemic pressures must be translated through intervening variables at the unit level."

Assuming that the analyses of these authors do indeed constitute "theories" of foreign policy, how can one present these theories as alternatives to "aspects" of international relations theories? What does it mean, theoretically, to say that "Neoclassical realists occupy a space between pure structural theorists and constructivists?" One is left to wonder.

In presenting theoretically informed case analysis, these authors are doing what a neorealist would expect from an investigation of foreign policy: explore the domestic basis of foreign policy while taking account of external factors. And they do a fine job of it. Thomas Christensen finds that Chinese leaders were limited in their ability to implement strategic policies by domestic constraints, which diminished their ability to mobilize necessary resources to implement these policies. Schweller argues that misperception of the distribution of power led Stalin to bandwagon with, instead of balancing Hitler. Zakaria concludes that state strength is a factor in the state's ability to exploit external opportunity. New theories of foreign policy requiring a new name? An alternative school to "aspects" of realism?

The problem here is the same as with all attempts at modifying "aspects" of a theory such as substituting "influence" for power, balance of threat for balance of power, misperception of power for real power. The modification is fine if one is merely accounting for exceptions rather than the norm. One cannot begin with neorealist (or any other theoretical) assumptions, from which one would then derive logical conclusions that are then employed to challenge the assumptions; if the assumptions are wrong, the conclusions are wrong, and a new alternative theory, not only of foreign policy, but also of international relations must be provided.

If states misperceive power some of the time, this poses little problems for neorealism. If perceived "threat" sometimes does not correspond to real material power, it is hardly surprising, but it would still be helpful to differentiate threat from power. If the level of "influence" is shown to occasionally deviate from the level of material power, then the distinction is helpful for explaining exceptions. If, on the other hand, one begins with a theory at the heart of which material power is the central variable, and arrives at the conclusion that such "deviant" behavior is the norm, then something is fundamentally wrong. The entire theory must be abandoned.

Material power is the primary variable for neorealism. It is the ultimate measure of influence. It may not be easily fungible, but the rules and norms of international behavior on most issues of interest to the powerful states are heavily biased toward them. If they are not, they can be ignored or changed. Power may be sometimes misperceived or misunderstood by governments, but for the theory to hold, the inferences must always derive from material power. If balancing is the expected tendency of states, it must be the balancing of power, not perceptions of power or threat. Specifying threat as an alternative to power would beg an entirely new theory of international politics, unless there was a high degree of correlation between power and threat.

This is not to say that such concepts as "threat" are not important in explaining international relations, as Stephen Walt does very well in his work. It is hard to ignore that perceived threat sometimes has more impact on the behavior of states than objective power. But is it the basis for concluding that states react by "balancing" threat, and what is the meaning of "balancing" if it is not measured by adding more objective power to one side? The expectation of balancing is derived precisely from the notion of material power, entailing equalization of power. How does one conclude that balancing is the expected reaction to "threat," and what does one mean by balancing in this case? In answering these questions, one would need an entirely different theory—not merely a modification of neorealism.

Foreign Policy Motives

To the extent that neorealism can account for some motives of states, it accounts for their basic drive to attain security and, beyond that, to attain some relative power as an instrument for implementing a state's other motives. These other motives, which are essential in understanding any state's foreign policy, can have a number of sources that require different theories. Certainly, these can include domestic politics, ideology, leaders' personal preferences, and moral considerations.

While neorealism has been often understood to ignore the role of domestic politics in the formation of foreign policy, it has been more often understood to leave no room for moral motives. Can morality be a factor, sometimes even a dominant factor, in a state's foreign policy?

Given the external opportunity, neorealism certainly does not preclude such a role. An example of a theory that envisions a domestic context allowing for such a role is Samuel Huntington's notion of the American Creed and its impact on American foreign policy.[15] One does not have to agree with Huntington's particular propositions about American foreign policy, but the point here is that it is possible to conceive of domestic circumstances propelling a role for national or subnational values in foreign policy—given the international opportunity, which, for neorealism, is usually abundant for powerful states. Indeed, some of the dominant approaches to American politics envision a dominant role for interest groups that are often driven by group (though not always national) values, such as the Christian Right, to name but one. Even ethnic groups in America (Polish, Jewish, Cuban, Arab) are driven less by their own domestic political and economic interests and more by group values when they advocate particular foreign policies toward their ancestral homelands. Nothing in neorealism precludes a theory, or an empirical finding, linking moral factors and the external behavior of states. Although this point is misunderstood even by some of the adherents of neorealism, the bigger misunderstanding in international debate has to do with the connection between description and prescription, the "ought" and the "is" in neorealist (and realist, more generally) theorizing.

Much of the criticism of neorealism assumes that the "national interest" that one describes is the same that one prescribes. Realists are often said to argue that "there is not and cannot be a moral relationship among states."[16] This presumed realist position is then explained as a theoretical "preference" that emerged following World War II and the beginning of the Cold War by theorists like Hans Morgenthau who escaped Hitler's Germany, and that American policy-makers "swallowed realism hook, line, and sinker." So now that we have a new generation of theorists and the Cold War has ended, new theoretical preferences should emerge.

This broad postulation of realism and neorealism particularly, is at odds with the way in which neorealism is conceived by its adherents: as descriptive enterprise explaining the way the world is organized, not as a prescriptive giving states advice on what to do.[17]

At the descriptive level, morality can certainly be a factor in shaping the motives of states, aside from the attainment of security. At the prescriptive level, no logic of neorealism prevents a neorealist who is engaged in a foreign policy debate, or deciding on supporting a political cause or a political candidate, from supporting or prescribing a moral course—even in areas where neorealism expects amoral state behavior. One often supports failing causes, not merely for one's own internal pleasures, but also for the chance that the case may be one of the numerous acknowledged exceptions.

Policies of the Powerful and the Weak

One of the key issues about the relationship between relative power and the motives of states is the extent to which relative power provides opportunities for states to implement interests that are not security-related, or are not merely a drive for power itself. It is useful for this purpose to examine the different calculations of powerful and weak states after the end of the Cold War.

For the world's sole remaining superpower, extraordinary opportunities emerged, and the role of domestic politics in the formation of foreign policy reached new heights. But the same could not be said for smaller powers. Certainly, neorealism could not predict even post–Cold War American behavior associated most closely with security policy: the American intervention to liberate Kuwait, and the survival and expansion of NATO. Here I will not address the latter case since others are doing so in this volume. Instead, I will limit my empirical discussion to the analysis of the former case as an example of post–Cold War U.S. behavior and the reaction of weaker states in the Middle East to this behavior.

No one seriously suggested that the Iraqi invasion of Kuwait presented a military threat to the U.S. The primary interest-driven argument on behalf of the American military response was that the invasion threatened the stability, and thus pricing of oil supplies, which are vital to Western economies. This too has been the argument for the ultimate increase in the U.S. military presence in the Persian Gulf following the Iraq–Kuwait war.

Yet, even pure calculations of direct benefits and costs undermine the validity of this argument. The U.S. spends more than $50 billion a year on military presence and planning each year.[18] What does the U.S. get in return for this investment? Beyond individual anecdotal cases, there is no solid evidence that U.S. military presence helps U.S. business, unlike what is assumed by regionalist theorists of imperialism. In 1989, the year before Iraq invaded Kuwait, European exports to the Middle East stood at $40.2 billion compared to $13.1 billion for the U.S.. In 1992, the year after the Gulf War, Europe's total exports was $57.2 billion compared to $19.9 billion for the U.S. This trend continued; in 2000, Europe exported $63.7 billion compared to $23.0 billion for the U.S.

American dependency on Persian Gulf oil in particular, and on oil imports in general is also much less than those of Europe and Japan. So, at a minimum, there is a peculiar divergence of approaches between the U.S. and its Western European allies that cannot simply be explained by the degree of dependence on oil.

Pure calculations of costs and benefits from oil are also telling. First, there is probably little connection between U.S. military presence and oil prices, as supply and demand are usually the biggest factors in oil pricing. Even if there was some connection between military presence and pricing, this relationship cannot possibly begin to account for the extent of the American commitment. In short, oil alone cannot explain the U.S. policy in the Gulf or the extent of U.S. military presence there.

Similarly, it is useful to consider the notion that oil alone explained U.S. intervention in the Iraq–Kuwait crisis of 1990–1991.[19] The assertion that U.S. political and military dominance in the region was necessary to secure the flow of oil is challenged by considerable evidence about patterns of trade in the Middle East; states in the region sell oil and import goods independent of ideology, because markets tend to be their guide. The behavior of Japan and some European allies, considerably more dependent on oil than the U.S., was illustrative here too. Their early reluctance to support a military initiative against Iraq, even with the U.S. carrying the bulk of the burden, generated American resentment. If interest in oil logically entailed Western intervention, how can this behavior be explained?

While no one would contest the continued importance of Gulf oil to Western economies, it is obvious from the earlier that the intrinsic value of oil, by itself, cannot explain either U.S. perceptions of threat in the Gulf or the perceived need for military force to address these threats. Indeed, the public and congressional debates in the U.S. after the events of September 11, 2001, which questioned the need to have military presence in Saudi Arabia, were an indication of the absence of a logical connection between oil alone and the need for military presence.

This is not to say that one could not make a case for the need for American intervention following Iraq's invasion of Kuwait, but it reveals that one can make an even more powerful case against such a need, using neorealist logic. Ultimately, one would have to conclude that the choice of this option was not predictable from neorealist propositions, and the answers must lie in the domestic realm of American politics, or other realms outside the scope of neorealism. Indeed, Kenneth Waltz himself did not believe that military intervention was necessary for vital American interests.[20] Americans, and the U.S. Congress, were divided on the need for such an intervention until operations commenced.

Certainly, neorealism entailed that such American behavior became more *possible* with the demise of Soviet Power. During the Cold War, such behavior would have been unthinkable. Even Saddam Hussein predicted six months before he invaded Kuwait, that the U.S. will have expanded opportunities following the decline of the Soviet Union: "It has become clear to everyone that the U.S. has emerged in a superior position in international politics. This superiority will be demonstrated in the US readiness to play such a role..." and "the undisciplined and irresponsible behavior will engender hostility and grudges if it embarks on rejected stupidities."[21] But between possibility and necessity, or even likelihood, lay a large unexplained gap.

This American behavior, which was unpredictable by neorealist criteria, and which could not be understood without reference to American politics, had the consequence of significantly affecting not only Middle East politics, but also the distribution of power in the region, and thus the structure of Middle East politics. One can only imagine how different Middle East politics would look today if Iraq prevailed in its invasion and managed to double its economy by swallowing Kuwait's economy. The preferences of superpowers, even the arbitrary ones, have far-reaching consequences for smaller states. In other words, the domestic politics of the U.S. are a critical variable in the international politics of the Middle East—odd as this may sound as a neorealist conclusion.

But neorealism has much to say about the behavior of smaller states. In the Middle East, the reactions to U.S. intervention were more predictable. Here ideology was set aside, previous coalitions were shelved, and the politics of self-preservation took center stage.

Prior to the Iraqi invasion of Kuwait, Egypt had been a partner with Iraq in the Arab Cooperation Council (together with Yemen and Jordan), Saudi Arabia had signed a nonbelligerence treaty with Iraq, and Syria, the only state to share with Iraq the Baath ideology, was one of the strongest opponents of U.S. policy in the Middle East—at a time when opposition to American policy in the region was running high.

Within days, Saudi Arabia, Egypt, and Syria found themselves joining the U.S.-led coalition against Iraq. It was the kind of behavior neorealists would have predicted. Regardless of Iraq's intention toward Saudi Arabia, Iraq put itself in a position to invade Saudi Arabia within days, without the presence of American troops. American forces could easily defend the Kingdom, but would find it more difficult to liberate it once invaded. The nonbelligerence treaty was rendered meaningless, once Iraq invaded another neighbor.

After Saudi Arabia agreed to the American plan, Egypt's decision became even easier. Always concerned about competitive Iraqi power, Egypt was not especially happy to contemplate a dramatic growth in Iraq's influence. Egypt stood to lose much economic aid ($2 billion/year) from the U.S. if it went the other way, and stood to gain new aid (from Saudi Arabia) if it went along. More importantly, Egypt understood this: the U.S. was the sole surviving superpower and it was bound to win its confrontation with Iraq. Could it afford to be on the losing side?

Although Syria received no American aid, it received Saudi aid, and its calculations were similar to that of Egypt's. Most of all, with Golan Heights still occupied by Israel and the prospect of war still looming, it could no longer count on significant Soviet support. Had it gone against the U.S., its fate would have probably been similar to Libya's and Iran's. After the Gulf War and the end of the Cold War, American influence in the Middle East has substantially affected the distribution of military and economic power within the Arab world and the relevance of this distribution. Prior to the 1967 war, military power was an instrument of influence within the Arab world, not so much for the ability it conferred to intimidate other Arab states, but mostly because it allowed states who had it, to claim the ability to balance Israeli military might. Egypt held a decisive advantage in this category until its peace with Israel, and Iraq claimed this capability for a brief surge of regional influence between the end of the Iraq–Iran war in 1988 and Iraq's invasion of Kuwait in 1990. Beginning with the mid-1970s, the rise of the oil states and weakened Arab militaries in relation to Israel following the 1967 Arab defeat increased the relevance of economic power in the Arab world, especially given the surplus capital that oil-producing states acquired and were able to employ as an instrument of policy; Saudi Arabia in particular arose as a more powerful state. Since the 1991 Gulf War, the open roles in regional security for the U.S. and Israel, and continued presence of U.S. troops in the region have further reduced the significance of the distribution of conventional power within the Arab world. This explains how small Qatar can be a thorn in the side of its big neighbor, Saudi Arabia, pursuing a policy that its fellow member in the Gulf Cooperation Council, presumably an alliance, finds threatening. Besides pursuing an independent foreign policy on sensitive issues to Saudi Arabia, such as improving relations with Israel, Qatari rulers have called pointedly for political reform in the Gulf, and holding elections that included women for the first time. Its television station, al-Jazeera, has become the most popular in the Arab world by virtue of its Western news style, and free disagreements on political questions in the Arab world that often offend its bigger neighbor. Although a member of the coalition against Saddam Hussein in 1990, Qatar's TV broadcast, among other things, a speech by Saddam Hussein that called for the overthrow of Arab monarchs. How does Qatar manage to stave off the anger of Riyadh? By allowing the deployment of American forces on its soil, which also reduced Washington leverage with the emirate when al-Jazeera was seen to be giving too much air time to Osama Bin Laden after the terrorist attacks on the U.S. on September 11, 2001.

Conclusion

Neorealism has much to say about foreign policy, but does not provide a theory of foreign policy. The drive for security, so essential in neorealist theory, and the importance of relative power in explaining the degree of opportunity that states have in the conduct of foreign policy are important factors in understanding any state's foreign policy. Moreover, to the extent that relative power is seen as a primary instrument of policy, the accumulation of power is also a motive, although not equally pursued by all states. But power and security alone cannot explain the varied motives of states, especially the powerful among them who have ample international opportunity. And without a theory that explains the motives of states, including the motives of their constituent components, it is not possible for neorealism to explain the specific foreign policies of most states.

Notes

1. Colin Elman, "Horses for Courses: Why *Not* Neorealist Theories of Foreign Policy?" *Security Studies*, Vol. 6, No. 1 (Autumn 1996), 7–53.
2. Robert W. Tucker, "The Radical Critique Assessed," *The Radical Left and American Foreign Policy*, Johns Hopkins University Press, 1971.
3. Kenneth N. Waltz, *Foreign Policy and Democratic Politics: The American and British Experience*, Boston: Little, Brown and Company (Inc.), 1967.
4. Kenneth N. Waltz, *Man, the State and War*, New York: Columbia University Press, 1959.
5. In an earlier work, I provided the following interpretation of Waltz' neorealism: from the simple assumption that states seek, at a minimum, self-preservation in a self-help anarchic environment, several general propositions could be inferred. First, when a state's security is at stake, this consideration dominates all others in determining that state's behavior. Second, states, when they are threatened, tend to attempt balancing the threatening power, alone if they can, or with others if necessary. Third, the relative military and economic power is a critical determinant of states' behavior; the more powerful states are more likely to achieve their

objectives. Fourth, a change in the distribution of military and economic power is likely to result in corresponding new alignments among states. Fifth, to the extent that superpowers are the most powerful states, their relations, their power in relation to each other, their competition, and their foreign policies can affect the behavior of smaller states in dominant ways; a regional superiority of power by one state could be negated by superpower involvement. Sixth, the number of superpowers, and the incremental differences in their power are significant in determining the behavior of states. (Shibley Telhami, *Power and Leadership in International Bargaining: The Path to the Camp David Accords*, New York: Columbia University Press, 1990, 33.)

6. Fareed Zakaria, *From Wealth to Power: The Unusual Origins of America's World Role*. Princeton: Princeton University Press, 1998.
7. By so doing, he opens himself to the criticism, which he anticipates (Kenneth N. Waltz, *Theory of International Politics*, Reading, Massachusetts: Addison-Wesley Publishing Company, 1979, p. 98), that capabilities are unit attributes. His response that, unlike variables such as ideology, distribution of capabilities are estimated by comparing units, loses much of its power if one re-posits ideology as "the degree of ideological similarity among states." But Waltz does not need to define the distribution of capabilities as a component of the structure. In an anarchic, self-help system where states seek self-preservation, it follows that relative capabilities dominate their relations. It also follows that different distributions (e.g., the number of poles) would have different consequences.
8. Jack Snyder, *Myths of Empire: Domestic Politics and International Ambition*, Ithaca, New York: Cornell University Press, 1991.
9. Fareed Zakaria. "Realism and Domestic Politics: A Review Essay," *International Security*, Vol. 17, No. 1: 177–98.
10. Robert W. Tucker, "The Radical Critique Assessed," *The Radical Left and American Foreign Policy*, Johns Hopkins University Press, 1971.
11. Robert Jervis, *System Effects: Complexity in Political and Social Life*, Princeton: Princeton University Press, 1997. Elsewhere, I have argued that changes in the distribution of regional power were behind Egypt's dramatic policy changes leading to its abandoning pan-Arabism in favor of bilateral agreements with Israel; while pan-Arabism worked to enhance Egyptian influence when Egypt was strong, it made it more dependent on other Arab states when Egypt was weak. Egypt went from being the Arab world's largest economy in the 1960s to being its sixth in the mid-1970s. (Shibley Telhami, *Power and Leadership in International Bargaining: The Path to the Camp David Accords*, New York: Columbia University Press, 1990.)
12. Fareed Zakaria, *From Wealth to Power: The Unusual Origins of America's World Role*, Princeton: Princeton University Press, 1998.
13. Gideon Rose, "Review Article: Neoclassical Realism and Theories of Foreign Policy," *World Politics,* Vol. 51 (October 1998): 153.
14. Besides Zakaria, they are: Thomas J. Christensen. *Useful Adversaries: Grand Strategy, Domestic Politics, and Sino-American Conflict, 1947–1958*,

Princeton: Princeton University Press, 1996; Randall L. Schweller, *Deadly Imbalances: Tripolarity and Hitler's Strategy of World Conquest*, New York: Columbia University Press, 1998; and William Curti Wohlforth. *The Elusive Balance: Power and Perception during the Cold War*, Ithaca: Cornell University Press, 1993.

15. Samuel P. Huntington, "American Ideals versus American Institutions," *Political Science Quarterly*, Vol. 97, No. 1 (Spring 1982).
16. Maxwell, Mary. *Morality Among Nations: An Evolutionary View*, New York: SUNY Press, 1990.
17. In leveling arguments against realism's view of morality, several assumptions are generally attributed to realists: (1) realists prescribe what they describe; (2) realists believe that the international environment does not allow for moral relations; (3) Realists believe that group morality is fundamentally different from individual morality; (4) realism pretends to describe and explain but ultimately it serves the interest of the powerful in that only the powerful can afford to take advantage of what realists describe; in this regard, realism, by avoiding normative questions, has "negative" moral consequences. Realists reply in a variety of ways. First, they point out that description and explanation are different from prescription, not only in studying world politics, but also in social science in general, and that realists do not necessarily condone what they describe. A second line of argument is that the same general (situational) criteria of moral consideration that applies within the state, also applies in international relations but that the international environment is harsher and, therefore, what is less common within the state is more common outside the state. Third, the connection between morality and international relations is not a unique question, but is a subset of a broader question about the connection between morality and behavior, and morality and explanatory theory. Still, there are some conceptual questions that require clarification before one assesses this debate.

There are several ways in which morality has been conceived in this debate. First, some scholars posit morality as altruism. Second, morality is conceived as representing the collective interests, to be differentiated from individual interests. Third, morality is identified with ethics; i.e. norms, laws, and customs, that regulate behavior beyond the immediate selfish ends of the individual actors. Fourth, morality is posited as advocated "values" that are not captured by descriptive and explanatory theories. Realists have addressed the second and third interpretation of morality in effective ways, but have not sufficiently addressed the first and the last. In particular, when morality as collective interests is seen as being in the long-term interests of the individual, realists can assume that society will adjust and (selfish) cooperation will evolve. This is not altruistic cooperation, but one driven by long-term interests. The question of norms (ethics) governing these long-term interests is addressed in a similar fashion as reflecting an evolving understanding of long-term interests; the realist interpretation of international regimes is one example of this view. But realists do have a problem reconciling the "ought" with the "is": if realists in fact behave in a way that does not correspond to the way the world is, then why bother? If they are capable of moral behavior, others surely are. If they and others behave in a way that does not correspond to what they describe, isn't there a gap to be explained. One way to address this issue is straightforward: theories describe how the world works most of the time. There are always exceptions. Those exceptions are accounted for by the arbitrary behavior of actors who pursue ends such as moral ones that are not captured by the theories. Realists have not accounted for these exceptions, either because these exceptions do not lend themselves to systematic explanations, or because they are outside of the realm of realist concerns.

18. This figure is from William W. Kaufman, *Assessing Base Force: How Much is too Much?* (Washington, D.C.: Brookings, 1992), 89.
19. For competing explanations of U.S. behavior during the Iraq invasion of Kuwait, see Shibley Telhami, "Between Theory and Fact: Explaining American Behavior in the Gulf War," *Security Studies*, Vol. 2, No. 1 (Autumn 1992): 96–121.
20. Kenneth N. Waltz, "A Necessary War?" in *Confrontation in the Gulf: University of California Professors Talk about the War*, Harry Kreisler, ed. (Berkeley: University of California Press, 1992), 59–65.
21. Saddam Hussein's speech to the Arab Cooperation Council in Amman, Jordan, February 27, 1990 (FBIS-NES-90-039). Saddam Hussein also argued in that speech: that "We believe that the world can fill the vacuum resulting from the recent changes and find a new balance in the global arena by developing new perspectives and reducing or adding to this or that force," and that the new balance of power will take about five years to develop.

CHAPTER 7

Structural Realism and China's Foreign Policy: Much (But Never All) of the Story

Avery Goldstein

Can structural realism provide a satisfactory explanation for China's foreign policy? China scholars have often criticized the work of social scientists, especially those relying on abstract theories, for ignoring the special features of the Chinese case.[1] Since structural realism *intentionally* sets aside the distinctiveness of particular cases, it would certainly seem to be an obvious target for this sort of argument. Such criticism, however, is both accurate and beside the point. The issue is not whether structural realism can or cannot provide an adequate explanation for China's foreign policy. It cannot, as even neorealism's founding theorist would readily concede. Rather, the important question is *how much* of the explanation can the international-structural causes it highlights provide? With this question in mind, the following chapter reconsiders China's foreign policy during and after the Cold War.

In *Man, the State, and War* and *Theory of International Politics*, Kenneth Waltz explained recurrent patterns of international behavior and outcomes by highlighting the causal significance of the system's structure—the constraints of anarchy emphasized in the former work, and constraints of polarity emphasized in the latter. Yet, he also indicated that however powerful these structural constraints may be, the explanation of a particular international outcome (e.g., the outbreak of a specific war) and the explanation of a particular state's behavior (e.g., its foreign policy) will be incomplete and often misleading if the analyst ignores causes intentionally set aside for the purposes of crafting a parsimonious systems theory.[2] That including a host of such causes—the personality of state leaders, parochial political interests of government bureaucrats, ideology, and domestic social, economic, and political structures—helps provide a fuller account of the foreign policy choices particular states make, is not proof of neorealism's fatal flaw, but rather another demonstration of some simple methodological points. A theory is an attempt to depict an aspect of the real world through abstraction and simplification; in making sense of its chosen domain of inquiry, every theory has a limited range of application; a theory with a wider range of application is more useful or powerful, but even a powerful theory provides only a partial account of reality.[3]

The example frequently cited to make the last point, makes it well. Newtonian mechanics is a powerful body of theory (whose limits modern physicists eventually exposed). Nevertheless, although its attraction provide a compelling explanation as to why leaves fall to the ground rather than ascend to the heavens, they are of little use in understanding the different paths followed by leaves as opposed to apples.[4] To explain such differences, of course, requires drawing on other theories that focus on aspects of the physical world that were set aside by Newton. The usefulness of aerodynamics for explaining the path of falling bodies complements rather than contradicts Newton's insights about gravitational attraction. Engineers, engaged in applied as opposed to theoretical science, draw on and combine the insights that abstract and simplified disciplinary research provides. One should expect it to be likewise with the study of China's foreign policy. In analyzing a specific empirical case, one is engaged in applied science, not theoretical science. Thus, to restate the point made earlier, the question is *not whether* neorealism can explain China's foreign policy, *but rather how much* of the explanation can the international-structural causes it highlights provide?

The obvious but not very informative answer is that the significance of international-structural as opposed to national and subnational causes has varied over time. The Chinese case is intriguing, however, because of the remarkable extent to which structural constraints can account for the broad contours of Beijing's foreign policy during the Cold War, and the extent to which their constraining influence was usually evident despite strong reasons (i.e., the presence of nonstructural causes) to expect China to behave otherwise. China's early post–Cold War foreign policy demonstrates, by contrast, that although international-structural causes continue to shape Beijing's decisions, the constraints they pose are no longer as tight, and the imperatives they establish are no longer as straightforward, as in the past.

This chapter is divided into two parts. Each indicates the usefulness and limits of neorealist balance-of-power theory for understanding China's foreign policy. In the first part, I examine China's Cold War foreign policy line, or what in the West is usually termed grand strategy—a vision about the way to advance national interests in light of the dominant forces shaping international politics.[5] The four-decade epoch of Soviet–American rivalry was one in which China faced strong external pressures that clarified national priorities and their policy implications. During this period, China's behavior generally conformed to the expectations one would infer from neorealist balance-of-power theory, but some significant anomalies serve as a reminder of the inevitably partial explanation any single theory provides. In the second part, I sketch the evolution of China's post–Cold War foreign policy line, assessing the interaction of changing domestic and international-structural causes in the early post–Cold War era that have conditioned Beijing's search for a foreign policy that serves its interests. By mid-1996, a policy package was emerging that reflects both the international influences structural realism highlights as well as the distinctive features of the post–Cold War Chinese case.

China's Foreign Policy Line During the Cold War

During the Cold War, China was one of several second-ranking powers, each of whom pursued its foreign policy interests within the tight constraints and resulting clear incentives bipolarity provided.[6] Given China's meager national wealth and the scope of the threat each of the superpowers represented, Beijing's foreign policy for most of the four decades after 1949 was driven by a survivalist logic that trumped other regime preferences. The imperatives of international structure derived not merely from the relatively clear implications of bipolarity, but also the tightness of its constraints for a state so closely involved in the system's superpower-dominated competitive politics.[7] The People's Republic of China (PRC) was born in the mid-twentieth century as a result of a struggle that prefigured a major recurrent theme of Cold War politics—civil war in which each superpower backed its ideologically preferred horse. Then, in the ensuing decades, China's borders served as the venue for the superpowers' three biggest Cold War foreign military operations (Korea, Vietnam, Afghanistan) as well as the site for several escalation-threatening crises between Beijing and the system's duopolists (the Taiwan Straits during the 1950s, the Sino-Soviet border in 1969, and

Indo-China in 1979). China, in short, had little opportunity to opt out of international politics during the Cold War and confronted a nearly constant challenge in attempting to ensure its precarious security as a lesser power in a bipolar world.

What was China's grand strategy as a tightly constrained second-ranking power? Under Mao Zedong's leadership, its Cold War approach was distinctively realist, sometimes to the point of caricature.[8] Mao Zedong relied on a few basic principles that had proved useful in the decades-long revolutionary struggle against better armed domestic and foreign adversaries: identify the main enemy, unite with all others who are willing to cooperate in dealing with this common threat, and do not allow secondary contradictions (e.g., conflicts about ideology, personality, etc.) to prevent flexibility on tactics as long as it serves your strategic objective. Such principles neatly sum up the counter-hegemonic coalition-building philosophy of most statesmen who practice realpolitik. For China after 1949, these ideas manifested in the initial "lean to one side" grand strategy. Strong disagreements with Stalin and a sense of resentment about his tepid support for Mao's Chinese Communist Party (CCP) notwithstanding, the Sino-Soviet alliance provided the PRC with the only available counter to a globally dominant U.S., whose military policy in the western Pacific, and whose track record of hostility toward the Chinese communist movement made it the principal external threat to the newly founded PRC.

Mao's realpolitik, counter-hegemonic notions also later informed what could have been termed the "lean to the other side" grand strategy of Sino-American entente initiated in the early 1970s. As the Soviet military buildup along its Asian frontier compounded the deep-seated political and ideological disputes between Beijing and Moscow, and as Washington demonstrated the limits of its military ambitions in Southeast Asia and then previewed its plans for retrenchment (the Nixon doctrine), China's leaders determined that the Soviet Union was the superpower posing the more serious threat. This new principal strategic concern dictated China's flexibility in improving relations with the U.S. (and other advanced industrial states) so that the counter-Soviet coalition would include partners more weighty than the handful of Third World regimes and revolutionary movements who sided with Beijing against the USSR.[9]

After Mao's death, China's grand strategy retained its basic orientation, identifying the Soviet Union as the main adversary, and the U.S. as the essential member of a countervailing coalition of diverse states. Indeed, if anything, in the immediate post-Mao years (1976–1980), China's realpolitik was at its zenith. Beijing basically dropped the ideological fig leaf (neo-Leninist claims about the "revisionist" roots of Soviet "socialist imperialism" that was required in the era of radical socialism) and simply sought to build a global United Front based on naked claims about the growing power of an aggressive Soviet enemy. Although the Sino-American alignment would loosen somewhat during the 1980s as China's apprehension about Soviet hegemony diminished, during the last decade of the Cold War China continued its strategic tilt to the U.S. side.

Beijing's decision first to turn to the Soviets and then to the U.S. highlights the extent to which international-structural constraints shaped China's foreign policy line. Yet there is a difference between observing the importance of structural constraints and ignoring the presence of different sorts of influences whose presence they may overshadow. Simply put, structure constrains, rather than determines, state behavior. Indeed, explaining several significant anomalies for a structural-realist interpretation of China's Cold War foreign policy requires the inclusion of causes operating at the national, rather than international, level. I say "significant" anomalies because it is not surprising, and easily demonstrated, that the complex and multifaceted foreign policy of any major power will display features that no single theory can explain. More telling is consideration of those features that are substantively important, closely linked with aspects of the state's foreign policy the theory claims to explain, and not easily reconciled with its logic. Structural realism provides a powerful explanation for China's Cold War strategic alignment with each of the superpowers, but is not as obviously helpful for answering questions such as: why did the Sino-Soviet split emerge after 1957 despite continuity in the bipolar, anarchic structure of the international system? Why did Beijing, at perhaps its moment of greatest weakness (following the disastrous Great Leap Forward), undermine its close relationship with Moscow despite the perception that the U.S. remained the principal external threat to China's security? Why did Beijing back away from its close alignment with the U.S. after 1981, despite continuing concern about the Soviet threat? In thinking about the impli-cations of these apparent deviations from the expectations of neorealist theory, several questions arise. To what extent do these deviations reflect choices made at moments international-structural constraints eased, times when preference rather than necessity could shape policy? Or, to what extent do these deviations reflect a stubborn insistence on acting according to national preferences despite the risks of ignoring powerful external constraints?

Sino-Soviet Alliance and Split

The history of the Sino-Soviet alliance illustrates both the usefulness and limits of structural realism for explaining China's Cold War foreign policy.[10]

In the years immediately after the founding of the PRC in 1949, China's close alliance with the Soviet Union was consistent with the neorealist expectation that a second-ranking power unable to self-reliantly counter the threatening capabilities of one of the bipolar system's duopolists, would find it necessary to ally with the other. China's early postwar threat perceptions reinforced this structural, power-balancing logic.[11] U.S. activism in the Far East during and after World War II as well as Washington's track record of hostility toward the CCP encouraged Mao and his associates to take the ideologically more palatable path, "lean to" the Soviet-led socialist side in the emerging Cold War and formalize an alliance with Moscow in February 1950. For leaders in Beijing, subsequent events—U.S. power projection on the Korean peninsula that threatened China's northeastern frontier, Washington's increasingly harsh anticommunist rhetoric that suggested support for recovering a China that had been "lost," a resumption of U.S. military and diplomatic support for what had been a moribund regime in exile on Taiwan—seemed to confirm the correctness of the decision.

Thus, at first blush the Sino-Soviet alliance appears to have been overdetermined, consistent with both the structural power-based logic of neorealism and national threat-based logic Steve Walt has used in applying the theory to particular cases. But other national-level forces challenged Sino-Soviet solidarity. Though temporarily overshadowed by the unusually tight structural constraints of early Cold War bipolarity, their significance, rather than changes at the level of the international system, best explains the emergence of the Sino-Soviet split. Potentially divisive influences, muted in Beijing only as long as the necessity of coping with a pressing U.S. threat to China's national survival loomed large, were: geography; ideology (used here as a broad label for historical memory, nationalism, and revolutionary marxism); the personality of China's undisputed leader, Mao Zedong; and, by the middle of the decade, the political implications of nuclear weapons technology.

Geography

However sensible the Sino-Soviet alliance appeared from the perspective of power balancing under bipolarity, it seemed less sensible from the perspective of geography. China shared a long, inconclusively defined, common border with the USSR, and its frontiers were mostly populated by minority peoples, often with kinsmen on the Soviet side, whose loyalty to Beijing was far from certain. The threat that local ethnic politics posed to the recently reestablished territorial integrity of China introduced a distinctive complication to the Sino-Soviet relationship. Moreover, whereas the threat U.S. power posed in East Asia after World War II was a matter of choice and a reflection of its unmatched global reach, the Soviet position in East Asia was a matter of geography, not policy, and because of proximity it would not be necessary for Soviet power to reach U.S. levels in order to be a potentially grave threat to China.

Ideas—Historical Memory

Historical legacies exacerbated the effects of geography. The USSR was the successor state to an empire that along with the West and Japan had seized Chinese territory and extracted humiliating concessions from the Qing Dynasty in its final decades. After a fleeting Leninist interlude when Moscow seemed prepared to atone for Romanov's China policies, the USSR carried forward most of the tainted historical legacy of imperial Russia. In addition, the Soviet leadership, especially Stalin, subsequently attempted to dictate the course of China's Communist revolution to serve Moscow's aims, nearly dooming the CCP's cause on more than one occasion.[12] Soviet policy toward the PRC after the Communist victory in the Chinese Civil War continued to reflect a determination that China subordinate its national interests to Moscow's international agenda. If geographic proximity created potential conflicts of interest and magnified the importance of Soviet capabilities, historical legacies ensured suspicion about Soviet motives.

Ideas—Nationalism

The nationalist prism through which the PRC's founding fathers viewed history increased the disruptive potential in Sino-Soviet relations. The CCP rose to power only after it had positioned itself as the champion of Chinese nationalism, able to deliver on the promises of unity, development, and international respect that had been put on the political agenda by its predecessor—the Kuomintang (KMT) of Sun Yat-sen and Chiang Kai-shek. The CCP's leaders risked jeopardizing their hard-earned nationalist credentials if they allowed Moscow to push them around after 1949. Even if one discounts the importance of the authoritarian CCP elites' regard for public reaction, the staunchly nationalist beliefs of those who had assumed control of the party by the end of the Civil War were sufficient to ensure they would jealously guard China's interests. For them, the lesson of history was clear. The road to ruin was paved with Soviet advice. Stalin's directives to the Chinese Communists had resulted in the near extermination of the movement not once, but twice (the 1927 White Terror and the collapse of the Jiangxi Soviet in 1934 that resulted in the disastrous retreat subsequently hailed as the Long March). Having survived the Comintern's meddling through World War II (largely because isolation enabled Mao to limit the influence of Stalin's supporters and to ignore Moscow's foolish suggestions), the CCP then had to fend off Stalin's recommendation that the Communists not press on to victory in the late 1940s, but rather settle for a division of China into a CCP northern and a KMT southern state—an arrangement that would have maximized Beijing's dependence on Moscow and enabled the USSR to retain many of the deals it had struck with Chiang's government.[13] After 1949, deference to Moscow's leadership of the alliance prevailed as long as the need to cope with the American superpower dominated China's strategic planning. Such deference, however, obscured a long history of rocky relations between the Chinese and Soviet communists, a problem for which the shared belief in Marxism was no panacea.

Ideas—Marxism

Rather than helping to smooth bilateral relations, the shared commitment to Marxism further complicated the Sino-Soviet alliance. In ways that Morgenthau's work suggests, ideological similarity unrealistically raised the expectations on both sides.[14] Business-like dealings according to the calculus of national interest were not good enough. Moscow expected Beijing's unswerving loyalty to maintain the solidarity of a hierarchic communist movement whose behavioral code emphasized leninist discipline. Beijing expected Moscow not simply to reward loyalty but to show a special generosity reserved for comrades. These expectations of solidarity and generosity were repeatedly tested. The initial negotiations to formalize the Sino-Soviet alliance saw each side fight hard to ensure its national interests. Then, in the Korean War, Stalin had the Chinese assume most of the risk and burden of fighting for the North's cause. And under both Stalin and Khrushchev, Soviet assistance to China (often loans not grants) was strictly limited—not only because Moscow needed to tend to its own recovery from World War II's devastation, but also (to Beijing's dismay) because it chose to devote scarce resources to a global competition with the U.S. in places like Egypt and India rather than further assist a China already on the socialist side of the ledger.

Mao Zedong

Mao's leadership was yet another potentially disruptive influence behind the edifice of Sino-Soviet unity. Like his closest comrades in the CCP leadership, Mao was a strong Chinese nationalist. He was also an unusually self-confident individual, especially after he succeeded in reviving the fortunes of a nearly defeated CCP and guiding it to a stunning national victory within little more than a decade. By the late 1940s, he had become a leader who brooked little criticism of his views. One needn't delve deeply into psychology to observe that Mao was not a figure who would easily serve in the role of "little brother" or "junior partner," the role he was consigned to play in the era of the Sino-Soviet alliance. Yet, whether it was the infuriating need to sit tight while waiting for his audience with Stalin in 1950, or the discomfiting need to deliver an address to the November 1957 International Congress of Communist Parties lauding unity under Moscow's leadership, as long as Soviet backing was necessary to cope with the serious threat the U.S. posed, Mao the master strategist swallowed his pride and kept his eye on the prize (in Maoist terminology, focusing on the "principal contradiction").[15] When Mao became convinced that this unpleasant charade was not providing the anticipated security benefits for China, however, his personal resentment accelerated the deterioration of Sino-Soviet relations. In short order, Mao shifted from loyal ally and faithful disciple to independent critic and ambitious rival, claiming that he and his party were the true champions of revolutionary socialism.

Military Technology

Finally, as the 1950s progressed, even as the structure of the international system remained unchanged, the revolutionary new military technology of nuclear weaponry strained the alliance in several ways. First, because the U.S. adversary was a nuclear power, it became ever riskier to live up to alliance commitments. Involvement might entail not just participation in a bloody war, but national annihilation. Knowing this, China's leaders reasonably worried that their Soviet partner would abandon them rather than run such a risk, a concern that Soviet behavior during the Taiwan Straits crises, especially the 1958 crisis, intensified. Second, as the Soviets began to deploy their own nuclear weapons, China's fear of abandonment also reflected the fact that the military importance of Soviet allies, even the biggest ally of them all, was questionable. The new nuclear logic in which possession of an absolute amount of destructive force together with the resolve to employ it were decisive, eclipsed the old conventional logic in which relative numbers of men and equipment were decisive.[16] Third, the logic of these new weapons created the opportunity for states otherwise unable to match the capabilities of the superpowers, and who doubted the reliability of external support, to provide for themselves by developing and deploying their own deterrent arsenals. Beijing's strong interest in an independent Chinese nuclear force conflicted with Moscow's concern that it might become entrapped in unwanted clashes with the U.S., further straining alliance solidarity.[17]

Structural Constraints and National Attributes

What does this cursory review of the forces in play during the period of China's "lean to one side" foreign policy line in the 1950s suggest about the usefulness of a neorealist explanation? China's strategic dependence on the Soviet superpower in the 1950s as well as China's reservations about its dependence are consistent with the expectations about behavior in a bipolar world that one would sensibly infer from neorealist balance-of-power theory. And in the Chinese case, distinctive national-level causes reinforced the usual structural incentives of anarchy that encourage a measure of self-reliance. Geography, history, nationalism, Mao's personal pride, and the emerging logic of nuclear strategy contributed to China's preference for a more independent foreign policy. For most of the 1950s, however, the necessity for external balancing continued to trump the preference for internal balancing.

But why, then, did China's policy begin to shift at the end of the decade? The world remained a bipolar anarchic arena, and China's capabilities had in no way dramatically increased relative to the superpower it feared most. Nevertheless, Beijing abandoned its deferential posture, and with increasing frequency questioned the wisdom of its comrades in Moscow. The alliance soon changed—from a tight-knit military partnership to a tenuous formality. This change is in part explained by the impact of the nuclear revolution on the role alliances can play in ensuring national security and in part by the easing of international-structural constraints on China.

Sino-Soviet Alliance and Extended Deterrence

As Moscow deployed a more credible missile-based nuclear deterrent after 1957, the key benefit from the alliance for China would be its extended deterrent effect. This benefit derived from the possibility, however slim, that Moscow (if only out of a self-interest in preserving the Soviets' international credibility) would run the grave risk of standing by its Chinese ally in the event that it faced an escalation-threatening crisis with the U.S. If extended deterrence was effective, it was because even as a remote pros-pect, the specter of nuclear war was sufficiently frightening to dissuade Washington from bold action against China.[18] For China to enjoy this benefit from Moscow's nuclear umbrella, a tenuous alliance was nearly as good as a very close one. A tenuous alliance would still constrain Washington, and a close alliance could not guarantee a diffident Soviet patron's reliability.[19]

Loosening Structural Constraints

The weakening of the Sino-Soviet alliance after 1957 also reflected a relaxation of the structural constraints China faced. By the late 1950s, the PRC's leaders confronted a less challenging international situation than in the immediate postrevolutionary years, not because the *polarity* of the system had changed, but rather because the *intensity of the threat* the U.S. represented (only partly determined by capabilities) had changed. The fear that U.S. aggression, aimed at either the industrial heartland of the northeast from the Korean peninsula or at the eastern seaboard from Taiwan, might be combined with internal subversion to topple the regime had diminished greatly. Beijing had consolidated its political position on the mainland, the Korean conflict had ended with a buffer state in place, and U.S. support for the KMT regime on Taiwan assumed a defensive rather than offensive posture after 1954.[20] During the second half of the 1950s, the focus of superpower competition in the Cold War was shifting from Asia to Europe, especially Berlin. No longer hardpressed by the threat one superpower posed, China was freer to act in ways that had the effect of weakening, though not severing, its connection to the other. Its foreign policy reflected the strong preference for self-reliance rooted in national attributes, and the necessity of dependence rooted in the structure of the international system less.

China's increasingly independent approach, a posture that courted serious risks for at least several years in the mid-1960s, would be abandoned by the end of the decade. With the Sino-Soviet border clashes of March 1969 threatening escalation to full-scale war, China again found itself tightly constrained by the international system's bipolar structure. Because China had not yet deployed a nuclear retaliatory force capable of striking the Soviet heartland, the harsh constraints of bipolarity meant that the PRC had to defuse the crisis by agreeing to negotiate under duress as Moscow rattled its nuclear saber, or to find an ally to stand with it against the threat Soviet power posed. Beijing did both. Sino-Soviet negotiations commenced and the two sides managed to keep incidents along their ever-more militarized border from escalating.[21] Meanwhile, Mao began the process of signaling that China was prepared to expand contacts with the U.S..[22] The resulting de facto Sino-American alignment against the Soviet Union during the last two decades of the Cold War again revealed the extent to which tight structural constraints induced China to sacrifice ideological preferences (especially at the outset, the highly touted Cultural Revolutionary themes of self-reliance and revolutionary purity) on the alter of strategic necessity.

The foregoing discussion suggests that the weakening of the Sino-Soviet alliance after the late 1950s may not pose a serious challenge to the usefulness of neorealist theory for explaining China's foreign policy. Two qualifications are in order, however. First, the analysis relies largely on circumstantial evidence. Such evidence, for example, makes it plausible to argue that China retained confidence in the dissuasiveness of even a troubled Sino-Soviet alliance because it continued to constrain U.S. decision makers and, therefore, that China understood its lingering importance after 1958. At least until the mid-1960s, Beijing was careful to keep the door open to reconciliation rather than opt for dissolution. And China's behavior after 1959 does suggest also an easing of the constraints of bipolarity. Prior to the border clashes with the Soviets in 1969, Beijing's fear of major war involving a superpower adversary seemed to have diminished. China did not undertake the sort of dedicated conventional force-modernization program that would have better enabled it to cope with local American threats in the short run (especially from Vietnam); instead, it diverted its limited resources to the long-term effort to deploy a credible nuclear deterrent. But determining the extent to which China's leaders believed that a weakened Sino-Soviet alliance was a strategically sufficient hedge against a reduced threat of major war with the U.S. requires access to contemporary documents that have thus far remained beyond public scrutiny. As Washington, Moscow, and Beijing continue to make more materials about Sino-Soviet–American relations available, the empirical warrant for this assertion will be easier to assess.

Second, demonstrating that China's undermining of the Sino-Soviet alliance may not have been completely foolish or exceedingly risky, and thus may be less impressive as a challenge to the usefulness of a structural-realist explanation, should not obscure the point that it is not easily reconciled with the theory. For most of the 1960s, China adhered to a foreign policy line that served national (i.e., mainly Maoist) preferences, and paid little heed to the necessities of a bipolar international structure. The error of post hoc ergo propter hoc reasoning looms large. It would be a bit more than slightly Procrustean to focus only on the reasons why a weak China might have believed it could get away with greater independence in a still bipolar world. It seems at least as plausible to argue that China's perilous foreign policy course in this period reflected either Chairman Mao's remarkable risk acceptance or his foolishness.[23] Only after Moscow's August 1968 military intervention in Czechoslovakia, its announcement of the Brezhnev doctrine to justify such actions to preserve "genuine socialism" in other countries, and border clashes along the heavily armed Sino-Soviet border that suggested the potential not only for similar Soviet meddling in Cultural Revolutionary China's murky elite political struggles but also for general war, did Mao finally, though tacitly, acknowledge that the risks of following his preferred course had become prohibitive. Neorealism nicely explains China's subsequent strategic entente with the U.S. as the constraints of bipolarity again tightened in 1969; it is much less helpful for explaining the degree to which Mao was willing to tempt fate during much of the 1960s. The Chinese experience, in short, reminds us that neorealism identifies systemic constraints that shape, rather than determine, state behavior, and that explaining a state's foreign policy often requires a grasp of those forces that a theory highlighting international-structural causes omits (e.g., Mao's risk acceptant personality and the strategic consequences of nuclear weapons).

International Structure and the Sino-American Entente

Even more than the Sino-Soviet alliance, the strategic entente between Washington and Beijing that developed in the 1970s conformed with the expectations of neorealist balance-of-power theory. The limits of a brief essay preclude a discussion paralleling the one just presented, but the essential points are simple. China perceived a rapid increase in Soviet power relative to the U.S., an increase whose significance was amplified by the diversion of U.S. capabilities to a peripheral struggle in Southeast Asia, and then a diminished American determination to maintain its strategic superiority. Moscow's international behavior after 1968 reinforced concern about the potential threat unchecked Soviet power might pose to an outgunned China armed with conventional forces that were obsolete and nuclear forces whose operational range could not yet threaten the heartland of European Russia. Threat perceptions in an era of rough Soviet–American parity and then power perceptions in an era of asserted Soviet dominance conditioned China's policy of alignment with the U.S. as counterweight. Unlike the Sino-Soviet alliance, the Sino-American collaboration was not plagued by tensions arising from geographic proximity, the echoes of unequal treaties the Qing Dynasty had signed, ideologically raised expectations, or personal rivalry. The one important bone of contention between Beijing and Washington was China's interest in reasserting sovereign control over Taiwan and displacing a regime long supported by the U.S.. This domestic imperative limited China's willingness to accommodate American preferences, but the need to maintain a strategic entente with the less threatening superpower in a bipolar world repeatedly prevented China from standing on principle.

The tightness of international-structural constraints on China, and the extent to which neorealist balance-of-power theory explains much of the PRC's foreign policy after 1969, was evident in the two most decisive breakthroughs in Sino-American relations. In 1972, Beijing demonstrated its willingness to substantially improve ties with Washington despite the latter's refusal to comply with China's longstanding demand that the U.S. sever its formal links with the Republic of China (ROC) regime in Taipei. And in 1979, renewed strategic concerns about Soviet assertiveness, especially on the eve of China's campaign against Moscow's Vietnamese ally, led Beijing to seek full diplomatic relations with Washington despite the U.S. insistence on maintaining a rather substantial "informal" relationship with the authorities in Taipei, including continued arms sales to the ROC's military. Although the pressure of the Soviet buildup along the Chinese border after the 1969 skirmishes, and Soviet activism in Southeast and Southwest Asia in the late 1970s, induced first Mao and then Deng Xiaoping to subordinate their preferences about the Taiwan issue to the necessity of parrying the potentially devastating threat its superpower neighbor posed, the importance of the Taiwan issue for China's foreign policy elite was never far below the surface. Throughout the 1970s and 1980s, China's willingness to overlook this thorn in its nationalist side varied directly with perceptions of the seriousness of the Soviet menace.[24]

As in its alliance with Moscow, the chief strategic benefit for China from cooperation with the U.S. was the way in which it compelled the Soviet adversary to consider the possibility that aggression against China might provoke the other superpower to react in an unpredictable, but potentially dangerous, fashion. The nature of this benefit was first illustrated by the Nixon administration's reported negative reaction to Soviet trial balloons in 1969 about preventive strikes against China's fledgling nuclear weapons facilities.[25] For Moscow's leaders, such a proposal may have seemed a logical follow-up to the quite similar proposal the U.S. had made to them in September 1964. Indeed, the Soviets could plausibly have argued such strikes were even more justifiable in 1969 since many analysts perceived China, having just experienced the height of its Cultural Revolutionary upheaval, as a country gone mad and one whose impetuous leaders would soon have a terrifying nuclear arsenal. But bipolarity encouraged a focus on relative gains for competing superpowers, not absolute gains for the good of the system. Permitting Moscow to defang China would relieve Soviet worries about a two-front war and might even result in a more compliant post-Mao leadership willing to return to the Soviet fold. Thus, Washington's self-interest in ensuring that Beijing remained a strategic complication for its superpower rival benefited China by reducing the likelihood of a Soviet assault.

Structural realism usefully highlights the international constraints that encouraged China to maintain its strategic alignment with the U.S. for nearly two decades after the Nixon opening in 1971. Structural realism does not, however, explain changes in the enduring Sino-American relationship in the 1980s. Despite the persistence of bipolarity, after 1981 China became less willing to subordinate national preferences (especially about Taiwan) to the strategic necessity of cultivating a close connection to the U.S.. Four reasons for this change seem plausible; none reflects a change in international structure per se. First, though bipolarity endured, its constraints eased. The Soviet threat was downgraded as China began to view the Soviet Union as strategically overextended. Second, domestic political change in the U.S. meant that China could free ride on the Reagan administration's strong interest in countering Soviet power, regardless of the state of Sino-American relations. Third, by the 1980s, China was beginning to deploy nuclear weapons with the range to threaten targets in European Russia. Fourth, Mikhail Gorbachev's foreign policy revolution reinforced China's growing sense of security and further reduced the need to nurture the strategic entente with the U.S.[26] The path that China might subsequently have followed had bipolarity endured became a moot point with the collapse of the Soviet empire and the accompanying structural transformation of the international system. The events that followed the 1989 Tiananmen Square suppression suggest that the domestic imperatives of a besieged Communist regime and the security a growing nuclear arsenal provided, would most likely have encouraged the drift toward strategic aloofness even under bipolarity. In the event, this was the path the country followed during the structural transformation that occurred in the opening years of the post–Cold War era.

Neorealist Expectations and China's Post–Cold War Foreign Policy[27]

What were the international-structural constraints that prevailed after the Cold War? First, anarchy endured, as did its consequences—insecurity and the self-help imperative. Second, the U.S. emerged as the world's preeminent global power. The Japanese economic challenge had stalled and the Russian inheritors of the Soviet military machine were presiding over its atrophy. Many analysts anticipated a transition to multipolarity sometime in the next century, but for the immediate future the system was effectively unipolar.[28] How would China cope with the novel challenge of unipolarity?

Neorealist balance-of-power theory predicts that self-regarding states will act (by arming themselves or allying with others) to counter the potential threat other states' unchecked capabilities pose. Under bipolarity, China's limited resources made self-reliance infeasible and induced it to side with one giant against the other, even while hedging against anarchy's ever-present fear of abandonment by mustering national capabilities (most dramatically its efforts to develop and deploy a nuclear deterrent). Under unipolarity how would China respond to the potential threat of unchecked American power? The dramatic decline of the former Soviet military essentially eliminated the Cold War alternative of siding with a peer competitor of the U.S. And, although China's small, but growing, nuclear arsenal provided security against the most dire threats U.S. power could pose, the PRC still lacked the full array of military and economic assets needed to deal with the U.S. on equal footing. China, it seemed, would have to accommodate an international system made in the U.S.

Unbridled American dominance of global economic institutions and regional security affairs would complicate China's ability to ensure national interests that went beyond mere survival. Washington's promotion of sanctions against the PRC after the Tiananmen suppression, and its insistence on stiff terms for China's accession to the World Trade Organization (WTO) demonstrated that conflicting interests and American power were a combination that could threaten Beijing's program of economic modernization that depended on access to and integration with the global economy. U.S. treaty commitments with Japan, Australia, and some of the ASEAN countries, as well as a revived informal security relationship with a democratizing Taiwan challenged China's interest in securing a favorable resolution of its disputes over sovereign claims in East Asia—South China Sea claims including the Spratly Islands, East China Sea claims disputing Japan's control of the Senkaku (for China, Diaoyu) Islands, and of course the PRC's claim to Taiwan and the smaller islands held by the ROC government.

As structural realists would anticipate, Beijing was determined to offset U.S. power and the difficulties it could pose for China. But structural realism, however accurately it may identify the incentives for action, provides limited guidance in predicting how specific states respond to these incentives. China's post–Cold War foreign policy has, in fact, reflected two different sorts or responses. At first, the regime adopted the straightforward approach of investing in its own capabilities and attempting to cultivate ties with others who shared its concerns about U.S. hegemony. Relatively soon, however, Beijing tacitly acknowledged the failure of this approach and opted for an approach emphasizing threat reduction and linkage politics—a more subtle foreign policy line, though one designed to serve the same purpose, enabling China to ensure its national interests in an anarchic system in which the U.S. dominated.

China's Post–Cold War Foreign Policy Line: Take One

During the transition to the post–Cold War era, from 1989 through 1991, China's leaders were focused on surviving the global collapse of communist regimes, a startling process that was especially alarming in Beijing inasmuch as it unfolded in the months following China's own massive antigovernment demonstrations suppressed only by resorting to lethal force in June 1989. Beleaguered at home, and besieged by criticisms and sanctions from abroad, in this period the regime saw politically motivated instability, rather than external military pressure, as the principal security threat. By 1992, the domestic crisis had passed, the first war of the new era (Desert Storm) had provided a startling indication of the extent of U.S. supremacy, and the Soviet Union had dissolved. China, like other countries began to adjust to the realities of the post–Cold War world. With counter-Soviet containment no longer the bedrock of Chinese (and U.S.) grand strategy, conflicting Sino-American interests once subordinated to this higher objective began to take center stage. The corrosive effect of previously muted disagreements is precisely what balance-of-power theory, including its neorealist version, predicts for allies deprived of their unifying common enemy.

For China, the prospect of an international system dominated by the U.S. was disturbing not just because of unmatched capabilities but also because of renewed American hostility toward the communist regime after the events of June 1989. Ironically, inasmuch as the U.S. had traditionally seen its defunct Soviet rival as the ideologically motivated great power, and inasmuch as China had abandoned its communist beliefs in all but name, ideology played an increasingly prominent role in Sino-American relations in the 1990s. The U.S. was easing into a grand strategy informed by the conviction that democracies do not fight democracies and that U.S. policy should promote enlargement of the democratic community on security, not just moral, grounds. China's leaders viewed such enlargement as a policy that put them in the crosshairs simply because they were communists. Whether the U.S. chose a China policy of containment designed to replicate in China the pressure-induced changes that such a strategy had allegedly produced in the Soviet Union, or a policy of engagement designed to rely less on the military stick and more on the society-opening economic wedge (in an earlier time, the CCP had labeled this the "sugar-coated bullets of the bourgeoisie"), the objective of hastening the arrival of a post-Communist regime in China was the same, and constituted the basis for fundamental conflict between Beijing and Washington. Concerned about the purposes to which the great power of a more hostile U.S. might be put, China (as neorealist theory would expect) intensified its program of military modernization and, to the extent feasible, attempted to cultivate improved relations with a Russia that was also nervous about American dominance.

The resumption of high-speed economic growth in 1992 provided the wherewithal to carry forward the program of reform and revitalization of the antiquated Peoples' Liberation Army (PLA) that had begun in the 1980s. At the same time, the desperation of former Soviet arms-producers provided an opportunity to supplement this intensified national effort with the purchase of relatively advanced, though not state of the art, Russian equipment. As a result, during the early 1990s, China was beginning to create a few better-equipped "pockets of excellence" within the PLA. Compared with China's military capabilities in recent decades, and in absolute terms, the achievements were substantial. In the arena of international security competition, however, relative capabilities are what counts. By this measure, China's self-strengthening was a long-term project in its early stages. Compared with the countries against whom it might have to match forces, including the U.S., China was not dramatically narrowing the gap.[29] Since armament could only slowly and modestly enhance China's security, neorealist balance-of-power theory would expect China to search for allies that might fill out its security portfolio. The most plausible candidate, both in terms of capabilities and (again ironically) a willingness to eschew the ideological litmus tests some in the West imposed, was Russia.

Commercial–military relations between China and Russia helped solidify their diplomatic ties, building on a rapprochement that had begun in the Soviet Union's twilight years. As the early post–Cold War honeymoon between Washington and Moscow ended by 1993, Beijing cultivated a Sino-Russian relationship whose central themes would be the rejection of U.S. hegemony and the endorsement of building multipolarity. In a series of summits between Presidents Boris Yeltsin and Jiang Zemin that culminated in the April 1996 announcement that the two countries had established a "cooperative strategic partnership," a shared concern about the way the U.S. was wielding its unprecedented power encouraged China and Russia to move closer together. Heading the list of concerns for Russia was the eastward expansion of NATO despite Russian objections; heading the list for China was the U.S. rejuvenation of its Cold War alliances in East Asia (especially with Japan) that seemed part of a de facto anti-China containment strategy.

To be sure, neither the Chinese nor the Russians were interested in a true anti-American alliance. The slight additional military benefit of an actual alliance (especially in light of Russia's rapidly declining power) would be more than offset by an unacceptably high economic cost. It would almost certainly undermine the two countries' development strategies that depended on integration with the advanced industrial West, especially the U.S. But, in a modified revival of the Cold War strategic triangle, a closer Sino-Russian partnership provided Beijing a source of leverage for improving relations with the U.S.[30] For China, the Russian card might not be an ace, but there were no aces available.

Neorealist balance-of-power theory readily accounts for China's initial effort to augment its own capabilities and to search for a strategically weighty international partner. For reasons the theory does not illuminate, however, these efforts were counterproductive. Despite its own efforts and limited cooperation with Russia, China remained militarily weak relative to the U.S. and, given its poor power projection capabilities, relative even to several of its neighbors with whom it had lingering disputes (Taiwan, Japan, and the increasingly cohesive and better-equipped states of ASEAN).[31] But the resumption of rapid economic growth that some worried might easily be translated into military power, had the effect of intensifying concern about a potential "China threat." This concern mushroomed with Beijing's more assertive international behavior in 1994–1996 when the PRC resorted to coercive diplomacy—first in support of its claims to disputed territory in the South China Sea and then to send a clear message about its willingness to use force to preclude Taiwan's independence.

Beijing viewed its muscle flexing, especially the military exercises and missile firings in the Taiwan Strait in mid-1995 and through early 1996, as simply a justifiable reassertion of sovereignty over *national* territory, but key regional actors interpreted the PLA's actions as a portent of China's general willingness to use force to pursue its *inter*national goals.[32] This reaction heightened the interest of the U.S. and its regional allies in reaffirming the American post–Cold War military commitment to East Asia. U.S. troops were not new to the region, nor were the alliances with Australia and Japan, whose revision had been initiated prior to new concerns about China. But with the Clinton administration reiterating that the U.S. would keep 100,000 troops in East Asia, and as the details of the U.S.–Australia and U.S.–Japan security arrangements emerged, diplomatic denials could not dispel Beijing's view that China was the source of instability against whom the U.S. and its allies were hedging their bets.[33] Worse still, if the trend of the mid-1990s continued, the anticipation of a growing China threat might well foster an encircling coalition headed by the U.S. that would make it more difficult for Beijing to resolve regional disputes to its satisfaction, and jeopardize foreign economic relations with valued trade partners worried about enriching a prospective adversary. Such a result would more than offset the benefits from selective purchases of Russian military equipment and the comforting rhetoric of Sino-Russian summit statements. Lacking the means to counterbalance what looked like a nascent anti-China coalition, Beijing began to shift to an approach that aimed to reduce its threatening potential.

The emerging strategy that has been evident since mid-1996 is one consistent with the logic of structural realism (especially the expectation that states will adjust the methods by which they pursue national interests in light of the costs external constraints impose) but not one readily inferred from it. In order to forestall collaborative efforts to contain China, Beijing set out to reduce the exaggerated perceptions of its capabilities and assertiveness while also increasing the value others would attach to China's development. The means to realize these objectives are embodied in what have become the two central features of Beijing's foreign policy line: (1) diplomacy designed to reassure others and transform their image of China from "threat" to "responsible participant," and (2) the forging of improved bilateral relations with each of the system's major powers, creating various sorts of "partnerships," designed to introduce the dynamics of multipolarity into what remains a unipolar system. These two elements directly respond to the recognized inadequacies of China's initial post–Cold War approach.

China's Post–Cold War Foreign Policy Line: Take Two

From "the Threat," to "the Responsible Participant"

China's diplomatic change after Spring 1996 addressed the fearful reaction to its growing capabilities and assertive regional behavior. To be sure, Chinese spokesmen had long argued that the "China threat theory" was absurd, that China's national defense buildup was purely defensive in nature, and that the notion that China needed to be contained was groundless.[34] They supported these positions by noting the very real limits on China's economic and military capabilities for the foreseeable future, China's lack of hegemonic intentions and strong normative inhibitions against the sort of aggressive international behavior that had victimized its own people over the past century and a half. They also pointed to the risk that acting on a mistaken belief in the existence of a China threat could create a self-fulfilling prophecy.[35] Yet no matter how well articulated, Beijing's propaganda effort to discredit "China-threat theory" failed to reassure regional and global actors. "Cheap talk" predictably mattered less than the uncertainties created by China's growing capabilities and assertive behavior. To more effectively change threat perceptions, China sought to cultivate a reputation as a cooperative and responsible actor, most notably through its new approach to multilateralism and its reaction to the international economic crisis that arose in East Asia during 1997.

In the early post–Cold War period, China had participated in multilateral diplomacy, but mainly in order to symbolize the PRC's status as a major power that must be included in deliberating matters of importance. It was a reluctant participant because of a strong concern that the U.S. and Japan could manipulate multilateral forums to put pressure on China.[36] But experience suggested that the original calculation of the costs and benefits of multilateralism, and the advantages for China of an emphasis on bilateralism or unilateralism, was misguided. Even in its dealings with relatively small powers in the South China Sea disputes, the PRC had not maintained the leverage it hoped for. When disputes intensified, regional adversaries whose unity China feared would manifest in multilateral settings, united anyway.

As a result, Beijing apparently concluded that accepting the constraints that come with working in multilateral settings was often preferable to the risk of isolation and encirclement that its aloof stance and assertive behavior were creating. A visible shift to a more receptive posture on multilateralism was expected to help dampen the "China-threat" perceptions that so worried Beijing. And prominently advertising China's continued participation was expected to foster the perception of responsible international behavior more convincingly than the repeated official denunciations of "China-threat theory."[37] Agreeing to the CTBT, cooperating with the effort to promote peace on the Korean peninsula, joining the international community in condemning the South Asian nuclear tests of 1998, increased flexibility on settling its differences with the ASEAN states, and negotiating agreement on the disputed borders with its former Soviet neighbors, were all reflections of Beijing's new multilateralism that served its national interest in changing perceptions of an aggressive China.[38] These efforts, moreover, promised tangible and not just reputational benefits for China. China's foreign policy elite now expects multilateralism to be a vehicle for countering American dominance. Security regimes, it is hoped, will simultaneously dilute the significance of U.S.-led East Asian military alliances and provide forums in which representatives of the developing world side with Beijing on the importance of upholding the principle of noninterference in the domestic politics of sovereign states.[39]

As with its shift on multilateral diplomacy, China's stance on currency devaluation during the East Asian financial crisis reflected the broader foreign policy goal of transforming the 1995–1996 image of China as an irredentist, revisionist, rising power, into the 1997–1998 image of China as a paragon of international responsibility. What would constitute an economically sensible Chinese reaction to the currency devaluations undertaken by major trading states in East Asia was debatable. But Beijing's announcement, and repeated assurances, that it would not devalue the Yuan to maintain the competitiveness of Chinese exports, paid significant international political dividends. Foreign analysts continued to speculate about the likelihood that China would ultimately devalue because declining exports were hurting the national economic growth at the same time that the regime was undertaking painful domestic reforms. The more others speculated about the difficulties China faces in holding the line, the greater was the payoff for Beijing in terms of a reputation for responsible internationalism that seemed to contrast with the narrowly self-interested approaches of others in the region, and also greater was the payoff for Beijing in terms of the increased credibility of its international promises that seemed to contrast with others' unfulfilled or broken promises. Even if the pressures built to the point that devaluation of the Yuan became an economic necessity, the longer China was able to delay the decision the more likely it would be able to portray the step as a result of the others' (e.g., Japan's) failure to assume their responsibilities while China shouldered more than its share.

Multipolar Methods in a Unipolar World

Efforts to alter the alarmist interpretation of China's growing power were only part of the PRC's new foreign policy line at the end of the 1990s. Beijing also sought to recast its bilateral relations with each of the world's major powers in ways that anticipated the eventual emergence of multipolarity, while recognizing the immediate need under unipolarity to reduce the chance that the U.S. and others would collaborate to oppose China. To accomplish this objective, in 1996 Beijing set out to build a series of "partnerships," a term first applied to the good relations it had recently cultivated with Moscow.[40] For China, the essential elements of a partnership are a commitment to promoting extensive economic intercourse, muting disagreements about domestic politics in the interest of working together on matters of shared concern in international diplomacy, and routinizing the frequent exchange of official visits, especially those by representatives of each country's military and regular summit meetings between top government leaders.[41]

Such partnerships are designed to create linkages that enhance the attractiveness of close relations with Beijing without requiring China to align firmly with any particular state or group of states. Asserting that the old categories of ally and adversary are a relic of power politics that prevailed only until the end of the Cold War, Beijing now seeks to improve ties with each of the world's other major powers in order to increase the price they would pay for taking actions that run contrary to China's interests.[42] Expanding trade with and investment in the China market and Beijing's cooperation on managing the security problems of weapons proliferation and terrorism, are the two most important benefits partners put at risk if they opt to press China on matters important enough to sour bilateral relations.[43]

Beijing values these Great Power partnerships not only because they allegedly promote international peace and mutually beneficial economic relations, but also, as repeatedly emphasized in discussing the first one established with Russia, because they serve China's interest in fostering the emergence of a multipolar international system in which the U.S. would no longer be so dominant. Chinese spokesmen emphasize that such partnerships are both a reflection of emerging multipolarity and (in an echo of the Western constructivist position on structure) a force accelerating this trend.[44] Moreover, cultivating such partnerships enables China to pursue this goal without resorting to the more directly confrontational (and under unipolarity, probably futile) alternative of straightforward counter-hegemonic balancing. Indeed, by eschewing alliances and cultivating such partnerships, Beijing not only avoids antagonizing others, and perhaps exacerbating concerns about its international intentions, it also gains a propaganda advantage insofar as it can now portray U.S. efforts to reinvigorate, expand, and redirect Cold War alliances in Asia and Europe as stubbornly anachronistic.[45]

Has China's shifting post–Cold War foreign policy conformed with the expectations of neorealist balance-of-power theory? The theory goes a long way toward explaining China's initial post–Cold War focus on increasing its own capabilities and improving ties with a weighty partner also concerned about the implications of a Pax Americana. But to what extent is the *current* Chinese strategy that emphasizes molding a more positive international image and cooperation rather than rivalry with the other Great Powers consistent with the expectations of structural realism? Structural realism indicates that states will be sensitive to costs that the system imposes and will modify policies if negative consequences accumulate. Indeed, though there was no change in international structure in 1996, China's foreign policy shifted as the inadequacies of its original balancing efforts became clear. China continued its effort to cope with the potentially dangerous consequences of unchecked U.S. power, but through a more subtle strategy. Even so, a structural-realist account of China's new realpolitik will take one only so far. To better understand the current foreign policy line and assess its durability, requires the inclusion of China's distinctive national attributes. Among the most important of these features that fall outside the purview of neorealist theory are: the priority assigned economic modernization; enduring historical legacies; the domestic political requirements of an insecure leadership with a shallow reservoir of legitimacy; and the country's nuclear inheritance.

Modernization

Because China is still a developing country, even if one with pockets of prosperity, the current regime continues to place top priority on the requirements of economic modernization. Modernization is not only a prerequisite for achieving world-class levels of influence, including military power, but also an absolute political necessity for a communist leadership that staked its reputation on achieving this longstanding objective of China's nationalist movement when it initiated the post-Mao reform program in late 1978. The requirements of modernization, in turn, encourage a foreign policy that facilitates access to the most useful sources of foreign investment and trade (thus, the interest in maximizing the range of good bilateral relations with the system's advanced industrial states, especially the U.S.),[46] access to scarce resources and essential trade routes beyond China's mainland (thus, the interest in multilateral arrangements that resolve, or at least set aside, conflicting sovereignty claims with neighbors, while buying the time it will take to develop a power projection capability that can serve as a coercive hedge against the failure of diplomacy).

History

Because of China's traumatic history of domination by foreign powers during the nineteenth and early twentieth centuries, the leaders in Beijing attach a high priority to respecting the legacy of the past. Among the hot-button historical memories, none is hotter than the half century of Sino-Japanese relations between 1895 and 1945.[47] The legacy of Japan's military action against and occupation of China runs through Beijing like a fault line. Japanese words and actions, even those with little real policy impact (e.g., subtle revisions in school textbooks, politicians' visits to war memorials, the occasional outrageous or careless comment about Japan's role in World War II by a right-wing politician expressing what is clearly the opinion of only a small minority of Japanese) intermittently shake the foundation of Sino-Japanese relations. These tremors exacerbate the territorial dispute over the Diaoyu (Senkaku) islands and ensure Beijing's sensitivity to any hint of a

Japanese role in a future Taiwan Straits crisis under the terms of the recently revised U.S.–Japan security guidelines. In a broader and more important sense, past experience limits the strategic options a government in Beijing will consider, in ways that confound structural-realist expectations based simply on assessing capabilities. As Tom Christensen has suggested, balance-of-power logic indicates that Japan should be viewed as a valuable strategic asset for a China concerned about its inability to counter the capabilities of the system's dominant state (certainly a more plausibly valuable counterweight than impoverished post-Soviet Russia).[48] Yet, Beijing instead focuses on suspected intentions as much as known capabilities, takes Tokyo's earlier record of anti-Chinese hostility as a reliable guide to future behavior, and alternates between worries about U.S. encouragement of an internationally more active Japan under the terms of the U.S.–Japan security treaty, and fears that a self-interested Japan will break the restraining bonds of its alliance and assume the role of an independent Great Power.[49]

A second major national historical legacy that constrains China's foreign policy is the unresolved Taiwan dispute. The determination to reestablish Beijing's sovereign control over the islands now controlled by the regime in Taipei sets a firm limit on Beijing's current effort to soften perceptions of the threat China's growing capabilities may pose. The disastrous economic, military, and diplomatic consequences of using force to uphold its claim to Taiwan mean that self-interest reinforces Beijing's proclaimed preference for a peaceful settlement of this dispute. But domestic political sentiment at both mass and elite levels means that the threat to use force, even if it carries very high costs, is in all likelihood not an idle bluff. No mainland Chinese regime can expect to survive the loss of Taiwan without a fight, certainly not the current regime whose legitimacy now rests almost entirely on its nationalist credentials.[50] "One-China" has become so engrained as part of the national myth of the country, and the CCP leaders have so publicly committed themselves to its realization, that the regime has little wiggle room if Taiwan takes steps that jeopardize reunification. Even if the strategy of reassuring others that China's international intentions are benign, encourages self-restraint, the conflicting national imperatives may well lead Beijing to decide that the use of military force is an unfortunate necessity.[51]

Political Insecurity

If the political insecurity of the regime suggests potential problems with the currently more cooperative foreign policy line, it also explains part of its appeal. There is a domestic political payoff to the extent that Beijing has recently been able to boost the regime's international reputation. For a regime that cannot now ensure international respect based simply on deference to the capabilities it commands, the current policy designed to polish China's reputation may be a sensible alternative. More active and cooperative participation in multilateral forums enables the PRC's leaders to benefit from what Iain Johnston labels "social backpatting," in which the desirability of praise is enhanced by the size of the group offering it.[52] Beijing's high-profile bilateral exchanges, which are an essential feature of Great Power partnerships, also enable the CCP leadership to claim it has earned for China the international status the country deserves, but was so long denied.

Nuclear Legacy

Finally, China's nuclear inheritance, a legacy of its most impressive Cold War military research and development effort, better enables the current regime to embrace the new foreign policy line of the late 1990s by providing a sturdy hedge against serious external threats to national security. Though small and crude, relative to the deterrents the other major nuclear powers possess, China's arsenal is sufficient to require those who might challenge its vital interests to confront the risk that they are triggering a chain of events whose outcome could be quickly catastrophic. Because the logic of nuclear deterrence is one in which national control and absolute amounts of punitive capabilities, rather than alliances and relative strength, are what counts, this logic works as well in the unipolar world as it did in its bipolar predecessor. With the ultimate guarantee in hand, China can more safely undertake its current experiment with multilateral approaches to resolving international problems and its attempt to manage Great Power threats by cultivating multiple partnerships that reduce tensions and discourage anti-China coalitions from forming.[53]

In sum, then, responding to systemic and national constraints, Beijing has recast rather than discarded the techniques of realpolitik. For China at the dawn of the twenty-first century, the historically familiar means for counterbalancing the system's dominant state are not promising. Classic "external balancing" is not feasible. There are no partners with the clout, and more importantly, with concerns about American power sufficiently strong to serve as the basis for an old-fashioned strategic alliance. In addition, the attractiveness of the U.S. as an economic partner for all major powers is an important offsetting consideration. Moreover, in the nuclear age, the effectiveness of alliances, both in terms of their military significance and their political viability, is questionable. Classic "internal balancing" is also not feasible. There is little prospect that China's economic and military capabilities will increase so rapidly that it can become a peer competitor of the

United States in the next few decades. Indeed, given the domestic development burdens Beijing faces, and given the nature of both economic and military competition in the era of advanced technology (in which increased funding is a necessary but not sufficient basis for modernization), China would be hard-pressed to close the gap with "the world's sole remaining superpower" even if the U.S. stood still. In a world where all nations, including the U.S., are sensitive to the imperatives of economic and military competition, China faces a stiff challenge in simply achieving more modest goals—remaining competitive with its neighbors in the East Asian region and significantly raising the price a still stronger U.S. will have to pay if it threatens China's interests in its own backyard.[54]

China's current foreign policy line is, then, an approach that makes the best of a strategically difficult situation. It is a response to the structural constraints of a unipolar, anarchic international system, a response whose logic is illuminated by structural realism, but whose content can only be understood in light of the specific features of the Chinese case. The evolution of China's foreign policy line after the Cold War, as in the preceding decades, confirms both the usefulness and limits of structural-realist accounts. Neorealist balance-of-power theory, a product of theoretical science, identifies important international-structural influences that constrain a state's foreign policy. And, as ever, the usefulness of the theory for understanding a particular case, the task of applied science, is demonstrated by exploring how the causes it identifies interact with the many it has set aside. The durability of the international system's present structure and the national attributes most important in shaping China's foreign policy will together determine whether Beijing's subtle realpolitik that emerged in the late 1990s continues or is supplanted by its historically more familiar, brash cousin.

Notes

1. On the long-running postwar debate about the role of area studies, see Robert H. Bates, "Area Studies and the Discipline: A Useful Controversy?" Chalmers Johnson, "Preconception vs. Observation, or the Contributions of Rational Choice Theory and Area Studies to Contemporary Political Science." Ian S. Lustick, "The Disciplines of Political Science: Studying the Culture of Rational Choice as a Case in Point." All in *PS: Political Science & Politics* 30 (June 1997): 2; Avery Goldstein, "The Domain of Inquiry in Political Science: General Lessons from the Study of China," *Polity* 21:3 (Spring 1989): 517–37; Thomas J. Christensen, "China's Rise and the Limits of Systemic Theorizing," paper prepared for the Workshop on IR Theory and the Study of Chinese Foreign Policy, Harvard University, June 19–20, 1998.

2. Kenneth N. Waltz, *Man, the State, and War: A Theoretical Analysis* (New York: Columbia University Press, 1959); Kenneth N. Waltz, *Theory of International Politics* (Menlo Park, CA: Addison-Wesley, 1979); Colin Elman, "Horses for Courses: Why *Not* Neorealist Theories of Foreign Policy?" *Security Studies* 6:1 (Autumn 1996): 7–53; Kenneth N. Waltz, "International Politics is not Foreign Policy," *Security Studies* 6:1 (Autumn 1996): 54–57; and Elman's response, pp. 58–61. See also the debate about the neorealist research program contained in the *American Political Science Review* 91:4 (December 1997).
3. See Martin Landau, *Political Theory and Political Science* (Atlantic Highlands, NJ: Humanities Press, 1972); Goldstein, "Domain of Inquiry."
4. See Waltz, *Theory of International Politics*, ch. 1 and pp. 121–23.
5. For discussion of the term "grand strategy" see Paul Kennedy, "Grand Strategy in War and Peace: Toward a Broader Definition," in Paul Kennedy, ed., *Grand Strategies in War and Peace* (New Haven: Yale University Press, 1991), p. 6; also Barry Posen, *The Sources of Military Doctrine: France, Britain, and Germany Between the World Wars* (Ithaca: Cornell University Press, 1984).
6. See Avery Goldstein, *Deterrence and Security in the 21st Century: China, Britain, France and the Enduring Legacy of the Nuclear Revolution* (Stanford: Stanford University Press, 2000).
7. On the relation between the closeness of involvement with a political system and the tightness of its structural constraints, see Waltz, *Theory of International Politics*, p. 128; also Avery Goldstein, *From Bandwagon to Balance-of-Power Politics: Structural Constraints and Politics in China, 1949–1978* (Stanford: Stanford University Press, 1991), pp. 111–13.
8. On Mao's realism, see Thomas J. Christensen, *Useful Adversaries: Grand Strategy, Domestic Mobilization, and Sino-American Conflict, 1947–1958* (Princeton: Princeton University Press, 1996); also Alastair Iain Johnston, "Cultural Realism and Strategy in Maoist China," Peter J. Katzenstein, ed., *The Culture of National Security: Norms and Identity in World Politics* (New York: Columbia University Press, 1996).
9. See the following three items in *Cold War International History Project Bulletin*, Issue 11 (Winter 1998), available online, http://cwihp.si.edu/pdf.htm: "Report by Four Chinese Marshals—Chen Yi, Ye Jianying, Xu Xiangqian, and Nie Rongzhen,—to the Central Committee, 'A Preliminary Evaluation of the War Situation' (excerpt), 11 July 1969," Document No. 9, trans. by Chen Jian and Li Di; "Report by Four Chinese Marshals—Chen Yi, Ye Jianying, Nie Rongzhen, and Xu Xiangqian—to the CCP Central Committee, 'Our Views about the Current Situation' (excerpt) 17 September 1969," Document No. 11, trans. Chen Jian and Li Di; "Further Thoughts by Marshal Chen Yi on Sino-American Relations," Document No. 12, trans. Chen Jian. See also the discussion and analysis in Goldstein, *Deterrence and Security in the 21st Century*, pp. 71–76.
10. For two detailed historical analyses of the alliance, see Donald S. Zagoria, *The Sino-Soviet Conflict, 1956–1961* (Princeton: Princeton University Press, 1962);

Lowell Dittmer, *Sino-Soviet Normalization and Its International Implications, 1945–1990* (Seattle : University of Washington Press, 1992).

11. On the role that threat perceptions play in conditioning balancing responses, see the writings of Stephen M. Walt, "Alliance Formation and the Balance of World Power," *International Security* 9:4 (Spring 1985): 3–43; *The Origins of Alliances* (Ithaca: Cornell University press, 1988); and his discussion of its effects on China's foreign relations in, *Revolution and War* (Ithaca: Cornell University Press, 1996), pp. 310–30.
12. The continuing flow of previously unreleased documents confirms the depth of the tensions between the Soviet and Chinese communists that actually began as early as the 1920s with disagreements over the best strategy for waging revolution in China. China's communist leaders were intimately familiar with the Soviet track record of bad, sometimes disastrous, advice to the CCP that was tailored to serve Soviet rather than Chinese interests. This history set the stage for Beijing's skepticism about the wisdom of accepting Moscow's foreign policy advice after 1949. On Sino-Soviet disagreements about revolutionary strategy in the 1920s and 1930s, see Benjamin Isadore Schwartz, *Chinese Communism and the Rise of Mao* (Cambridge: Harvard University Press, 1951); Chalmers A. Johnson, *Peasant Nationalism and Communist Power: The Emergence of Revolutionary China, 1937–1945* (Stanford, CA: Stanford University Press, 1962). For evidence of Stalin's reluctance to back the CCP in its final push to power after 1945, see Brian Murray, "Working Paper #12: Stalin, the Cold War, and the Division of China: A Multi-Archival Mystery," *Cold War International History Project Document Library*, http://cwihp.si.edu/cwihplib.nsf. For Mao Zedong's recounting of Soviet (i.e., mainly Stalin's) mistaken China policies, see Mao Zedong, "Tong Sulian Zhu Hua Dashi You Jin de Tan Hua" (Mao's Talks with Soviet Ambassador to China, Yudin), July 22, 1958, in *Mao Zedong Waijiao Wenxuan* (Beijing: Shijie Zhishi Chubanshe, 1994), pp. 325–27; Mao Zedong, "Guanyu Guoji Xingshi de Jianghua Tigang" (Outline of Speech on the International Situation). Mao Zedong, "Guanyu Guoji Xingshi de Jianghua Tigang," December 1959, in *Jianguo Yilai Mao Zedong Wengao*, Vol. 8 (Beijing: Zhongyang Wenxian Chubanshe, 1993), pp. 599–600. See also Zhang Shuguang, *Deterrence and Strategic Culture: Chinese-American Confrontations, 1949–1958* (Ithaca: Cornell University Press, 1992), p. 19; Sergei N. Goncharov, John W. Lewis, and Litai Xue, *Uncertain Partners: Stalin, Mao, and the Korean War* (Stanford: Stanford University Press, 1993), pp. 23, 25, 72, 77, 78.
13. For Mao's list of grievances about the Soviet role in China's revolution, see Mao Zedong, "Tong Sulian Zhu Hua Dashi You Jin de Tan Hua," pp. 322–33; also Goncharov, Lewis, and Xue, *Uncertain Partners.*
14. See Hans Morgenthau, *Politics Among Nations* 5th ed. (New York: Knopf, 1973), p. 184; also Walt, *Origins of Alliances.*
15. See Zagoria, *Sino-Soviet Conflict*; Mao Zedong, "Tong Sulian Zhu Hua Dashi You Jin de Tan Hua," esp. p. 327.

16. On China's fear of strategic marginalization, see Christensen, *Useful Adversaries.*
17. See Goldstein, *Deterrence and Security in the 21st Century,* Chs. 3 and 4.; also Goldstein "Discounting the Free Ride: Alliances and Security in the Postwar World," *International Organization* 49:1 (Winter 1995): 39–72.
18. It was the slimness rather than the possibility that worried Beijing, however, fostering a determination to acquire an independent deterrent capability. On the complex relationship between rational deterrence theory and the practice of extended deterrence, see Jervis Robert, *The Meaning of the Nuclear Revolution* (Ithaca: Cornell University Press, 1989). Goldstein, *Deterrence and Security in the 21st Century.*
19. Even during the open, often bitter, disagreements between Beijing and Moscow in the early 1960s, prudent decision makers in Washington had to worry about Soviet reaction to military strikes aimed at China. Both the Kennedy and Johnson administrations were aware of the deep Sino-Soviet split, but wondered and worried about Soviet reactions when considering preventive strikes against China's nuclear weapons development infrastructure. Moscow's cool reaction to informal trial balloons about such strikes did not diminish U.S. inhibitions against taking this dramatic step. Occasional efforts to sound out Moscow's reaction were apparently rebuffed on each occasion, have long been rumored, and are now substantiated in the growing record of declassified documents. See Goldstein, *Deterrence and Security in the 21st Century,* pp. 103–10; *National Intelligence Estimate 10–61,* August 8, 1961, "Authority and Control in the Communist Movement," *Foreign Relations of the United States,* Vol. XXII: *China; Korea; Japan,* #49 (available online at http://www.state.gov/www/about_state/history/frusXXII/); "Editorial Note" *FRUS,* Vol. XXII, #164; "Memorandum from the Assistant Secretary of Defense for International Security Affairs (Nitze) to Secretary of Defense McNamara," May 11, 1963, *FRUS* Vol. XXII, #177; "Editorial Note," *FRUS,* Vol. XXII, #180; "Highlights from Secretary of State Rusk's Policy Planning Meeting," October 15, 1963, *FRUS,* Vol. XXII, #191. On the Johnson administration's rekindled interest in preventive strikes one month before China's first nuclear weapons test, see McGeorge Bundy, "Memorandum for the Record," September 15, 1964, National Security Archive electronic Briefing Book No. 1, *The United States, China, and the Bomb,* http://www.seas.gwu.edu/nsarchive/NSAEBB/NSAEBB1/nsaebb1.htm., document 3.
20. China's perception of the risks it faced were evident in the 1958 Taiwan Straits Crisis as Mao acted on his belief that he could manipulate tensions without triggering a general war. See Christensen, *Useful Adversaries.*
21. Richard Wich, *Sino-Soviet Crisis Politics* (Cambridge: Harvard University Press, 1980). For a review of the border clashes in light of recently declassified documents, see Christian F. Ostermann, "East German Documents on the Sino-Soviet Border Conflict, 1969," *Bulletin, Cold War International History Project: The Cold War in Asia, Issues* 6–7, pp. 186–93.

22. See "Report by Four Chinese Marshals—Chen Yi, Ye Jianying, Xu Xiangqian, and Nie Rongzhen,—to the Central Committee, 'A Preliminary Evaluation of the War Situation' (excerpt), 11 July 1969"; "Report by Four Chinese Marshals—Chen Yi, Ye Jianying, Nie Rongzhen, and Xu Xiangqian—to the CCP Central Committee, 'Our Views about the Current Situation' (excerpt) 17 September 1969"; "Further Thoughts by Marshal Chen Yi on Sino-American Relations"; Goldstein, *Deterrence and Security in the 21st Century*, pp. 71–76.
23. The Hundred Flowers Campaign, the Great Leap Forward, and the Cultural Revolution offer plenty of evidence of Mao's recklessness on the domestic front. Yet, on both domestic and foreign policy, Mao would eventually accommodate reality and agree to policy adjustments as dangerous consequences accumulated. Mao thus alternated between the prudence of a hard-boiled realist, and the impulsiveness of a romantic ideologue. On Mao as a realist, see Christensen, *Useful Adversaries*; Christensen, "China's Rise and the Limits of Systemic Theorizing," Johnston, "Cultural Realism and Strategy in Maoist China." On Mao as a romantic ideologue, see Shu Guang Zhang, *Mao's Military Romanticism: China and the Korean War, 1950–1953* (Lawrence, Kansas: University Press of Kansas, 1995); Michael M. Sheng, *Battling Western Imperialism: Mao, Stalin, and the United States* (Princeton: Princeton University Press, 1997).
24. See Robert S. Ross, *Negotiating Cooperation: The United States and China, 1969–1989* (Stanford: Stanford University Press, 1995).
25. Recently declassified notes of Henry Kissinger confirm that the United States subsequently assured China that this remained the American position. See William Burr ed., *The Kissinger Transcripts: The Top Secret Talks with Beijing and Moscow* (The New Press, 1999) (excerpts available at the National Security Archive website http://www.seas.gwu.edu/nsarchive/.
26. Sino-Soviet rapprochement began in Brezhnev's last years. The process accelerated with the accession of the Gorbachev leadership group who made clear its determination to improve Sino-Soviet relations by meeting what had become Beijing's three conditions for normalization (leave Afghanistan, reduce military presence on the common border, discontinue support for Vietnam's expansionism in Indo-china). See Goldstein, *Deterrence and Security in the 21st Century*, p. 89, n. 74.
27. In addition to cited material, this section draws on approximately 25 hours of interviews with Chinese foreign policy elites undertaken in Beijing between June 27 and July 15, 1998. For more information about the affiliations of those interviewed (though not the identity of individuals), and their responses, please contact the author.
28. For contrasting perspectives on unipolarity and its implications, see Christopher Layne, "The Unipolar Illusion: Why New Great Powers will Rise," *International Security* 17:4 (Spring 1993): 5–51; Charles Krauthammer, "The Unipolar Moment," *Foreign Affairs: America and the World* 70:1 (Winter 1991): 23–33;

and especially William C. Wohlforth, "The Stability of a Unipolar World," *International Security* 24:1 (Summer 1999): 5–41.

29. See Avery Goldstein, "Great Expectations: Interpreting China's Arrival," *International Security* 22:3 (Winter 1997/1998): 36–73, reprinted in Michael E. Brown, Owen R. Cote, Jr., Sean M. Lynn-Jones, and Steven E. Miller, eds., *The Rise of China* (Cambridge, MA: MIT Press, 2000).
30. See Lowell Dittmer, "The Strategic Triangle: An Elementary Game Theoretical Analysis," *World Politics* 33:4 (July 1981): 484–515.
31. Analysts and foreign policy elites who focused on China's purchase of advanced fighter aircraft (Su-27), submarines (Kilo-class) and destroyers (Sovremennyi) tended to ignore, or at least downplay, the fact that such equipment purchases were not sufficient to reverse the imbalance in fighting power between China and its plausible adversaries in the most likely theaters of operation, let alone turn the PRC into a peer military competitor of the United States. Those who pointed alarmingly to the emergence of new military units designed for combined arms warfare, tended to gloss over the fact that such units remained a small fraction of the PLA, and that many were neither adequately trained nor equipped. On the military and economic aspects of the exaggeration of Chinese capabilities, see Goldstein, "Great Expectations." For discussion of the military modernization efforts of regional actors, see Desmond Ball, "Arms and Affluence"; "SE Asians Arming Up to Protect Their Resources," *Reuters*, January 29, 1996, clari.tw.defense, ClariNet Communications Corp.
32. On the complex calculations driving the three principals in the 1995–1996 Taiwan Straits crisis, see Robert S. Ross, "The 1995–96 Taiwan Strait Confrontation: Coercion, Credibility, and the Use of Force," *International Security* 25:2 (2000): 87–123. Chas. W. Freeman Jr., "Preventing War in the Taiwan Strait; Restraining Taiwan and Beijing," *Foreign Affairs* 77:4 (July–August 1998): 6–11; Thomas J. Christensen, "Chinese Realpolitik," *Foreign Affairs* 75:5 (Sep–Oct 1996): 37–52.
33. Interviewees emphasized that this was China's clear understanding. For the official U.S. position, see *United States Security Strategy for the East Asia-Pacific Region* (Washington: Department of Defense, Office of International Security Affairs, February 1995, November 1998).
34. See Chi Haotian, "Zou Fuhe Woguo Guoqing Bing Fanying Shidai Tezheng de Guofang Xiandaihua Jianshe Daolu" ("Follow the path of modernizing national defense suited to our national conditions and the characteristics of our times"), *Qiushi* 188:8 (April 1996): 10.
35. For representative official statements, see "Jieshou Meiguo Youxian Xinwen Dianshiwang Jizhe Caifang, Jiang Zemin Changtan Zhongmei Guanxi ji Taiwan Deng Wenti" (Giving An Interview to an American CNN Reporter, Jiang Zemin Speaks Freely about Sino-American Relations, Taiwan, and Other Questions), *Renmin Ribao*, May 10, 1997 (*Renmin Ribao* articles available online at http://www.snweb.com/gb/people_daily/gbrm.htm); "Jiu Zhongmei Guanxi,

Taiwan Wenti, Zhongguo Renda Zhidu deng Wenti: Qiao Shi Jieshou Meiguo Jizhe Caifang" (Qiao Shi takes questions from American reporters on Sino-American relations, the Taiwan problem, the national people's congress system, etc.), *Renmin Ribao*, January 17, 1997; "Chi Haotian Zai Riben Fabiao Yanjiang, Zhuozhong Chanshu Zhongguo Guofang Zhengce" (Chi Haotian's Lecture in Japan Setting Forth China's National Defense Policy), *Renmin Ribao*, February 5, 1998; Wang Jisi, "Shiji Zhi Jiao de Zhongmei Guanxi" (Sino-American Relations at the Turn of the Century), *Renmin Ribao*, March 1, 1997.

36. See "Analyst Interviewed on APEC's Prospects," *Chuon Koron*, December 1995, pp. 30–44, FBIS-EAS-95-232, Daily Report. Han Hua, "Zhang Yishan [Chinese Foreign Ministry Official] on China's Multilateral Diplomacy," *Wen Wei Po*, January 7, 1997, p. A2, FBIS-CHI-97-009. Most of those I interviewed emphasized the prevalence of this fear about multilateralism.
37. Referring to Jiang Zemin's report to the fifteenth CCP Congress in September 1997, Liang Shoude noted, "This is the first time China has announced that it would take vigorous part in multilateral diplomatic activities. It is a major change in China's diplomacy" (Liu Di, "Deng Xiaoping's Thinking on Diplomatic Work and China's Diplomatic Policy—Interview with Liang Shoude, Dean for College of International Relations for Beijing University," *Ta Kung Pao*, November 2, 1997, p. A6, FBIS-CHI-97-310, Daily Report). See also Alastair Iain Johnston and Paul Evans, "China's Engagement with Multilateral Security Institutions," unpublished ms., p. 44. See Masashi Nishihara, "Aiming at New Order for Regional Security—Current State of ARF," *Gaiko Forum*, November 1997, pp. 35–40, FBIS-EAS-97-321, Daily Report.
38. See Thomas J. Christensen, "Parsimony is No Simple Matter: International Relations Theory, Area Studies, and the Rise of China," unpublished ms., February 26, 1998, pp. 35–36; Johnston and Evans, "China's Engagement with Multilateral Security Institutions," pp. 33–34. At every opportunity China proudly points to the April 1996 five-nation treaty (among China, Russia, Kazakhstan, Kyrgyzstan, and Tajikistan) on military confidence building measures in the border areas as "the first multilateral treaty signed to build confidence in the Asia-Pacific region" and cites it as a "powerful rebuttal of the 'China threat theory,'" evidence that "instead of being a 'threat,' China actually plays a constructive role in preserving peace and stability in its peripheral areas" (Xia Liping, "Some Views on Multilateral Security Cooperation in Northeast Asia," *Xiandai Guoji Guanxi*, December 20, 1996, No. 12, pp. 12–15, FBIS-CHI-97-074; "Five-nation Agreement Provides Model in Peaceful Conflict Resolution," *Jiefang Ribao*, April 27, 1996, p. 4, FBIS-CHI-96-145, Daily Report). In June 2001, the "Shanghai Five" (so-named because of the site of their original meeting) added a sixth member, Uzbekistan, and formalized its existence as the Shanghai Cooperation Organization. In March 1997, when the "Inter-Sessional Support Group on Confidence-Building Measures of the ASEAN Regional Forum (ARF)" was held in Beijing, it was emphasized that "China has placed

importance to (sic) this three day meeting because it's the first on multilateral dialogue and cooperation hosted by China" ("ARF Support Group Meeting Ends in Beijing," *Xinhua*, March 8, 1997, FBIS-CHI-97-067, Daily Report).

39. Xia, "Some Views on Multilateral Security Cooperation in Northeast Asia." On the clash of sovereignty concerns and the principle of transparency in arms control, see "Wo Caijun Dashi Zai Lianda Yiwei Qiangdiao, Ying Fangzhi Ba Caijun Mubiao Yinxiang Fazhanzhong Guojia" ("Our Disarmament Ambassador at the General Assembly's First Session Emphasizes, [We] Should Guard Against Making the Developing Countries the Target of Disarmament"), *Renmin Ribao*, October 16, 1997.
40. See "China: Qian Qichen on 'Constructive' Strategic Partnerships," *Xinhua*, November 3, 1997, FBIS-CHI-97-307, Daily Report; Lu Jin and Liu Yunfei, "New Analysis: From Beijing to Washington and From Moscow to Beijing—a Revelation of New-Type Relations Between Major Powers," *Xinhua*, November 9, 1997, FBIS-CHI-97-313, Daily Report.
41. For discussion of these bilateral relationships, see Avery Goldstein, "The Diplomatic Face of China's Grand Strategy: A Rising Power's Emerging Choice," *The China Quarterly*, 168 (December 2001); Avery Goldstein, "An Emerging China's Emerging Grand Strategy: A Neo-Bismarckian Turn?" in John Ikenberry and Michael Mastanduno, eds., *The Emerging International Relations of the Asia-Pacific Region* (New York: Columbia University Press, forthcoming). While relations with the United States, Europe (separately with Britain, France, and Germany as well as with the EU), and Russia have been put on solid footing, a decisive breakthrough in the status, if not the substance of Sino-Japanese relations remains elusive because of the interplay of disagreements about the historical legacy of World War II and domestic politics in each country.
42. Elsewhere I have labeled this part of a neo-Bismarckian grand strategy, indicating the similarity in overarching purpose while recognizing the important differences between the foreign policies of nineteenth-century Germany and late twentieth-century China. The similarity is the attempt to reduce the likelihood that the system's other major powers will cooperate against a rising but not yet dominant state. The differences are many, but perhaps most importantly the diminished importance of formal military alliances and the much diminished likelihood that Great Power war will be a prominent feature of international politics (Goldstein, "An Emerging China's Emerging Grand Strategy").
43. On the opportunity costs, others will confront if they fail to maintain their partnerships with China, see Shi Nangen, "1997: A Fruitful Year in China's Multi-Dimensional Diplomacy," *Beijing Review*, No. 7, February 16–22, 1998, p. 7, FBIS-CHI-98-053, Daily Report; see also "Prospects of China's Diplomatic Activities in 1998," *Beijing Central People's Radio*, January 25, 1998, FBIS-CHI-98-028, Daily Report. Some of my interlocutors explicitly mentioned controversial arms and technology transfers as one of the few cards China could use as leverage in its international bargaining with the advanced West.

44. See "Yici Yiyi Zhongda Yingxiang shenyuan de Fanwen—Zhuhe Jiang Zhuxi Fang E Yuanman Chenggong" (A Trip of Great Significance and Far-Reaching Influence—Congratulations on President Jiang's Completely Successful Russian Visit), *Renmin Ribao*, April 27, 1997; "Iraq Crisis Revealed Collapse of U.S. Global Authority: Chinese Analysts," *Agence France-Presse*, March 9, 1998, Clari.China.; Tang Tianri, "Relations Between Major Powers Are Being Readjusted," *Xinhua*, December 15, 1997, FBIS-CHI-97-351, Daily Report.
45. See Zhao Gangzhen, "Daguo Guanxi, 'Huoban Re,'" ("Big Power Relations", "Partnership Fever"), *Renmin Ribao*, April 21, 1998. Chinese Defense Minister Chi Haotian told U.S. Defense Secretary William Cohen during his January 1998 visit to Beijing "that at present, relations between major powers are undergoing a strategic readjustment. In the new situation, neither expanding military alliances [i.e., NATO] nor strengthening military alliances [i.e., U.S. alliances with Japan and Australia] is conducive to maintenance of peace and security" ("China: Expanding Military Contacts Part of Diplomatic Strategy," *Xinhua*, February 20, 1998, FBIS-CHI-98-051, Daily Report.)
46. Several interviewees emphasized that after his "southern tour" in Spring 1992 re-accelerating economic reform, Deng Xiaoping directed the foreign policy establishment that good relations with the United States were an absolute necessity, and that China must be prepared to make some compromises in order to improve Sino-American relations. This directive has remained an important guideline ever since.
47. Half a century on, China's leaders continue to contrast Japan's slow and reluctant expressions of regret about its wartime activities with postwar Germany's quick and unhesitating renunciation of those undertaken by its Nazi predecessors. My interviewees consistently repeated this familiar Chinese claim. For the views of foreign analysts that emphasize the depth of the changes within Japan, see Peter J. Katzenstein and Nobuo Okawara, "Japan's National Security: Structures, Norms, and Policies," *International Security* 17:4 (Spring 1993): 84–118; Thomas U. Berger, "From Sword to Chrysanthemum: Japan's Culture of Anti-Militarism," *International Security* 17:4 (Spring 1993): 119–50.
48. See Christensen, "Chinese Realpolitik"; "China's Rise and the Limits of Systemic Theorizing." The constraining force of this historical legacy was revealed again at the November 1998 summit in Tokyo when disagreements about how to address the events of World War II apparently prevented Sino-Japanese relations from moving to the next level of major power partnership.
49. A focus that sets aside non-structural factors that mold threat perceptions also would miss the reasons why any such Chinese interest in strategic cooperation would not likely be reciprocated. For reasons of geography as well as the history of an earlier era during which imperial China was hegemonic in East Asia, Japan remains more concerned about future Chinese intentions than about current U.S. capabilities. Moreover, as with the Russian case, Japan would be loathe to alienate its most valuable economic partner especially in an era of economic difficulty.

50. None of the interviewees doubted that military force would be used if necessary to prevent the loss of Taiwan. One interviewee with close ties to the military pointed out that force would be used even though the PLA expects it would lose the battle that would inevitably involve the United States. He emphasized that the CCP regime could survive if it fights and loses, but not if it concedes without a fight.
51. See Freeman, "Preventing War in the Taiwan Strait." China's leaders must also worry about demonstration effects in Tibet, Xinjiang, and Inner Mongolia should it backtrack on its refusal to abandon sovereign claims. Each of the territories poses distinct problems, and none shares many similarities to the Taiwan case, but Beijing is most likely risk averse in this issue area, especially after witnessing the unraveling of the multiethnic Soviet state in the early 1990s.
52. See Alastair Iain Johnston, "Socialization in International Institutions: The ASEAN Regional Forum and IR Theory," unpublished paper prepared for the Penn-Dartmouth conference on "The Emerging International Relations of the Asia-Pacific Region," May 8–9, 1998, Christopher H. Browne Center for International Politics, University of Pennsylvania.
53. A key question, to which there are not yet clear answers, is why China agreed to end its testing program and sign the CTBT in the summer of 1996. If the decision reflected a belief that nuclear weapons were not essential to China's security, then the position I have staked out is contradicted. If, as seems more likely, the decision reflected a belief that China's final series of tests ensured it of at least a minimal deterrent capability, then accession to the CTBT is consistent with both the importance of maintaining the nuclear guarantee and a willingness to trade off military capabilities (in this case, at least slowing, if not crippling, warhead modernization) for diplomatic gains.
54. On the challenges facing China as it tries to increase its military capabilities relative to its most plausible adversaries, see Goldstein, "Great Expectations"; Andrew J. Nathan and Robert S. Ross, *The Great Wall and the Empty Fortress: China's Search for Security* (New York: W.W. Norton, 1997); cf. Richard Bernstein and Ross H. Munro, *The Coming Conflict with China* (New York: Alfred A. Knopf, 1997). On the lower barriers to acquiring a capability to complicate U.S. foreign policy decisions in the Western Pacific, see Thomas J. Christensen, "Posing Problems without Catching Up: China's Rise and Challenges for U.S. Security Policy," *International Security* 25:4 (Spring 2001): 5–40.

CHAPTER 8

America Deals with North Korea: A Realist's Approach

Robert L. Gallucci

I propose to offer some observations drawn from our most recent past in dealing with North Korea—those that seem to emerge from the American negotiations with the Democratic People's Republic of Korea (DPRK) over the last seven years. Let me offer three observations, and then suggest what implications or lessons seem to follow. First, it seems to me, that we do not know with any confidence what the North Korean grand strategy is. We do not know even if, looking ahead five, ten, or fifteen years, the DPRK has a consistent goal or coherent strategy for dealing with the South, with the U.S. of America, with Japan, or with the rest of the world. Since we do not know what the North Korean strategy is, we really do not know which of the two kinds of approaches to North Korea is more nearly correct. One approach assumes that North Korean strategy has been aimed at deterrence in the purpose of defense. North Korea, by this interpretation, is looking at the growing strength of South Korea over decades, the loss of protection from its principal ally, the Soviet Union, and a reorientation of its other ally, China, and concludes that it needs a way to counter, to check, to deter, the U.S. in alliance with the Republic of Korea (ROK), its enemy to the south. It needs a way, as Vice Foreign Minister Kang Sok Ju used to say to me, to stop the U.S. from strangling North Korea.

If North Korea is simply looking for a way to stop an overwhelming onslaught from the South, then the North Korean nuclear weapons and ballistic missile programs might simply be part of this strategy. Moreover, it would be quite reasonable to conclude, since both programs were, and are "for sale," that the North is prepared to abandon these programs. If the North thought it could use the sale of these programs to buy a new relationship with the U.S., with South Korea, with Japan, and with the rest of the world, and if the price for which the North could sell these programs was high enough to meet their needs for defense, to boost their sagging economy, and to help them to some level of economic reform, then it would be reasonable to look favorably upon the process that we are engaged in with the North. It is not important at what point the North decided upon this strategy; what is important is that it's a defensive strategy. That is one view. And it would be good news, particularly if it were true.

Another view, another school of thought, would be that the North Korean strategy was, is, and most importantly, always will be aimed at creating the opportunity for the North to overwhelm the South and unify the peninsula at the first opportunity that should be presented—and almost certainly by the use of force. If this is the fundamental strategy, the goal of the DPRK, then the nuclear weapons and the ballistic missile programs are not designed for deterrence in a defensive strategy; rather they are, for deterrence in an offensive strategy. They are designed to undercut the alliances between the U.S. and Japan, and the U.S. and the ROK. According to this view, if the day comes when the North can successfully engage the South with its conventional forces, they will have the capability to deter the U.S. from executing its alliance obligations and even deter the Japanese from extending support. According to this view, the long-range purpose of the North Korean strategy is offensive, the purpose of these weapons systems—the nuclear weapons and the ballistic missiles—is offensive, and they were not, are not, and will not be for sale. They may be for rent, they may be for lease, but they are not for sale. According to this approach, the North will never give them up and we ought to recognize that.

So the initial part of the first observation is that since we do not know what North Korean strategy is, there certainly may be more Kum Chang Rhee's, more caves and caverns, and we certainly cannot tell whether our negotiating partner is acting in "good faith," or as I have learned, Koreans like to say, "sincerely."

The second part of the first observation about our ignorance of North Korean strategy is that we do not know if North Korea is essentially and fundamentally deterred from a military offensive, no matter what the circumstances. That is very important.

I note that the U.S. and the ROK, to the best of my knowledge, have concluded that their combined forces will prevail in any conceivable engagement with North Korean forces. The issue here is what we think they think. One view, again, is that the North Koreans can see the U.S.–ROK advantage as clearly as we can, because it is that clear. And that therefore deterrence on the Korean peninsula is extremely stable; it is secure and we really do not have to worry about a strike out of the blue from the North. But there is another view. If the North should see certain collapse, if the regime leadership should see inevitable absorption into the South in the distance, it may opt for preventive war; or if there should be a catastrophic incident of some kind, the regime may see imminent collapse, the possibility of intervention from the South, and thus the virtue of a preemptive strike. In other words, the concern is that the regime may calculate that an engagement, even a large-scale engagement, will leave it in a better circumstance than would either the collapse or absorption scenarios.

The second observation is that just because we understand the value of a unified Washington–Tokyo–Seoul approach to North Korea, it does not mean that we will always achieve one. It seems clear that Japan, South Korea, and the U.S. have substantial common interests and common objectives, but very often different perceptions and perspectives. Examples abound. Many in the U.S. understood that the South Korean attitude toward our direct negotiations with the DPRK was not always positive. And there were times when, quite frankly, Americans regarded Kim Young Sam's approach to the negotiations as vacillating, difficult, and driven by domestic politics rather than national security calculations: seeking retribution rather than resolution. I myself was struck by the "thermostatic" quality of the South Korean response. It seemed that when we really wanted to negotiate and were trying to "warm up" a little bit with the North, President Kim would turn down the thermostat and cool us off. And then, as soon as we decided that we needed to get tougher, perhaps seeking international sanctions, he would want to soften the approach, avoid confrontation, and encourage negotiations with the North. We had a hard time getting on the same wavelength.

That was then, and this is now. Now we look at President Kim Dae-jung's policy, and note that it has become known as the Sunshine Policy toward the North. We see it as consistent, open, flexible, resilient in the face of provocation, and significantly reflecting much less of a concern about the threat from the North. This is a different policy. It is clearly consistent with the approach that the U.S. and the Japanese have agreed upon. We are working trilaterally, and generally moving in the direction of engagement with the North. But one thing that is missing is a shared focus on the threat from the North, particularly with respect to the separate elements of the threat. We do not all agree on how to assess the threat from nuclear weapons, the threat from ballistic missiles, and the conventional threat.

I was in Japan right after the North Korean ballistic missile test on the last day of August 1998. I would say that the Taepo-Dong test "got Japan's attention," and there was quite a lot of concern that there would be another test in 1999. I think it is fair to say that the concern about North Korean ballistic missiles in Tokyo was much greater than in Seoul. As a matter of fact, there was, dare I say, some admiration in Seoul for a missile fired over Japan. "Pretty good," some South Koreans thought, "Not bad."

The U.S., as you have noticed, has been deeply concerned about the North Korean nuclear weapons program for a long time, and I think, more so than South Korea. The U.S. focused almost exclusively on nuclear weapons in the Agreed Framework. Since then, the U.S. has also focused on ballistic missiles. You will see that focus reflected in the rationale for a national missile defense by the U.S. Some here are prepared to antagonize Russia, China, Europe, and the rest of the world, and expend billions of dollars, all to deal principally with a threat from North Korean ballistic missiles. Moreover, the Perry Report, which sets the course for future policy, has the nuclear weapons and ballistic missile programs of North Korea as the focus of American concern.

Why is that interesting? It is interesting because that troubles the South Koreans. There is in South Korea, I think, a continuing, latent fear that the U.S. would sell out the South if it could do so and achieve its strategic objectives with respect to ballistic missiles and nuclear weapons. And that is important because it is the new manifestation of the old concern about the North Korean wedge dividing the ROK and the U.S. There is a concern that the U.S. will forget that the essential issue is the political confrontation between North and South, that the U.S. in its policy prescriptions will forget the absolute necessity of keeping the North–South dialogue central to its objectives, that the U.S. will instead focus on the objectives it has with respect to the threat that could reach the continental U.S. So there are really different perspectives here, certainly emphasized, between South Korea, Japan, and the U.S., and these differences can occasionally lead to tensions.

The third observation is that domestic support for engagement with North Korea is shallow at best in the U.S., and is difficult to plumb, for me at least, in the ROK. This is particularly true if by "engagement" we mean something more than negotiating. Victor Cha, a faculty member at Georgetown University's School of Foreign Service, has noted that we should mean something more by "engagement," specifically, a positive attitude toward inducements. We would expect to work through the use of "carrots" as well as the threat of negative consequences.

But for the U.S. Congress, for the media in the U.S., and for a fair number of American people, negotiation with rogues—and we have defined North Korea as a rogue state—is a borderline traitorous and immoral act. For many, if engagement in negotiation means concessions, it means compromise, and this means compromising the national security, because this is a national security issue. Making concessions is equated to being blackmailed; the U.S. becomes a victim, rather than a Great Power. The negotiator–diplomat is characterized as engaging in appeasement. Such an approach is said to be counterproductive, giving the "wrong signal." According to this view, negotiation and engagement with North Korea sustains the most evil regime left on earth; it is naive and wrong.

The point is that there is no reservoir of support for a policy of negotiation; and that may be an understatement. Even the Perry Report rejects the concept of "buyouts." Buyouts are described as incompatible with American values and unwise in dealing with North Korea. This is the report whose fundamental policy prescription is engagement. Somehow, then, we need to engage, but not to have buyouts. The negotiator is to be pitied.

So we must be wary in the U.S., and maybe in the ROK too, of our ability to sustain domestic support for the policy we would presume to pursue, call it engagement or sunshine. We should be wary of the vulnerability to domestic attack, the shallowness of domestic support.

What are the implications of these observations? First, from the recognition that we have a fundamental ignorance of North Korean strategy, I conclude that we have to be very careful to avoid making the Agreed Framework—the one arrangement that we now have with the North that seems to have some durability—an end in itself. Since we do not know what North Korean calculations are, the Framework must remain a means to an end. The implication is that if there are credible concerns about possible secret nuclear sites in the North, we should abandon the Agreed Framework if we cannot resolve those concerns. That has to be, in my view, our stated policy. It has to be the way we approach the North. The Agreed Framework is not a mechanism for continuing a good relationship with North Korea. It is a mechanism designed to deal with a nuclear weapons program. If the Framework is not working, it ought not be sustained.

The second part of the first point on ignorance goes to the durability of our deterrent relationship. Quite simply, no matter what else may arise to cause tension in our allied relations, and no matter what may be said about North Korean nuclear weapons or ballistic missile capability, we need to have, and to project, an unambiguous, shared commitment to the defense of the South.

The second implication, from the recognition of the divergence of allied perspectives, is that we cannot consult too much. We do have consultative mechanisms, more formal mechanisms now among the three and they must be maintained. The reassurance from the U.S. must go beyond the security of the ROK. There must be a consistent emphasis on the part of American policy makers, both privately and publicly, on the need to keep the goal of a political dialogue between the North and the South as a central feature in the American strategy of dealing with the DPRK.

The third implication, from the observation about the shallowness of domestic support for an engagement policy, is that we have to be clearer, and in a sense more honest about what we can expect from the policy. There should be clarity on the limits and uncertainties of this policy of engagement; I do not think we are "coming clean" now. For example, we should be clear that the implications of trade, relaxing sanctions, giving food aid, and pursuing track-two diplomacy wherever possible, could well be the cause the collapse of the regime in the North as this new economic and political openness, this sunshine, turns out to be more than the North's repressive regime can tolerate. The model that we have followed elsewhere, where sunshine has brought down repressive Communist regimes, might well be repeated in this case, very nearly the last one on earth.

That is one possible outcome. But another possible outcome is that by engagement we will be propping up this regime and saving it from the natural course of decline that other Communist regimes have followed. We may be sustaining this economy, this totalitarian state, the worst of all Stalinist regimes. This engagement may be entirely counterproductive in terms of the long-term future that we would like to see on the peninsula. So, the virtue of a policy of engagement may be limited to stopping the North's nuclear weapons and ballistic missile programs by negotiated restraints and limited "buyouts." But the policy may not promote, indeed, it may delay the emergence of a democratic regime. We should be honest about that.

Second, we should be clear about the stakes. Those of us who were involved in the 1993–1994 negotiations were privately very clear about what was at stake. We felt the burden on our shoulders. But I do not think that we ever quite adequately conveyed that publicly. We thought that in the absence of successful negotiations, failing to negotiate something like the Agreed Framework meant that North Korea would pursue a nuclear weapons program. Moreover, it would be a serious nuclear weapons program: three reactors, one at 5 megawatts, one at 50 megawatts, and one at

200 megawatts. We can calculate the plutonium production of these reactors, and it comes to about 150 kilograms of plutonium per year. That is enough for about 30 nuclear weapons. Such a program would be bigger than India's, bigger than Pakistan's, and bigger than what most people calculate as Israel's. That is what we were trying to stop.

The third point, then, is that we had no other acceptable way to prevent this outcome. We ought to be clear, in other words, about options and outcomes so that we can evaluate what "carrots" buy. It is on this point that I have a complaint with the Perry Report. It still seems to me that in the absence of a willingness to conclude the Agreed Framework, to provide 5 or 6 billion dollars in light water reactors and heavy fuel oil worth about 50 million dollars a year, there was and is no other way to stop the North's nuclear weapons program except by the use of force and the conduct of a war. The third approach, to hunker down, enhance deterrence and defense, is fine. But recognize that an enhanced defensive and deterrent posture would mean accepting a huge nuclear weapons program mated with an extended range ballistic missile program in North Korea; recognize that if we rely on deterrence and maybe theater and national missile defense, instead of a war or a policy of engagement, we must accept North Korea as a nuclear weapons state with a ballistic missile delivery system.

It is important to understand that North Korea is not obliged to give up these programs. We can deplore the ballistic missile program in North Korea, but there are many other countries that decided they wanted ballistic missiles for their own defense and deterrence, and those nations test them occasionally. There are a number of other countries that decided they wanted to have nuclear weapons programs and pursued them as well. One might say that North Korea made the mistake of joining the NPT, so they would be violating their international undertakings if they pursued nuclear weapons development. But one should recall that the North was going to withdraw from the Treaty in 1993. Moreover, if the North stayed in the Treaty and accepted safeguards, it could be a member in good standing of the Treaty regime and still produce 150 kilograms of plutonium each year. There's nothing in the NPT barring plutonium production in large quantity. The North could even transfer some of that plutonium under safeguards to other NPT parties, such as Iran, Iraq, and Libya, and not violate any international undertakings.

So the question is, when a country is pursuing ballistic missile development and export, and nuclear weapons–related activity, how do you get it to stop? If the decision is not to use force, because a war would be costly, then negotiation and engagement may be the only course. Sometimes sanctions may be an option, if the leverage exists, and if those who have it are prepared to use it. I do not think sanctions would have stopped the North. We ought to be prepared to discuss all this openly. We ought also be prepared to say that this is not the regime we would like to see in North Korea, but it is the regime we have to work with in North Korea.

I conclude by proposing that we embrace engagement, intelligently as the Perry Report recommends, and that we embrace Sunshine, courageously as Kim Dae-jung has advocated. But let us also be clear that in foreign policy, just as in domestic policy, there is no free lunch: the policy comes with a price that we should expect to pay, and with risks that we must be prepared to take.

Note

This text was derived from remarks presented by Robert L. Gallucci at "The Forum on Promoting International Scientific, Technological and Economic Cooperation in the Korean Peninsula: Enhancing Stability and International Dialogue" in Rome, Italy on May 31, 2000. The views presented are the author's own, and do not necessarily represent those of the U.S. government.

CHAPTER 9

Why States Believe Foolish Ideas: Nonself-Evaluation by States and Societies

Stephen Van Evera

Socialization and Self-Evaluation

Kenneth Waltz argues that states are socialized to the international system because they will be injured or even destroyed if they fail to adapt to it.[1] I believe this claim is correct but should be qualified. Most states are indeed socialized to the international system, but their socialization is often slow and sometimes minimal because states widely fail to evaluate their own ideas and policies. Organization theorists note that organizations are poor self-evaluators; I argue here that states suffer the same syndrome.

This failure to self-evaluate impedes national learning and allows misperceptions to flourish. Myths, false propaganda, and anachronistic beliefs persist in the absence of strong evaluative institutions to test ideas against logic and evidence, weeding out those that fail. As a result national learning is slow and forgetting is quick. The external environment is perceived only dimly, through a fog of myths and misperceptions.

States that misperceive their environment in this way are bound to fail to adapt to it, even when the penalties of such a failure are high. Blind to the incentives they face, they will respond inappropriately, even if they accept in principle the need to adapt.

The following two sections frame reasons why self-evaluation is hard for organizations and outline ways that parallel problems inhibit evaluation in governments and whole societies. The next two sections discuss tactics used by opponents to inhibit or prevent evaluation and frame conditions that are more and less conducive to self-evaluation. The last two sections look at cases that shed light on this theory and offer some concluding thoughts.

Why Organizations Cannot Self-Evaluate

Aaron Wildavsky contends that organizations evaluate their own policies and beliefs poorly because they often turn against their own evaluative units, attacking or destroying them.[2] Evaluation promotes innovation and change. This threatens the jobs and status of incumbent members of the organization. Hence incumbents often seek to hamper or prevent evaluation and to punish evaluators. These incumbents tend to dominate the organization's decision making, so evaluation finds itself with stronger enemies than friends within the organization. Hence self-evaluation is often timid and ineffective.[3]

In essence, the organization suffers an autoimmune disease of the brain. It attacks its own thinking–learning apparatus if that apparatus does its job. As a result the organization thinks poorly and learns slowly.

Private companies hire outside management consultants to get around this problem. Outside consultants know less about company operations than company insiders but are less inhibited from telling what they know. Companies hire them less for their special expertise and more because they can expose problems that members of the organization, if tasked to evaluate, will pretend not to see. Their ability to speak freely is often the main value that outside consultants provide.

The obstruction of evaluation takes several forms. Targets of evaluation may simply move to threaten or destroy the organization's evaluative units. Threats are often enough to inhibit evaluation, making evaluative units into "selective evaluators" that dilute their judgments to avoid making enemies.[4]

Alternately, targets of evaluation can create competing units to produce pseudo-evaluation and disinformation that drowns out the voice of evaluation.[5] Or they can refuse to cooperate with evaluators. Specifically, they can withhold or doctor data that evaluators need for their evaluation, or they can bargain for leniency in exchange for data. Or they can threaten evaluators with social ostracism or co-opt them with personal friendship.

Evaluative units also fail if they lack an evaluative ethos. This happens if members of the evaluative unit omit evaluation from their own definition of their professional mission, or if they do not recognize the importance of evaluation, or if their emotional loyalties lie with those they assess.

Often these problems cannot be solved without creating others. Outside evaluators may need help from experienced organization insiders to assess competently. If these insiders are excluded, the evaluators may make mistakes of ignorance. As a result, it may be impossible to exclude insiders from the evaluation team, despite the danger that they will corrupt the evaluation.

Finally, evaluative units themselves may be hard to evaluate. As a result, others may not be aware when self-evaluation fails; so nothing is done to correct the failure, and it persists. Because nonevaluation is underestimated, it is more pervasive.

In short, organizations nonself-evaluate because obstacles to organizational self-evaluation are formidable. Wildavsky summarized: "I started out thinking it was bad for organizations not to evaluate, and I ended up wondering why they ever do it. Evaluation and organization, it turns out, are to some extent contradictory terms."[6]

Nonself-evaluation is not universal. Organizations that face a competitive environment, such as most private firms, must do some self-evaluation to survive. This puts a minimum limit on how little evaluation the organization can get away with. Those falling below the minimum limit are destroyed. But nonevaluation can reach extremes if organizations face little market or other environmental discipline—as with most government agencies.

Why States Cannot Self-Evaluate

Most political science literature on national misperception relies heavily on psychological explanations.[7] However, the failure to self-evaluate is a cause of national misperception that arises more from institutional dynamics than human psychology. This highlights the value of adding organization theory to the tools we use to understand national misperception.

Nonself-evaluation explains national misperception in two ways. First, government *bureaucracies* nonself-evaluate. At a minimum, agencies with evaluative responsibilities are not invited to evaluate—they are kept out of the loop, their opinions are not sought. At a maximum, government agencies actively suppress their own internal evaluative units and are discouraged from evaluating the beliefs and policies of other agencies. As a result, official misperceptions persist that would fall under scrutiny. Thus before World War I, German navy chief, Admiral Alfred von Tirpitz, censured and silenced those German naval officers who dared to reassess his mistaken strategic calculations,[8] and French army officers were punished or purged for criticizing unwise and offensive official doctrines.[9] In the U.S., General Billy Mitchell was court-martialled for demonstrating the value of airpower at sea, and

State Department "China Hands" were purged in the 1940s and 1950s for accurately reporting the weakness and corruption of China's Chiang Kai Shek government.[10] During Vietnam, the CIA was deterred by the military and White House officials from accurately reporting Vietcong troop strength. (Accurate reports would have raised questions about the military's performance and White House, policy.)[11] Meanwhile false evaluators often prosper. Many U.S. officials responsible for corrupting U.S. intelligence—for example, for the erroneous "bomber gap" estimates of the mid-1950s, for miscalculations about Vietnam, and for politicizing CIA intelligence in the 1980s—were later reappointed or promoted.[12]

Government organizations suppress inside evaluation partly to protect bureaucratic incumbents and also for other reasons. Inside dissenters can hamper policy implementation by leaking unfavorable information on the policy to outsiders. This breaks the agency's monopoly of information, enabling informed criticism of the policy from observers outside the agency. This can empower external opposition that may kill the policy in the cradle. Fearing such leaks, agency leaders will confine policymaking to "team players" that favor the policy from the outset. Agency leaders will also hesitate to order internal analyses of the policy, fearing that the analysis will be leaked and then taken out of context in public debate. For example, a technical analysis might show curable problems with a policy, but might be used by external policy opponents to suggest that the policy is infeasible. Fearing such a chain of events, the agency leader never asks for the technical analysis in the first place. The question "How would that study's results look in the *New York Times*?" often deters needed internal assessments.

Confining policymaking to team players and limiting internal analysis prevents leaks that could stymie the policy's implementation, but it allows the policy to escape hard questions during its formulation. Thus nonevaluation stems partly from tension between the demands of policy formulation and policy implementation. Sound policy often cannot be made without dissent but cannot be implemented with too much of it either.

Second, the *whole society* can also suffer the nonself-evaluation syndrome: the national process of evaluating public policy is damaged by a scaled-up version of the same dynamics that afflict organizations. Academe, the press, and other nongovernmental evaluative institutions often fail to evaluate because evaluation makes enemies that often have the power to defeat or deter it. Government agencies or officials that are targets of evaluation can attack or deter evaluators by finding ways to cut their funding. They can drown out evaluation by setting up sham evaluative units to generate disinformation and pseudo-analysis. They can co-opt evaluators with special perquisites. They can domesticate evaluators that need their data by releasing this data only to congenial analysts. They can conceal their strategies and policies, leaving evaluators without a clear target to assess. They can shift rationales and arguments, hoping to exhaust evaluators by presenting a moving target. They can smear the reputations of evaluators by releasing defamatory state-collected information. They can threaten to deny evaluators hoped-for state employment. And in countries where civil liberties are unprotected, government agencies can of course use police state measures—prison, torture, murder, and the like—to punish and deter evaluators.

Governments are not the only actors that impede or destroy evaluation. Any strong actor or group can do it. Since the 1960s Cuban–American extremists have silenced American voices that questioned their views, often by violence or threat of violence.[13] The American tobacco industry has used the threat of expensive lawsuits to silence critics who point to the industry's many misdeeds.[14] And U.S. business firms often punish Wall Street investment houses whose stock analysts rate their stock poorly by moving their underwriting and bond business elsewhere. As a result, Wall Street stock analysts glowingly recommend most stocks and almost never name companies they would sell.[15] Like the children in Garrison Keillor's mythical Minnesota town, all stocks are miraculously above average!

However, states are the most important anti-evaluators. States have the greatest power to curb evaluation, and the blunders they make in the absence of evaluation have the greatest consequences.

Thus societies, being very large organizations, suffer the same pathology that damages organizational learning. Nongovernmental units that evaluate public policy are usually weaker than those they evaluate. Those they evaluate usually resent and resist evaluation. Hence policy evaluators are often destroyed, deterred, out-shouted, or co-opted. The whole society opposes the national thinking and learning apparatus, just as its bureaucratic components oppose their evaluative subunits.

Moreover, the defects in evaluation of national beliefs and policies are often underestimated by those not close to it. As a result, too little is done to compensate for poor evaluation, or to improve it. Academics have a monopoly on academic expertise. As a result, outsiders often cannot tell how little evaluation academe actually produces so they fail to criticize academe for its failure to evaluate. Professors are therefore free to immerse themselves in irrelevant research on obscure topics—a common academic pastime, especially in the social sciences—without being criticized for their irrelevance. They can be as irresponsible as they wish, a freedom that many fully exploit.

In short, impediments to self-evaluation operate on a national as well as organizational scale. Public policy analysis seldom reaches the standards achieved the professions and natural sciences because policy evaluation is crushed, deterred, or co-opted. As a result, policy debate often assumes an inane character. Key hypotheses and assumptions are unspecified and untested, and facts are assumed without proof. Charlatans who purvey disinformation on behalf of special interests often have the loudest voice and the last word. Thus Ernst Cassirer once noted the "deep chasm" between the customs of scientific and political inquiry:[16]

> When it comes to political action man seems to follow rules quite different from those recognized in all his mere theoretical activities. No one would think of solving a problem of natural science or a technical problem by the methods that are recommended and put into action in the solution of political questions. In the first case we never aim to use anything but rational methods.... But in man's practical and social life the defeat of rational thought seems to be complete and irrevocable.

In politics, Cassirer notes, "modern man is supposed to forget everything he has learned in the development of his intellectual life. He is admonished to go back to the first rudimentary stages of human culture." In political dialogue "rational and scientific thought openly confess their breakdown."[17]

Evaluation is weak because social knowledge affects the distribution of social and political power. Hence the creation of social knowledge is politicized. Elites suppress evaluation because it often threatens their social or political positions. Society needs evaluation to formulate effective state policies but smothers it to protect the social and political order from challenge. Thus in 1939 the American sociologist Robert Lynd wrote:[18]

> A world foundering disastrously because of its inability to make its institutions work is asking the social sciences: "What do you know? What do you propose?" And, unfortunately for the peace of mind of the social scientist, these questions are not asked with complete dispassion; not infrequently they are loaded in the sense of, "Tell us what we want to hear, or else—!"... The social scientist finds himself caught, therefore, between the rival demands for straight, incisive, and, if need be, radically divergent thinking, and the growingly insistent demand that his thinking shall not be subversive.... [The university professor] lives in a world which, by and large, is not asking, "Is Smith trying to get at the facts? Is he trying to be fair and constructive at the same time that he is unwilling to pull his punch?" but which asks, "Are you for us, or against us?"

Likewise Hans Morgenthau noted that societies destroy those who question the myths that support the power and authority of dominant groups:[19]

> In all societies certain social problems cannot be investigated at all, or only at grave risk to the investigator. The basic philosophic assumptions by which society lives are beyond scientific investigation, for to question them is tantamount to questioning the worth of society itself, its justice, its rationality, its very right to exist. . . . [Evaluative social science becomes] a political threat to the defenders or the opponents of the status quo or to both; for the social conventions about power, which political science cannot help subjecting to a critical—and often destructive—examination, are one of the main sources from which the claims to power, and hence power itself, derive.

Evaluation often serves no interest except the general interest. Hence even oppositions and out-groups will not evaluate: instead they, like their opponents, issue self-serving propaganda. As a result the "free marketplace of ideas" often creates a confusion-sowing competition among charlatans that generates more darkness than light. Thus Marxist critics of capitalist foreign policies crafted their criticism less to explain reality than to strengthen the case for socialist rule. For example, in their studies of imperialism V. I. Lenin and Rosa Luxemburg endorsed the false economic notions of nineteenth-century American and European imperialists because this helped them argue that capitalism fostered imperialism, hence was warlike, and so was inferior to socialism.[20] Their writings were less "evaluation" than self-serving propaganda, crafted to advance socialist claims to power. Finding truth was a secondary concern.[21]

In sum, states misperceive partly because national evaluative machinery is weak or defective, evaluation meets powerful resistance, and it often profits no one capable of doing it. As a result, state decisions are often taken without serious analysis, on the basis of simplistic analogies or misinformation. Careful assessment of key ideas is never done.

Nonevaluation is a permissive condition that allows militaristic and nationalistic myths to survive. If evaluation is effective, such ideas are challenged and filtered out. More often evaluation is weak; this allows such myths to persist once they gain a footing. Nonevaluation also is a prerequisite for diversionary war—that is, wars begun by elites to stir public support for the regime.[22] This ploy succeeds only because the public is unaware that the war is a political ruse. Better evaluation would unmask the ruse, making it ineffective. Other kinds of war-causing misperceptions—false optimism, conflict spirals, deterrence failure stemming from acts of appeasement that grow from underestimates of others' hostility, and so forth—are also reduced by strong policy evaluation and thus are fostered by nonevaluation. If misperception is a major cause of war, so also is nonevaluation.

A political science literature has developed on the topic of government learning—that is, of when and how states improve their understanding of the world.[23] The tone of this writing is unduly optimistic about the possibility of government learning because it omits the problem of nonevaluation. Nonevaluation is a powerful retardant to government learning and a powerful cause of government forgetting. It makes states inherently prone to overlook what they once knew; to accept and to act on false and even silly premises; and hence to make policy blunders. It would be good if governments could create and conserve knowledge. But evaluation is a prime engine of learning—perhaps a prerequisite for learning—and governments are reflexively hostile to evaluation. Hence government learning is almost an oxymoron. Governments can learn, but only poorly and unreliably, and they often forget at an even faster rate.

Tactics Used Against Evaluation

What specific mechanics are used to inhibit evaluation? Evaluation is often suppressed by direct attack on evaluators. Thus before World War I, dissident German scholars were disciplined or fired from universities,[24] and critics of official policies were hounded from the German navy.[25] French officers who criticized the French army's doomed offensive war plan saw their writing suppressed and their careers destroyed.[26] In Germany, after the war the historian Hermann Kantorowicz was attacked by his colleagues for debunking the myth that Britain had organized an aggressive encirclement of Germany before 1914, and his work was suppressed.[27] Later the historian Fritz Fischer saw his government funding cut and was denounced for "national masochism" in the press after publishing studies that exposed German responsibility for World War I.[28]

In Japan before World War II, government analysts who warned against confrontation with the U.S. were fired and arrested.[29] Academics who questioned Japan's expansionism were dismissed, and publishers were forbidden to publish authors who failed to toe the official line.[30]

During the 1950s, American scholars who displeased the Taiwan government were attacked by the China lobby and its U.S. allies. The lobby forced the Institute of Pacific Relations to close.[31] Prominent China specialists were smeared with false charges of pro-communist sympathy and were investigated by the Congress.[32] Ross Koen believes that the lobby achieved "the virtual destruction of the public and governmental reputations and influence of many of the foremost private China specialists in the U.S."[33]

French journalists were intimidated, arrested and fined, beaten, or expelled from Algeria if they covered the seamier side of French operations in the Algerian war of independence (1954–1962).[34] The French press bent to this pressure, omitting coverage of many ugly stories.[35]

The Indian government purged and replaced Indian military officers who correctly warned in 1961 that China would resist India's incursions in the Himalayas.[36] And after these incursions provoked China to rout India's forces, the Indian government raided the offices of the publisher of Neville Maxwell's *India's China War*, which had exposed the government's prewar blundering.[37] A folly caused by attacking evaluators can often be concealed by punishing or deterring later evaluators.

In the U.S. many television journalists lost their jobs during the blacklisting of the McCarthy period. And Congress has investigated the major television networks for airing documentaries that offended powerful special interests.[38]

Needless to say, evaluators in communist dictatorships have fared far worse. Josef Stalin, Mao Zedong, Pol Pot, and Kim Il-sung routinely jailed, tortured, and murdered critics who questioned their policies until all were terrified into silence.

Evaluators that are not attacked may be ignored. Ibn Khaldun, the great Arab historian of antiquity (1332–1406), was until recently largely forgotten in the Arab world and was only rediscovered by Arabs via Western scholars. Like all great historians Khaldun had sinned by criticizing his own people. After his rediscovery, his works were banned in Iraq for their supposed criticism of Arabs.[39] The writings of Karl von Clausewitz have been widely ignored by modern militaries, who find his arguments for defensive tactics and civilian control uncongenial; the less insightful but more agreeable writings of Antoine Jomini are much more widely read at military academies.[40] Historians who deviated from official post-1918 German innocence propaganda, such as Bernadotte Schmitt, were unread in Germany after World War I.[41] During late 1950s, top U.S. policymakers never gave a proper hearing to government analysts who warned that U.S. policies would soon provoke a Chinese attack on U.S. forces in Korea.[42] And during the 1960s the works of renowned Vietnam expert Bernard Fall were unknown to Secretary of Defense Robert McNamara for many years; although Fall taught in Washington, the Defense Department preferred to import a more congenial expert from England.[43]

Alternately, evaluators may find their message suppressed. Lord Lansdowne, Conservative Party leader in the British House of Lords, had difficulty finding a British newspaper willing to publish his peace proposal in 1916.[44] The 1971 film *The Sorrow and the Pity*, which exploded the treasured French myth of a strong French resistance by showing that many French acquiesced to Germany's World War II occupation, was banned from French television.[45]

Japan's Colonel Iwakuro Hideo returned from a 1941 fact-finding mission to the U.S. to report that the U.S. had vast industrial superiority over Japan. Japan's Chief of Staff Sugiyama Gen burned the report, explaining that its conclusions were at variance with the supreme will of the state.[46]

Saburo Ienaga found that the Japanese education ministry refused to approve his high-school history text in 1963 because it was "excessively critical of Japan's position and actions in World War II." Ienaga had sinned by truthfully noting "atrocities by Japanese troops," speaking of the "reckless war," and accurately arguing that "the war was glorified as a 'holy cause.' " The ministry claimed this did "not give students a proper understanding of this country's positions and actions in the war."[47]

Evaluation is sometimes defeated by starving it of information. During World War I, the British war Cabinet was kept in the dark by military leaders; this often made civilian control over war policies impossible. Thus before the disastrous British offensive at Passchendaele in 1917, the Cabinet tried to assess General Douglas Haig's proposed campaign but Haig concealed vital facts, including realities of German strength and the fact that the French and Haig's own Intelligence Staff had advised against his plan.[48] Likewise, in Japan, cabinet ministers were denied access to data on Japanese military strength during the 1941 government debate over war with America, so discussion proceeded in a factual vacuum.[49] And once at war, the military services kept the Japanese government ignorant of military developments: Prime Minister Tojo was not even told of the navy's defeat at Midway until a month later.[50]

Post hoc evaluation is frustrated by concealing archives. For decades, the German government hid archives showing that Bismarck had helped to instigate the 1870 Franco-Prussian war,[51] and the U.S. state department has often withheld documents showing the U.S. in a bad light from its declassified documents series.[52]

Targets of evaluation also starve it of information by concealing their aims and strategies; this leaves evaluators with no target to assess. Thus in August 1914, the German government issued a formal ban on any publication discussing German war aims or peace terms in other than vague and general terms.[53] Those concerned about German policy had no policy to judge.

Opponents of evaluation can disrupt it by proliferating competing pseudo-evaluations. Governments and private interests operate internal propaganda organs and fund-friendly external think tanks that publish congenial policy analysis. These institutions clog the debate with disinformation and sow confusion. Often their analysis ignores contrary analysis instead of answering it, so the public debate becomes a contest of volume. As studies pile up, outsiders find it harder to intrude because the amount of "literature" to master before one qualifies as an expert becomes unmanageable. Thus Herbert Gans notes how news sources can manipulate the news by "news saturation"—"the proliferation of so much information by the source that some of it cannot help but turn into news, concurrently placing less well organized sources with more accurate information at a disadvantage."[54]

For example, after 1918, the German government funded hundreds of corrupt studies claiming German innocence for World War I that drowned more serious analyses of the war's origins.[55] And in the U.S. since the 1980s, the fossil fuel industries have organized a noisy public relations campaign to obscure the near-consensus among scientists that significant human-caused global warming is underway. As a result the U.S. public exaggerates scientific disagreement about the basic facts of the matter.[56]

Finally, evaluators can be co-opted or domesticated, their evaluation tempered or suppressed with their consent. Thus the famed journalist Walter Lippmann observed that journalists' pursuit of the truth can clash with their "desire to be on good terms with the powerful," who are "dispensers of many kinds of favor, privilege, honor and self-esteem."[57] Joel Primack and Frank von Hippel likewise argue that scientific criticism of U.S. government policies has sometimes been silenced by including scientists on advisory boards whose reports remain confidential. Participating scientists gain access to official secrets and the corridors of power, but lose their right to comment in public. If the government heeds their advice then evaluation has succeeded, but if their views are ignored, evaluation has been silenced.

Conditions Conducive to Self-Evaluation

What conditions most conduce to policy evaluation, and which are least conducive? Prospects for evaluation heavily depend on having a large system of free universities. These universities must be autonomous from the state and be well protected by traditions of academic freedom. They must be so numerous that orthodoxies cannot easily gain hegemony in particular disciplines, but instead will always face challenge from dissenting views. Evaluation will be weak where these conditions are missing—where universities have little autonomy and are few in number. Wilhelmine Germany, Nazi Germany, Imperial Japan, and the Soviet Union score badly on these dimensions; modern Britain scores better, and the modern U.S.—with its huge system of highly independent schools—scores very well.

A large system of free universities is not enough by itself, however. Academics must also have an evaluative ethos—a sense that their duties include evaluating important official or popular beliefs. This ethos is often missing: instead many scholars hold policy-relevant studies in disregard while dwelling on esoterica. In its absence, a large university system can become a self-contained community in which academics serve as markets for one anothers' writings and ideas. If this market is large enough, academics can forego the need to address the wider society; their internal market sustains them. Large academic community size then operates to inhibit evaluation by giving scholars a guaranteed audience that tolerates irrelevance and obscurantism. Scholars that seek to avoid addressing reality can retreat by addressing this audience.[58]

Evaluation is better when publics and elites are socialized to value evaluation. Contrarily, a hyper-patriotic public climate can deter evaluation by conditioning potential audiences to condemn evaluators as unpatriotic. Critics of official mistakes become, in the public mind, opponents of flag and country; this deters such critics to begin with.

The effectiveness of evaluation varies with issue area. Evaluation is best when the expertise required to evaluate the policy or belief is grounded on a well-developed science. It is worst if this expertise is grounded on poorly developed science. Thus in the U.S., evaluation has been most effective when policies have turned on hard-science issues—for example, the danger that smoking causes cancer, or that chlorofluorocarbons released into the atmosphere will destroy the ozone layer.[59] The basic methods of the hard sciences have proven effective and withstood scrutiny. As a result evaluation grounded in hard science is often done well, and its results are difficult to ignore because they rest on proven methods. Evaluation grounded on social science stands on a weaker foundation: social science remains a primitive enterprise, lacking proven methods and cumulative traditions. As a result evaluation grounded in social science is often done poorly, and even when done well it lacks the prestige to persuade others to accept its conclusions.

Evaluation is weaker in issue areas where policymakers have a monopoly of information and expertise. For example, evaluation of national defense and security policy is impeded in all societies by barriers of secrecy and classification. Secrecy shields information from hostile powers, but also inhibits evaluation by analysts inside and outside of government by starving them of data. Domestic policies that turn on widely available information and expertise are evaluated more effectively.

Evaluation is better when it threatens politically weak interests and protects strong interests. Unfortunately this is rarely the case, especially when important policies are evaluated. Important policies tend to affect important interests; these interests can mobilize large resources to defeat evaluation. As a result more important policies are often less well-evaluated. Thus Holger Herwig suggests a perverse law whereby "those events that are most important are hardest to understand because they attract the greatest attention from mythmakers and charlatans."[60]

Evaluation is better when evaluators are skilled in political action. Policy evaluation requires academic/scientific ability, but its success depends as well on expertise in political combat and public relations. Evaluative institutions will be subjected to political attack and they must have effective strategies for coping. They must infuse their personnel with an ethos that anticipates and accepts the hardship that these attacks create. They should recognize that the results of evaluation must be publicized effectively; unpublicized studies have no results. This requires a grasp of public relations techniques and willingness to use them. Evaluative institutions perform poorly unless their leaders recognize and address the combat nature and the public nature of the enterprise. (This recognition is often missing among academics, weakening their efficacy as evaluators.)

Evidence from Cases

How common is policy nonself-evaluation? Where does it most thrive, and what conditions produce it? How much national misperception can it explain? Light is shed on these questions by policymaking in Germany, France, Italy, Britain, and the U.S. in the last century, especially during the two world wars. Wartime is a good venue for study because the stakes of wartime decisions are very high, so evaluation failure cannot be ascribed to the inattention that leaders often give to secondary issues. If we find evaluation failure, therefore, we can infer that a pathology such as nonevaluation—not mere inattention—was at work.

What do we find? Policymaking by the belligerent powers in the two world wars was quite poor despite the gravity of the issues and the high cost of error. The belligerents made large errors without carefully assessing their options. Frequently, even rudimentary analysis would have exposed these errors but was omitted. Governments often later failed to reassess their wartime decisions in search of lessons. Individuals who did evaluate were often attacked and punished for their trouble. And some who might have evaluated—especially academics—sometimes drifted into dreamy irrelevance, studying questions of no importance while central issues were unaddressed. Things were worst in the more authoritarian states (Germany, Japan, and Italy) and best in the U.S., but even there things were not satisfactory.

The German foreign policy debate before World War I saw frivolous arguments pass unchallenged to become the basis for policy, while German scholars further poisoned the debate instead of steering it toward solid ground.[61] The German press was filled with articles that glorified war and offered fatuous but unanswered arguments for empire. The public was assured that war was a fine experience—the "noblest and most sacred manifestation of human activity"[62]—and told that "we Teutons" must "no longer look upon war as our destroyer . . . at last we must see it once more as the savior, the physician."[63] Expansionists wrongly warned that without colonies Germany would "suffocate in her small territory."[64] If Germany did not expand, one magazine ludicrously warned, "we shall be so dwarfed that we shall become a second Belgium."[65] Expansionists also exaggerated the value of empire by falsely claiming that conquests could serve as markets, fields for investment, and areas for resettlement of German "surplus population." And they purveyed a myth of British geopolitical momentum to highlight the need for a big navy: Germans were warned that Britain and Russia were achieving immense growth, thereby destroying the "balance in the world," which must be checked by a German battle fleet.[66] Germany was portrayed as being in relative economic decline[67]—even though Germany actually had Europe's fastest-growing economy.[68]

German scholars were largely silent in response to this nonsense, offering little in the way of answer or assessment. Their silence reflected the fact that scholars who disputed official dogmas risked their careers. As Charles McClelland notes, any scholar "who ran against the current of accepted orthodoxy . . . had great difficulties making a good career in Imperial Germany."[69]

In-government policy assessment in Germany was likewise suppressed. Admiral Tirpitz censured critics of his ideas within the navy and restricted the right of the admiralty staff to discuss strategic planning.[70] German diplomats abroad likewise knew that their careers would suffer if they disputed views that were fashionable in Berlin.[71]

German policy evaluation in wartime was no better, as Germany's crucial 1917 decision to escalate its U-boat campaign illustrates. This decision probably cost Germany the war but German leaders barely looked before they leaped. The German navy knew that unlimited U-boat warfare would bring the U.S. into the war but argued that this would not matter. Admiral Tirpitz' successor, Eduard von Capelle, preposterously declared that the military significance of American intervention would be "zero, zero, zero!"[72] Even in early 1918, Tirpitz announced that "America's help is a phantom."[73] In fact U.S. entry on the Allied side probably decided the war for the Allies; without it Germany could well have won.

The German navy's rosy hopes for the unlimited U-boat campaign were based on the assumption that Britain would surrender after five months of U-boat blockade. This claim rested in turn on a host of flimsy notions, including: the assumption that Britain would not respond by convoying its merchant fleet (an obvious countermeasure); would fail to requisition neutral shipping; and would be discouraged into surrender although its American ally would shortly come powerfully to its assistance.[74] Advocates of escalation also overlooked possible British food stockpiles, which neutral sources estimated as being enough for one year. They forgot that Britain could begin importing goods that took less shipping space—flour instead of grain, canned meat instead of livestock. They overlooked that Britain had secured the English Channel from submarines, and thus was no longer really an island—it could import goods by rail through French, Spanish, Portuguese, or Italian ports.[75] They assumed that Britain's decision to surrender would be independent of America's joining the war on her side.[76] Later German historian Gerhard Ritter found it "utterly baffling" that trained naval officers could produce such incompetent analysis.[77]

German leaders accepted these judgments. After the war, the German secretary of state confessed that the possibility that the war could last two more years despite the U-boat blockade "was not being considered seriously by anyone at that time [of the U-boat decision]."[78] Chancellor Bethmann-Hollweg had believed that American entry into the war would mean nothing more than America's "delivering food to England, providing some financial help, and sending some aeroplanes and a corps of volunteers."[79] He never scrutinized the navy's dubious claims.[80]

Even after the war, German naval officers denied that the U-boat campaign was mistaken. In 1919, Admiral Koch argued that the U-boat campaign had failed because doves at home had stabbed it in the back; Britain might have sued for peace had it not been for the peace resolution of the German socialists and British awareness of Austrian peace sentiments.[81] German officials could speak such nonsense because German policy ideas faced no meaningful evaluation, even *post hoc*, from inside or outside of government.

German academics were cheerleaders for Germany's follies throughout the war. Instead of evaluating official arguments they echoed and amplified them. In October 1914, 93 of Germany's leading scholars published a manifesto untruthfully proclaiming German innocence for starting the war, for violating Belgian neutrality, and for committing atrocities in Belgium. In 1915, 352 professors signed another petition demanding vast annexations and endorsing unlimited submarine warfare.[82] The renowned sociologist Max Weber sang the war's praises.[83] Only a handful of academics raised their voices against German policies, and they were punished for it. One, Professor Georg Nicolai, finally fled to Denmark fearing for his life. Another, Professor Georg Mehlis, was drafted and killed in action soon after he published an article against the war.[84]

In allied countries neither war aims nor military tactics were analyzed carefully. Clear war aims were never specified.[85] Critics of French and British offensive tactics were purged from the army,[86] and scapegoats were blamed for successive failures. The reputations of the generals survived successive failures. In France, General Joffre kept his command even after France's horrendous defeat in the August 1914 Battle of the Frontiers. The British government blamed Britain's 1915 defeat at Neuve Chapelle not on its generals—where it belonged—but on British munitions workers, who allegedly spent their days drinking in pubs instead of making shells for General French's forces.[87]

Those responsible for failure were seldom called to account. A. J. P. Taylor notes that during the war "none of the statesmen who had blundered into war was discredited by his blunders. Asquith, Viviani, Bethmann, remained national leaders. . . . The generals who had failed to fulfil their confident promises of victory were discredited even less. . . . Those British generals who prolonged the slaughter kept their posts and won promotion; any who protested ran the risk of dismissal."[88]

Nor did the British army assess its conduct of World War I in retrospect. As Brian Bond notes, there was "no inclination [in the British army] to profit from the dreadful experience by studying [its] lessons," and "virtually no official attempt was made to garner the experience of the First World War while it was still fresh," something Bond finds "astonishing." Only in 1932 was a War Office committee set up to study the lessons of the war.[89] Meanwhile General Haig, who led the ruinous British failures at the Somme and Passchendaele, was made an earl and received 100,000 pounds from parliament.[90]

The French also made little effort to learn from their errors after the war. Most striking was their disinterest in assessing the flaws of Plan 17, the French war plan of 1914. That plan was premised on the strange assumption that Germany would lack sufficient troops to move beyond the Meuse river on its advance through Belgium. After the war, no French officer or historian even tried to explain this grave intelligence blunder[91]—doubtless from fear of retribution by the still-powerful blunderers.

The myth of the offensive survived the war. In the 1920s, many generals still preached the power of the offense, and denied that the defense had actually had the advantage during the war. In his memoirs Germany's General Ludendorff wrongly claimed: "Of the two [policies], the offensive makes less demands on the men and gives no higher losses."[92] In Britain, the army's faith in offensive doctrines during the war was not seriously assessed until 1927, when Winston Churchill published data in his *World Crisis* showing that attackers had taken significantly greater losses than defenders during the war. These facts, noted Churchill, "do not appear to have been at all appreciated in even the most expert circles" even nine years after the war, and "no true impression has ever reached the public."[93] In other words, the slaughter at Passchendaele and the Somme went unanalyzed for years after the battles happened.[94] The lives these battles consumed were wasted twice—by the battle and then by the failure to learn from it.

General Alfred von Schlieffen's disastrous 1914 German war plan was celebrated as a brilliant showpiece for decades after World War I, especially in Germany. A generation of Schlieffen's disciples and admirers, and most historians, thought it a clever scheme ruined in execution by others who lacked the courage to carry it through as Schlieffen had conceived it.[95] Schlieffen himself was written about as the supreme German strategist.[96] The Schlieffen myth was not scrutinized until Gerhard Ritter finally published *The Schlieffen Plan* in 1956, 42 years after the fact.[97]

Admiral Tirpitz's failed strategic ideas remained popular with interwar German naval leaders[98] and won new fans in the German air force. The Luftwaffe was so taken with Tirpitz' "risk" theory—which held that a large German fleet could intimidate Britain into neutrality, a notion clearly disproven by events during 1898–1914—that it argued for creating a long-range bomber force as an analogue to Tirpitz' "risk" fleet. Luftwaffe chief, Herman Goering, even termed the proposed bomber force a "risk fleet."[99]

Weimar German scholars made no effort to asses the policies that had led Germany to war and defeat.[100] Instead they parroted the patriotic line—denying German responsibility for the war and repeating the "stab in the back" myth that blamed Germany's defeat on leftists at home. Conservative German publishers conspired to reinforce these messages, commissioning hundreds of books that echoed these and other belligerent themes.[101]

The Weimar government hampered evaluation of past German policies by massively concealing or doctoring documents and other records that implicated Germany in 1914 or otherwise made Germany look bad.[102]

It also deployed pseudo-evaluation in the form of scholars who appeared to be independent but were in fact paid employees of the German foreign ministry, hired to iterate official arguments.[103]

Britain's appeasement policy in the late 1930s was not informed by an assessment of German intentions or the effect of appeasement on allied continental strategy. None of the top British leaders read *Mein Kampf*.[104] The British press paid scarcely any heed to Nazi ideology, making little effort to explain it to British readers.[105] Chamberlain took no brief to Munich that surveyed the Czechoslovak question; nor did he ask if a truncated Czechoslovakia could remain independent, or what the strategic effect would be for the West if Czechoslovakia were lost, or how the national composition of Czechoslovakia could be ascertained.[106] A. L. Rowse concludes of British leaders:[107]

> That they did not know what they were dealing with is the most charitable explanation of their failure; but they might at least have taken the trouble to inform themselves. . . . To be so uninstructed . . . was itself a kind of dereliction of duty.

The Axis powers scarcely evaluated the policies that brought them to ruin in World War II. Hitler never requested an evaluation of how German forces could fight the U.S. before his disastrous decision to declare war on them in 1941.[108] By Hitler's own absurd estimate, Germany's Luftwaffe and U-boat forces were strong enough to keep any American troops from landing in Europe.[109] Hitler also offered nonsense economics to justify his expansionism—"Our economic situation is such that we cannot hold out more than a few years. . . . We have no other choice, we must act."[110]

After Hitler's rise, German academics showed little resolve to assess the ideas that shaped Nazi policies. The Nazi regime savagely suppressed criticism, but suppression was barely necessary where German scholars were concerned since they had scant impulse to evaluate. As Oscar Hammen notes, German historians "needed little 'coordination' " under the Nazis—they were quite willing to silence themselves or even to endorse the regime's ideas.[111]

In Japan, fatuous analogies instead of analysis governed policy. Foreign Minister Matsuoka Yosuke thought Japan's expansion was "as natural as the growth of a child. Only one thing stops a child from growing:—death."[112] General Sato Kojiro explained that Japan was like a tree, and "a tree must have its roots." Britain had roots in Africa, India, Australia, and Canada; the U.S. had roots in North, Central, and South America. Now Japan must have roots in Asia to escape its "potted plant" existence, or it would shrivel and die.[113] That such ideas were vastly wrong was shown by Japan's fabulous post-1945 economic success with no such "roots."

Before Pearl Harbor, Japan's government never seriously studied Japan's chances of winning a war against the U.S.[114] It made no overall estimate of Japan's power and had no master plan for the conduct of the war.[115] It failed to analyze the likely effect of attacking Pearl Harbor on American will to defeat Japan.[116] The Japanese navy never seriously discussed the implications of its proposed advance into Southeast Asia—which triggered the war with the U.S.—with top government officials.[117] The Japanese army made no real effort to assess the military strength of the U.S.,[118] and suppressed whatever assessment was done.

Robert Butow notes that Tojo and his colleagues often made decisions without fully exploring their consequences and that "conclusions seem to have been based more on intuition than on reason."[119] Saburo Ienaga notes the decision for war betrayed "casual assumptions," "shoddy analysis," and "extreme lack of objectivity in planning."[120]

This poor thinking developed in a Japanese government that never had to answer critics. Instead it suppressed criticism of its expansionist policies to a point where antiwar criticism disappeared from public dialogue.[121] Evaluation became so dangerous that it almost never happened. Fatuous policies—and national ruin—were the result.

In Italy, Mussolini's imperial program was barely analyzed and Italian foreign policy ideas did not bear much relation to reality. The Italian government made little effort to assess Italian military capabilities, or the capabilities of Italy's adversaries, or the value of empire to Italy.

Many of Mussolini's arguments for expansion had been falsified by events even before they were made. Fascist leaders claimed that a wider empire would enrich Italy—even though Italy's existing colonies needed large subsidies.[122] They claimed that millions of Italians could be resettled in the proposed East African colonies—Mussolini talked of sending ten million emigrants to the empire—even as Italian settlers in East Africa fell year by year, from 146,000 workers in 1936, to 23,000 in 1939, to just 854 agricultural families in May 1940.[123]

These errors reflected a total failure to study the situation. The Fascist government never assessed the feasibility of sending settlers to Africa,[124] and it planned the annexation of Albania in 1938 without making any survey of the colony's potential profitability. Denis Mack Smith notes that Mussolini's imperial ideas were "effective as propaganda" but "would not have borne close and serious investigation."[125] They survived because they faced no such investigation.

Italian estimates of national military strength were equally deluded. Italian authorities thought the Italian air force was second to none, and that Italy was impregnable. Mussolini claimed the Italian air force was leading the world, and spoke of blacking out the sun with the sheer numbers of his aircraft.[126] Fascist propagandists claimed Italy's air force was stronger than the RAF and that one Italian air squadron could destroy any British fleet in the Mediterranean.[127] In 1939, official Italian figures showed Italian air strength at 8,530 planes; in fact Italy had only 583 bombers and fighters, nearly all of which were inferior to British planes.[128]

Fascist writers claimed that Italy had one of the strongest armies in Europe, and a navy and air force that had reached perfection. They boasted that Italy had "little or nothing to learn" from Germany or anyone else in military matters.[129] In fact at the end of World War II, Italy still lacked a real tank, and it produced more aircrafts in World War I than World War II.[130] Italy's peak artillery production rate in World War II was less than one-sixth its peak rate in World War I.[131] In the 1930s, Fascist propagandists claimed Italy could mobilize a 12-million-man army: in fact it mobilized only three million men, who carried rifles designed in 1891.[132] As Denis Mack Smith concludes, in Fascist Italy "myth-making became the one essential art of government, more important than statesmanship or farsightedness or even effective administration."[133]

In short, the history of policymaking in the belligerent European and Asian states of the two world wars is a record of recurrent folly. The belligerents repeatedly made blunders that could have been exposed by minimal objective analytic scrutiny, had it been allowed. These blunders were common among the democracies, even more common among the authoritarian states. Thus the realist image of these wars—that they grew from collisions among rational-acting states whose misperceptions reflected the opaqueness of the international environment—is incorrect. The belligerents misperceived a rather transparent world because they had no functioning analytic apparatus. This occurred because the belligerent governments and societies punished evaluation, often quite savagely. If so, these cases indicate that nonevaluation is pervasive. Even the large incentive for rational calculation posed by the perils of total war may be unable to overcome it.

Conditions for evaluation have been better in the U.S. than elsewhere, and the quality of policy evaluation in the U.S. has accordingly been higher than in the belligerent states discussed earlier. But measured against an absolute standard it leaves much to be desired. The quality of analysis achieved by the professions or the hard sciences is seldom achieved in the evaluation of major public policies, especially foreign and security policies.

Striking instances are found where important U.S. policies were never evaluated. For example, in the 1930s U.S. officials simply assumed the strategic importance of China and Southeast Asia to the U.S.; no study of their importance was done. On this flimsy basis the U.S. pursued a collision course with Japan.[134] Amazingly, before intervening in Vietnam, in 1965 U.S. officials made no systematic assessment of Vietnam's importance to the U.S.[135] The Reagan administration did no careful analysis before announcing its 1983 Strategic Defense Initiative (or SDI, also known as "Star Wars").[136]

Instances of the suppression or deterrence of evaluation in the U.S. are also abundant. During World War I, a sizable number of U.S. college teachers were fired for expressing antiwar views; the American Association of University Professors even announced in 1918 that it did not endorse guarantees of freedom of expression on campus "in a time so critical."[137] As noted above, many U.S. government China analysts lost their jobs in the 1940s and 1950s for honestly reporting the corruption of China's Chiang Kai Shek government. Pentagon leaders once fired a budget analyst for informing Congress about defense cost overruns, and another time engineered the firing of a former top official from his private sector job after he criticized current defense budget priorities.[138] Undersecretary of Defense Donald Hicks bluntly threatened in 1986 to deny Defense Department funding "even for basic research" to outside institutions that housed scholars who criticized Defense Department programs—a chilling threat to the many U.S. universities that receive Defense Department research funding.[139] Such stories could be multiplied many times.

Finally, evaluative lassitude is pronounced among American scholars, as observers of academe have often remarked. Thus Hans Morgenthau once lamented that American political science is guilty of a general retreat from evaluation. Instead, he noted, it hides in "the trivial, the formal, the methodological, the purely theoretical, the remotely historical—in short, the politically irrelevant."[140] External hostility would be a badge of achievement for social science—"a political science that is mistreated and persecuted is likely to have earned that enmity because it has put its moral commitment to the truth above social convenience and ambition."[141] Instead political science ducks criticism by producing obscure and irrelevant research. "History and methodology, in particular, become the protective armor which shields political science from contact with . . . political reality." Morgenthau observed a "new scholasticism," in academe—the pursuit of an "intellectual exercise, frequently executed with a high degree of acumen and sophistication, that tells us nothing we need to know about the real world." Scholars maintain their reputations by "engaging in activities that can have no relevance for the political problems of the day"; instead they substitute a "fanatical devotion to esoteric terminology and mathematical formulas, equations, and charts, in order to elucidate or obscure the obvious." As a result, in the study of international affairs "prudence and truth are bent to the purposes of power, and . . . superstition takes the place of rational knowledge." Social science resembles "a deaf man answering questions which no one has asked him."[142]

Many others have echoed Morgenthau's criticisms. Russell Jacoby laments the retreat toward irrelevance of American social science, despite the infusion of people with backgrounds in social criticism into universities.[143] Jacoby observes that even the New Left intellectuals, now ensconced in the academic world they once opposed, produce writing that is "largely technical, unreadable, and—except by specialists—unread."[144] For them professionalized social science has "served as a refuge" from social assessment.[145] Robert McCaughey notes that specialists on international affairs were conspicuously absent during the 1960s Indo-china War debate, in which their expertise was highly relevant.[146] David Ricci complains that during 1959–1969 only one of the 924 articles that appeared in the three leading political science journals dealt with Vietnam, and only 6 percent dealt with policy analysis in the broadest terms.[147] Patricia Wilner reports that during 1936–1982 only 5.1 percent of articles in the official sociology journal, *American Sociological Review*, addressed critical political and social events such as the Cold War, McCarthyism, and protest movements.[148] Todd Gitlin criticizes his fellow sociologists for expressing themselves in "inward-turning, indecipherable prose" that revealed that they "cannot be bothered to clarify matters for the reader who is not among the adept."[149] David Newsom, a foreign policy practitioner, complains that academics who publish on international relations "disappear behind a curtain of jargon" and "speak to each other rather than to a wider public." As a result "much of today's scholarship is either irrelevant or inaccessible to policymakers."[150] An appalled Martin Anderson notes the "trivial substance of much academic research and its blissful irrelevance to the vital problems of the world."[151] Commenting on scholars of East Asia, Richard Samuels laments "the reluctance of many political scientists with Japanese language expertise to engage in prescriptive research."[152]

This academic lassitude stems partly from fear of punishment for evaluating but more from a lack of evaluative ethos. Far more than nonacademics are aware, vast areas of American social science are infused with a contempt for policy assessment.[153] In many university departments those whose research veers into areas of policy importance are viewed as second-rate intellects, and those who write for the public are dismissed as mere popularizers.[154] The department majority assumes that these lesser minds address the real world because they lack the brilliance needed to ascend to more lofty theoretical heights. Academic evaluators accordingly find that their work often brings them little respect or reward from colleagues. We can only wonder how the American people would react if they understood the contempt with which their problems and concerns are treated by university faculties who are expensively supported by their tax and tuition dollars.

Nevertheless, evaluation in the U.S. is better than elsewhere. This is seen in the confined nature of most large American foreign policy blunders. Big mistakes have been common, but at some point most were recognized and reversed. Thus the U.S. erred by being disengaged from Europe before World Wars I and II, but it reversed the error by joining those wars and by later organizing NATO and deploying troops to Europe during the Cold War. The U.S. erred by attempting to conquer North Korea during the Korean war but it abandoned this goal after China intervened in the war. The U.S. blundered into Vietnam but eventually cut its losses and accepted failure. This record contrasts sharply with the relentless pursuit of error by Germany, Japan, and Italy earlier in this century. Once set on a course of folly, these powers usually stayed firmly on it. They learned little or nothing from their successive failures. Only total defeat could set the state on a new course.

Conclusion

Inquiry about politics is harder in the natural sciences because the investigator must overcome both the question and an established order that often fears the answer. As a result, state policies are often adopted on the basis of a less careful analysis than their importance warrants, leaving wide room for mistakes and misperceptions. Forces of knowledge destruction are often stronger than those favoring knowledge creation. Hence states have an inherent tendency toward primitive thought, and the conduct of public affairs is often polluted by myth, misinformation, and flimsy analysis.

A major risk of war lies in the tendency of policymakers to underestimate this phenomenon and assume instead that states are intelligent actors. It is safer for policymakers to assume that both their own state and their adversaries are prone to folly and to buffer their policies against this fact. They should rarely adopt policies that demand a large measure of sophistication and subtlety because such policies will often exceed their own state's analytic capacity. Adversaries should be assumed to be slow to learn, blunder-prone, and hard to deter. Ill-considered actions by adversaries should be anticipated. Nonevaluation injects folly into the warp and woof of international politics; policymakers should accept this reality and plan accordingly.

Nonevaluation has been noticed before but was explained in psychological terms. For example, Irving Janis has argued that the psychology of small-group dynamics, which he labels "groupthink," causes decision-makers to abandon their independence of mind and conform to the dominant view in the group. As a result the dominant view is never carefully examined even if it is woefully flawed.[155] Martha Wolfenstein, addressing another piece of the problem, argues that people who warn of disaster face hostility, even if they are proven right, because those who suffer the disaster interpret it as personal punishment and interpret warnings as threats of punishment.[156] Hence we see the "kill the messenger" syndrome—those who bring useful bad news are punished for it.

Nonevaluation theory differently argues that groupthink dynamics reflect the simple tendency of people, for rational self-serving reasons, to make life hard on those who criticize their performance. Evaluators understand this tendency and are deterred by it—they silence themselves from fear of retribution. And nonevaluation theory explains the "kill the messenger" syndrome as occurring because warnings of disaster threaten the reputation of leaders or officials who allowed the danger to arise, and may threaten other government incumbents by raising the need to address the disaster by innovation, with its attendant possibility of personnel shakeups. In this view the working out of self-interest in the context of bureaucratic power-politics, not psychological dynamics, explains the nonevaluation phenomenon.[157]

Several prescriptions emerge from the list of conditions conducive to evaluation outlined here. One solution lies in infusing academic professions with a stronger evaluative ethos. At a minimum, active hostility toward policy studies should be abandoned. More positively, academic professions could formally recognize and reward evaluative work in hiring, tenuring, salary, and prize-giving decisions. A second solution lies in developing nonacademic institutions that assume the mission of encouraging, protecting, and rewarding evaluative work. During the past two decades such a movement has taken hold on a small scale, embodied in the growth in Washington of institutions dedicated offering legal and financial protection for "whistle blowers" in government.[158] The concept behind these organizations could be applied more broadly, and institutions could be developed to serve as counterweights against the pressures that will otherwise operate to still evaluation.

Notes

1. Kenneth N. Waltz, *Theory of International Politics* (Reading, MA: Addison-Wesley, 1979): 127–28.
2. Aaron Wildavsky, "The Self-Evaluating Organization," *Public Administration Review*, Vol. 32, No. 5 (September/October 1972): 509–20.

3. Wildavsky notes that "evaluators must become agents of change acting in favor of programs as yet unborn and clients that are unknown," so their clients are inherently weaker than their opponents. "Self-Evaluating Organization": 510.
4. Wildavsky, "Self-Evaluating Organization": 516.
5. Wildavsky, "Self-Evaluating Organization": 514.
6. Wildavsky, "Self-Evaluating Organization": 509.
7. Prominent examples include Robert Jervis, *Perception and Misperception in International Politics* (Princeton, NJ: Princeton University Press, 1976); Irving L. Janis, *Groupthink: Psychological Studies of Policy Decisions and Fiascos*, 2nd ed. (Boston: Houghton Mifflin, 1982); Richard Ned Lebow, *Between Peace and War: The Nature of International Crisis* (Baltimore: Johns Hopkins University Press, 1981); Deborah Welch Larson, *Origins of Containment: A Psychological Explanation* (Princeton: Princeton University Press, 1985); Yaacov V. I. Vertzberger, *The World in Their Minds: Information Processing, Cognition, and Perception in Foreign Policy Decisionmaking* (Stanford: Stanford University Press, 1990); Ole R. Holsti, *Crisis Escalation War* (Montreal: McGill-Queens University Press, 1972); and Ralph K. White, *Nobody Wanted War: Misperception in Vietnam and Other Wars*, rev. ed. (Garden City, NY: Anchor, 1970).
8. Holger H. Herwig, "The Failure of German Sea Power, 1914–1945: Mahan, Tirpitz, and Raeder Reconsidered," *International History Review*, Vol. 10, No. 1 (February 1988): 68–105 at 74, 85, 104.
9. For examples, see B. H. Liddell Hart, "French Military Ideas Before the First World War," in Martin Gilbert, ed., *A Century of Conflict, 1850–1950* (London: Hamilton Hamish, 1966): 136, 142–45; and Richard K. Betts, *Soldiers, Statesmen, and Cold War Crises* (Cambridge: Harvard University Press, 1977): 187.
10. See Ross Y. Koen, *The China Lobby in American Politics* (New York: Harper and Row, 1974): 160–93; E. J. Kahn, Jr., *The China Hands: America's Foreign Service Officers and What Befell Them* (New York: Penguin, 1976); and David Halberstam, *The Best and the Brightest* (Greenwich, CT: Fawcett Crest, 1973): 462–76. As a result many leading American Asia experts were out of the government or the country when their expertise was needed to assess the situation in Vietnam in the early 1960s. John Paton Davies, among the most knowledgeable of these experts, was living in Peru making furniture; ibid.: 462.
11. Thomas Powers, *The Man Who Kept the Secrets: Richard Helms and the CIA* (New York: Pocket Books, 1979): 240.

    The legion examples of the penalizing or firing of "whistle-blowers" in government also illustrate nonevaluation. On the suppression of whistle blowers see Myron Peretz Glazer and Penina Migdal Glazer, *The Whistleblowers: Exposing Corruption in Government and Industry* (New York: Basic Books, 1989). Also relevant is the Bureaucracy Task Force, *The Whistle Blowers: A Report on Federal Employees Who Disclose Acts of Government Waste, Abuse and Corruption* (Washington, D.C.: U.S. Government Printing Office, 1978).
12. John Prados, *The Soviet Estimate: U.S. Intelligence Analysis and Soviet Strategic Forces* (Princeton: Princeton University Press, 1986): 49–50; Sam Adams,

"Vietnam Cover-Up: Playing War With Numbers," *Harper's* (May 1975): 41–73 at 71 (box, "Moral of the Tale," re: Daniel Graham, Edward Procter, and William Hyland); and Melvin A. Goodman, "Ending the CIA's Cold War Legacy," *Foreign Policy*, No. 106 (Spring 1997): 128–43 at 143.

Counterexamples where evaluation was tolerated or rewarded in government can be found. For example, U.S. General George Marshall bluntly criticized his superiors' policies several times during his long career but nevertheless won promotion. Mark A. Stoler, *George C. Marshall: Soldier-Statesman of the American Century* (Boston: Twayne, 1989): 36–37, 65. More telltale, however, is that Marshall's peers assumed he would be fired after these confrontations. They were wrong in the specific instance but right on the way things usually work.

13. See e.g. Cynthia Brown, "Strong-Arming the Hispanic Press: Cuban extremists Shape the News—With Threats and Bombs," *Contents* (July/August 1980): 51–54; Human Rights Watch, "Dangerous Dialogue: Attacks on Freedom of Expression in Miami's Cuban Exile Community," *Americas Watch/Fund for Free Expression*, Vol. 4, No. 7 (August 1992); and Human Rights Watch, "Dangerous Dialogue Revisited: Threats to Freedom of Expression Continue in Miami's Cuban Exile Community," *HRW/Americas and Free Expression Project*, Vol. 6, No. 14 (November 1994).
14. William Glaberson, "'60 Minutes' Case Illustrates a Trend Born of Corporate Pressure, Some Analysts Say," *New York Times*, November 17, 1995: B14; and James C. McKinley, Jr., "CBS Said to Fear Unusual Legal Challenge to '60 Minutes' Tobacco Report,"; ibid.
15. Michael Siconolfi, "Incredible 'Buys': Many Companies Press Analysts to Steer Clear of Negative Ratings," *Wall Street Journal*, July 19, 1995: 1; Diana B. Henriques, "The Pleasure of 'I Told You So,' *New York Times*, August 8, 1998: El; and Gretchen Morgenson, "Flying Blind in a Fog of Data," *New York Times*, June 18, 2000: 3–1.
16. Ernst Cassirer, *The Myth of the State* (Garden City, NY: Doubleday & Co., 1955): 1–2.
17. Cassier, *Myth of the State*: 2.
18. Robert S. Lynd, *Knowledge for What? The Place of Social Science in American Culture* (Princeton: Princeton University Press, 1939): 7, 10.
19. Hans J. Morgenthau, "The Purpose of Political Science," in James C. Charlesworth, ed., *A Design for Political Science: Scope, Objectives, and Methods* (Philadelphia: American Academy of Political and Social Science, 1966): 63–79 at 69, 72.
20. Luxemburg's ideas closely track the nonsense economic arguments advanced by U.S. imperialists during 1899–1900 for annexing the Philippines. Summarizing Luxemburg is Benjamin J. Cohen, *The Question of Imperialism: The Political Economy of Dominance and Dependence* (New York: Basic Books, 1973): 34–49 especially 43–44. Summarizing the economic ideas of U.S. imperialists is David Healy, *U.S. Expansionism: The Imperialist Urge in the 1890s* (Madison: University of Wisconsin Press, 1970): 42–46, 159–77.

21. Another criticism of the "free marketplace of ideas" is Benjamin Ginsberg, *The Captive Public: How Mass Opinion Promotes State Power* (New York: Basic Books, 1986). Ginsberg argues, similarly to the main argument of this chapter, that the ideas "free market" in fact resembles a monopoly because intellectual resources are heavily skewed, leaving some groups as producers and others as captive consumers of ideas.
22. On diversionary war see Jack S. Levy, "The Diversionary Theory of War: A Critique," in Manus I. Midlarsky, ed., *Handbook of War Studies* (Boston: Unwin Hyman, 1989): 259–88.
23. Reviewing this writing is Jack S. Levy, "Learning and Foreign Policy: Sweeping a Conceptual Minefield," *International Organization*, Vol. 48, No. 2 (Spring 1994): 279–312.
24. Gordon A. Craig, *Germany 1866–1945* (New York: Oxford University Press, 1978): 203–04. Even the nationalist historian Hans Delbrück was almost fired in 1899 for voicing a difference with the Kaiser's policies, Ibid.: 203.
25. Herwig, "Failure of German Sea Power": 85.
26. Liddell Hart, "French Military Ideas Before the First World War": 144–45; Jan Karl Tanenbaum, "French Estimates of Germany's Operational War Plans," in Ernest R. May, ed., *Knowing Ones Enemies: Intelligence Assessment Before the Two World Wars* (Princeton: Princeton University Press, 1986): 150–71 at 164; and Alfred Vagts, *A History of Militarism: Civilian and Military*, rev. ed. (New York: Free Press, 1959): 222, 352.
27. Holger H. Herwig, "Clio Deceived: Patriotic Self-Censorship in Germany After the Great War," *International Security*, Vol. 12, No. 2 (Fall 1987): 5–44 at 34–36; Imanuel Geiss, "The Outbreak of the First World War and German War Aims," in Walter Lacqueur and George L. Mosse, eds., *1914: The Coming of the First World War* (New York: Harper & Row, 1966): 71–87 at 73; and Jerzy Marczewski, "German Historiography and the Problem of Germany's Responsibility for World War I," *Polish Western Affairs*, Vol. 12, No. 2 (1971): 289–309 at 301.
28. James Joll, "The 1914 Debate Continues: Fritz Fischer and His Critics," in H. W. Koch, ed., *The Origins of the First World War: Great Power Rivalry and German Aims* (London: Macmillan, 1972): 13–29 at 15–16; and Imanuel Geiss, "Origins of the First World War," in Imanuel Geiss, ed., *July 1914: The Outbreak of the First World War: Selected Documents* (New York: W. W. Norton, 1967): 9–53 at 12.
29. Michael A. Barnhardt, *Japan Prepares for Total War: The Search for Economic Security, 1919–1941* (Ithaca: Cornell University Press, 1987): 170–71, 199–200, 268.
30. Thomas R. Havens, *Valley of Darkness: The Japanese People and World War II* (New York: W. W. Norton, 1978): 23.
31 Koen, *China Lobby*: xiv, 133–59.
32 Koen, *China Lobby*: 117–31.
33 Koen, *China Lobby*: 131. Michael Schaller notes that "an entire generation of government China experts was professionally destroyed. The purge of these

diplomats . . . ensured that a long time would elapse before the next generation of China specialists emerged. Until then the blind would lead the blind." Michael Schaller, *The United States and China in the Twentieth Century* (New York: Oxford University Press, 1979): 130.

Remarkably, Ross Koen's own book was also attacked and suppressed, an event that nicely illustrated its argument. His book was first printed in 1960 but the China Lobby, with assistance from allies inside the U.S. government, enjoined its distribution and it was not republished until 1974. See Richard C. Kagan, "Introduction," in Koen, *China Lobby*: ix–x; and Stanley D. Bachrack, *The Committee of One Million: "China Lobby" Politics, 1953–1971* (New York: Columbia University Press, 1976): 167–72.

34. Phillip Knightley, *The First Casualty: The War Correspondent as Hero, Propagandist, and Myth Maker* (New York: Harcourt, Brace Jovanovich, 1975): 358–69.
35. Knightley, *First Casualty*: 358–59.
36. Richard Ned Lebow, *Between Peace and War: The Nature of International Crisis* (Baltimore: Johns Hopkins University Press, 1981): 166–69.
37. Neville Maxwell, *India's China War* (Garden City, NY: Anchor, 1972): 480–81.
38. CBS was investigated after it aired *The Selling of the Pentagon* and *Hunger in America* in the 1970s. Herbert J. Gans, *Deciding What's News: A Study of CBS Evening News, NBC Nightly News, Newsweek, and Time* (New York: Vintage, 1980): 261–62. Gans speculates that these investigations "further eroded the enthusiasm of network management for exposé documentaries," ibid.: 262. Likewise, Howard K. Smith was forced out of CBS in the early 1960s because southern affiliate stations objected to his views on civil rights, and Edward R. Murrow was eased out of CBS in 1961 for stirring controversy. Gans, *Deciding What's News*: 259; and David Halberstam, *The Powers That Be* (New York: Dell, 1979): 209–24.
39. Bernard Lewis, *History—Remembered, Recovered, Invented* (Princeton: Princeton University Press, 1975): 78–79. Other examples of ignored evaluation are found in Joel Primack and Frank von Hippel, *Advice and Dissent: Scientists in the Political Arena* (New York: New American Library, 1974): 10–97.
40. Stephen M. Walt, "A Search for a Science of Strategy: A Review Essay on *Makers of Modern Strategy*," *International Security*, Vol. 12, No. 1 (Summer 1987): 140–65 at 153–54.
41. H. W. Koch, "Introduction," in Koch, *Origins of the First World War*: 1–12 at 5. Schmitt's important book on World War I origins, *The Coming of the War: 1914* was never even translated into German. Herwig, "Clio Deceived": 26.
42. Alexander L. George, "Findings and Recommendations," in Alexander L. George, *Avoiding War: Problems of Crisis Management* (Boulder: Westview Press, 1991): 545–66 at 555. See also Allen S. Whiting, "The U.S.–China War in Korea," in ibid.: 103–25 at 106–07, 113.
43. Bernard Brodie, *War and Politics* (New York: Macmillan, 1973): 214–15. Brodie notes the "one practically unvarying principle" about the use by government of

outside expert consultants: "[T]hey must be known to be friendly to that policy on which they are consulted. They may be critical of details or of the current execution of that policy, but not of the fundamentals"; ibid.: 214.

44. Fred Charles Iklé, *Every War Must End*, rev. ed. (New York: Columbia University Press, 1991): 79.
45. Anthony P. Adamthwaite, *The Making of the Second World War* (London: George Allen & Unwin, 1977): 24.
46. Kimitada Miwa, "Japanese Images of War with the United States," in Akira Iriye, ed., *Mutual Images: Essays in American–Japanese Relations* (Cambridge: Harvard University Press, 1975): 125–27.
47. Saburo Ienaga, *The Pacific War, 1931–1945: A Critical Perspective on Japan's Role in World War II* (New York: Pantheon, 1978): 255–56.
48. A. J. P. Taylor, *The First World War* (Harmondsworth: Penguin, 1966): 190–91.
49. Ienaga, *Pacific War*: 39; and Nobutaka Ike, ed., *Japan's Decision for War: Records of the 1941 Policy Conferences* (Stanford: Stanford University Press, 1967): 130. Foreign Minister Togo Shigenori later remarked "I was astonished at our lack of statistical data," and noted the "absurdity of our having to base our deliberations on assumptions, since the high command refused to divulge figures on the numbers of our forces, or any facts relating to operations"; ibid.
50. Ienaga, *Pacific War*: 39.
51. William Carr, *The Origins of the Wars of German Unification* (London: Longman, 1991): 179–80.
52. For an egregious example see Warren I. Cohen, "At the State Dept., Historygate," *New York Times*, May 8, 1990: A29.
53. Imanuel Geiss, *German Foreign Policy 1870–1914* (Boston: Routledge & Kegan Paul, 1976): 176.
54. Gans, *Deciding What's News*: 121.
55. Herwig, "Clio Deceived": 21–23.
56. Ross Gelbspan, *The Heat is On: The High Stakes Battle over Earth's Threatened Climate* (Reading, MA: Addison-Wesley, 1997): 33–62. Allies of these interest groups also pressed the U.S. Congress to defund government research on climate change; ibid.: 56, 68, 74, 76.
57. Ronald Steel, *Walter Lippmann and the American Century* (New York: Vintage, 1981): 572. For example, British Prime Minister Lord Palmerston (1855–1858, 1859–1865) bought favorable press coverage by awarding consular appointments to the sons of friendly journalists. Jack Snyder, *Myths of Empire: Domestic Politics and International Ambition* (Ithaca: Cornell University Press, 1991): 205.
58. Observing this dynamic in the United States is Russell Jacoby, *The Last Intellectuals: American Culture in the Age of Academe* (New York: Basic Books, 1987): 112–237.
59. Offering examples of successful evaluation in hard-science policy areas is Primack and von Hippel, *Advice and Dissent*: 128–235.
60. Herwig, "Clio Deceived": 7.

61. On prewar German thinking see Fritz Fischer, *War of Illusions: German Policies from 1911 to 1914*, trans. Marian Jackson (New York: W. W. Norton, 1975); idem, *Germany's Aims in the First World War* (New York: W. W. Norton, 1967); and Geiss, *German Foreign Policy 1871–1914*.
62. Otto von Gottberg in *Jungdeutschland-Post* in January 1913, quoted in Fischer, *War of Illusions*: 193. Gottberg gushed to readers about the "great and happy hour" when war would erupt, and the "secretly jubilant expectation" that would sweep Germany at that time; ibid.
63. The *Politisch-Anthropologische Revue* in November 1912, quoted in Fischer, *War of Illusions*: 194.
64. *Nauticus* in 1900, quoted in Volker R. Berghahn, *Germany and the Approach of War in 1914* (London: Macmillan, 1973): 29. Heinrich von Treitschke wrote that "the question whether we can become an overseas Power involves our existence as a Power of the first rank. If we cannot, we face the horrible prospect that England and Russia will divide the world between them." William Roscoe Thayer, ed., *Out of Their Own Mouths: Utterances of German Rulers, Statesmen, Savants, Publicists, Journalists, Business Men, Party Leaders, and Soldiers* (New York: D. Appleton & Co., 1917): 46–47.
65. *Die Zukunft*, quoted in Harmut Pogge von Strandmann, "Germany and the Coming of War," in R. J. W. Evans and Harmut Pogge von Strandmann, eds., *The Coming of the First World War* (New York: Oxford University Press, 1990): 87–123 at 109.
66. Admiral Tirpitz, quoted in John A. Moses, *The Politics of Illusion: The Fischer Controversy in German Historiography* (London: George Prior Publishers, 1975): 25. The publicist Axel Ripke likewise declared in 1913: "The saying that 'the world is rapidly becoming English' has so far proved true; and it is up to the Germans alone to put a stop to this prophecy." Fischer, *War of Illusions*: 233.

    Paul Kennedy notes that the German naval buildup was "based on premises which sheer commonsense, not to mention a considerable amount of contemporary British and German writings on strategy, contradicted." These premises survived from "the lack of informed civilian probing into strategic matters, such as existed in the English press and parliament." Paul Kennedy, *Strategy and Diplomacy 1870–1945* (Aylesbury: Fontana, 1983): 151–52.
67. See e.g. Heinrich Class, summarized in Roger Chickering, *We Men Who Feel Most German: A Cultural Study of the Pan-German League, 1886–1914* (Boston: George Allen & Unwin, 1984): 215.
68. Paul M. Kennedy, "The First World War and the International Power System," *International Security*, Vol. 9, No. 1 (Summer 1984): 7–41 at 12, 14 (tables 4 and 7). Among world powers only the United States economy grew faster than the German economy during 1880–1914; ibid.
69. Charles E. McClelland, *The German Historians and England: A Study in Nineteenth-Century Views* (Cambridge: Cambridge University Press, 1971): 195.
70. Herwig, "Failure of German Sea Power": 74.
71. Lebow, *Between Peace and War*: 126–27.

72. Ludwig Reiners, *The Lamps Went Out in Europe*, trans. Richard and Clara Winston (New York: Pantheon, 1955): 218. Finance Minister Hergt explained: "The Americans cannot swim and cannot fly; they will not come"; ibid.
73. Reiners, *Lamps Went Out*: 218.
74. Reiners, *Lamps Went out*: 218; and Iklé, *Every War Must End*: 46–47. In April 1917, after the campaign had been underway for three months, Germany's General Ludendorff thought Germans need not worry about American mobilization potential, since the blockade would force England to make peace within three months; ibid.: 45.
75. Reiners, *Lamps Went Out:* 218.
76. Iklé, *Every War Must End*: 47.
77. Gerhard Ritter, *The Sword and the Scepter: The Problem of Militarism in Germany*, 4 vols. (Coral Gables: University of Miami Press, 1969–1973): 3:120.
78. Iklé, *Every War Must End*: 44.
79. Klaus Epstein, "Gerhard Ritter and the First World War," in Koch, *Origins of the First World War*: 286–306 at 300.
80. Arthur S. Link, *Wilson the Diplomatist* (New York: New Viewpoints, 1974): 79. In fact, there was no trace of the famine in England that the German Navy predicted—the British were never even forced to ration food. Meanwhile the United States shipped two million men to France without losing a single soldier at sea during the whole war. Reiners, *Lamps Went Out*: 219.
81. Iklé, *Every War Must End*: 49.
82. Willis Rudy. *Total War and Twentieth-Century Higher Learning: Universities of the Western World in the First and Second World Wars* (Rutherford: Fairleigh Dickinson University Press, 1991): 41–43.
83. Weber extolled the war in 1916: "Had we not been prepared to risk this war, then we should never have bothered to found the Reich and should have continued to exist as a nation of small states." von Strandmann, "Germany and the Coming of War" 87.
84. Rudy, *Total War*: 52–54.
85. Taylor, *First World War*: 62. On allied aims see A. J. P. Taylor, "The War Aims of the Allies in the First World War," in Richard Pares and A. J. P. Taylor, eds., *Essays presented to Sir Lewis Namier* (London: Macmillan, 1956): 475–505.
86. On France see note 26.
87. Taylor, *First World War*: 83. The government solved the problem by closing pubs in the afternoon—a custom that lasted 70 years.
88. Taylor, *First World War*: 61, 84.
89. Brian Bond, *British Military Policy Between the Two World Wars* (New York: Oxford University Press, 1980): 34, 36.
90. Taylor, *First World War*: 108. The British official military history of the war, published between 1922 and 1948, heavily whitewashed Haig's mistakes. Its author General James Edmonds baldly admitted that "the whole truth cannot of course be told." Tim Travers, *The Killing Ground: The British Army, the Western Front and the Emergence of Modern Warfare 1900–1918* (London: Allen & Unwin, 1987): 221. See also ibid.: xxii, 6, 10, 24–26, 203–50, especially 203–04, 215–16.

91. Hajo Holborn, "Moltke and Schlieffen: The Prussian-German School," in Edward Mead Earle, ed., *Makers of Modern Strategy: Military Thought from Machiavelli to Hitler* (Princeton: Princeton University Press, 1971): 172–205 at 200.
92. Quoted in Winston S. Churchill, *The World Crisis. 1916–1918. Part I* (London: Thornton Butterworth Limited, 1927): 49.
93. Churchill, *World Crisis. 1916–1918. Part I*: 37, 53.
94. Churchill's book was attacked by military critics when he finally published it in 1927. The British official historian had doctored casualty figures to conceal the catastrophic results of the British offensives. Using this doctored data, group of leading British military officers and experts in 1928 published *The World Crisis by Winston Churchill: A Criticism*, claiming that Churchill was wrong to claim the attacking allies suffered persistently greater casualties than the defending Germans during the offensives. See Brodie, *War and Politics*: 19.
95. Gerhard Ritter, *The Schlieffen Plan: Critique of a Myth* (London: Oswald Wolff, 1958; reprint ed., Westport, CT: Greenwood Press, 1979): 48, also 9; and Brodie, *War and Politics*: 11–12.
96. B. H. Liddell Hart, "Foreword," in Ritter, *Schlieffen Plan*: 3–10 at 3.
97. Ritter, *Schlieffen Plan*: 4. B. H. Liddell Hart later marvelled: "In light of Schlieffen's papers, and of the lessons of World War I, it is hard to find reason for the way he has so long been regarded as a master mind, and one who would have been victorious if he had lived to conduct his own Plan." "Foreword," in Ritter, *Schlieffen Plan*: 9.
98. Herwig, "Failure of German Sea Power": 86–94.
99. Edward L. Homze, *Arming the Luftwaffe: The Reich Air Ministry and the German Aircraft Industry, 1919–39* (Lincoln: University of Nebraska Press, 1976): 55–56.
100. The spirit behind this silence was expressed by the head of Germany's naval archives, who privately explained that "history is not to be written for the purpose of tearing down but for building up. Therefore, with marked failures, much must be done to cover them with love, because history must be constructive." Keith W. Bird, "The Origins and Role of German Naval History in the Inter-War Period 1918–1939," *Naval War College Review* (March–April 1979): 42–58 at 47. Such attitudes led to major idiocies in Nazi-German naval policy. For example, despite World War I experience showing the great military value of U-boats, Germany entered; World War II with only 27 ocean-going U-boats—far too few to wage effective undersea war against Britain. Herwig, "Failure of German Sea Power": 94.
101. See Gary D. Stark, *Entrepreneurs of Ideology: Neoconservative Publishers in Germany, 1890–1933* (Chapel Hill: University of North Carolina Press, 1981): 148–234.
102. Herwig, "Clio Deceived": 15–18, 29–33, 37–40.
103. Herwig, "Clio Deceived": 21–22.
104. A. L. Rowse, *Appeasement* (New York: Norton, 1961): 116–17, quoted in Klaus Knorr, "Threat Perception," in Klaus Knorr, ed., *Historical Dimensions*

of National Security Policy (Lawrence: University Press of Kansas, 1976): 82–83.

105. Benny Morris, *The Roots of Appeasement: The British Weekly Press and Nazi Germany During the 1930s* (London: Frank Cass, 1991): 6.
106. A. J. P. Taylor, *The Origins of the Second World War*, 2nd ed. (Greenwich, CT: Fawcett, 1961): 169.
107. Quoted in Knorr, "Threat Perception": 82–83.
108. Iklé, *Every War Must End*: 19.
109. In April 1941, quoted in William L. Shirer, *The Rise and Fall of the Third Reich: A History of Nazi Germany* (New York: Simon & Schuster, 1960): 875.
110. To his generals on August 22, 1939, quoted in Shirer, *Rise and Fall of the Third Reich*: 530.
111. Oscar J. Hammen, "German Historians and the Advent of the National Socialist State," *Journal of Modern History*, Vol. 13, No. 2 (June 1941): 161–88 at 187. Alice Gallin, a student of interwar German academe, argues that German scholars accepted Nazi rule even more supinely than most sectors of German society: "I found cells of resistance [to the Nazis] in the army, the intelligence circles, the labor unions, and the churches, but none in the universities." *Midwives to Nazism: University Professors in Weimar Germany 1925–1933* (Macon, GA: Mercer University Press, 1986): 4.
112. In October 1937, quoted in R. J. C. Butow, *Tojo and the Coming of the War* (Stanford, California: Stanford University Press, 1961): 107.
113. In 1921, quoted in Butow, *Tojo and the Coming of the War*: 24.
114. Ike, *Japan's Decision for War*: 130.
115. Asada Sadao, "The Japanese Navy and the United States," in Dorothy Borg and Shumpei Okamoto with Dale K. A. Finlayson, eds., *Pearl Harbor as History: Japanese-American Relations 1931–1941* (New York: Columbia University Press, 1973): 225–59 at 256.
116. Bruce M. Russett, *No Clear and Present Danger: A Skeptical View of United States Entry into World War II* (New York: Harper and Row, 1972): 55.
117. Asada, "Japanese Navy and the United States": 251.
118. Fujiwara Akira, "The Role of the Japanese Army," in Borg and Okamoto, *Pearl Harbor as History*: 189–95 at 194.
119. Butow, *Tojo and the Coming of the War*: 155,315.
120. Ienaga, *Pacific War*: 141. Japan's naval planners ignored the navy's lack of transports to carry oil to Japan, its lack of escorts, and its lack of experience in sea-control operations. They failed to consider the scanty fortifications of Japan's South Pacific islands, or its lack of airpower to defend them. Nor did Japan's leaders analyze Japan's own role in creating its political encirclement. Charles E. Neu, *The Troubled Encounter: The United States and Japan* (New York: John Wiley & Sons, Inc., 1975): 189; and Butow, *Tojo and the Coming of the War*: 315.
121. Ienaga, *Pacific War*: 17–18.
122. Denis Mack Smith, *Mussolini's Roman Empire* (Harmondsworth: Penguin, 1977): 32.

123. Smith, *Mussolini's Roman Empire*: 33,109.
124. Smith, *Mussolini's Roman Empire*: 109, 33, 150.
125. Smith, *Mussolini's Roman Empire:* 65.
126. Smith, *Mussolini's Roman Empire*: 174–75.
127. Smith, *Mussolini's Roman Empire*: 177. In fact the Italian air force was "at the level of a Balkan state," as one Italian air force chief noted; ibid.: 175.
128. Smith, *Mussolini's Roman Empire*: 177. In fact, Mussolini did not know how many planes Italy had, nor could he easily find out; in 1939 he had to conduct an inventory by instructing the Fascist prefects of each region to count the aircraft on each military airfield. Ibid.: 197; and Donald Cameron Watt, *Too Serious A Business: European Armed Forces and the Approach to the Second World War* (Berkeley: University of California Press, 1975): 117.
129. Smith, *Mussolini's Roman Empire*: 169–70.
130. Smith, *Mussolini's Roman Empire*: 172, 178.
131. Smith, *Mussolini's Roman Empire*: 172.
132. Smith, *Mussolini's Roman Empire*: 169, 172.
133. Smith, *Mussolini's Roman Empire*: 94.
134. John Mueller, "Pearl Harbor: Military Inconvenience, Political Disaster," *International Security*, Vol. 16, No. 3 (Winter 1991/1992): 172–203 at 195.
135. Leslie H. Gelb with Richard K. Betts, *The Irony of Vietnam: The System Worked* (Washington, D.C.: Brookings, 1979): 190. Bernard Brodie writes that "many grave and highly consequential decisions concerning Vietnam were made on the basis of assumptions or premises which would not withstand any kind of logical scrutiny but were simply never challenged!" Brodie, *War and Politics*: 279.
136. McGeorge Bundy, *Danger and Survival: Choices About the Bomb in the First Fifty Years* (New York: Random House, 1988): 570.
137. Rudy, *Total War and Twentieth-Century Higher Learning*: 57–59.
138. The budget analyst was A. Ernest Fitzgerald, fired in 1969; the former Pentagon official was Lawrence Korb, fired by the Raytheon corporation in 1986. A. Ernest Fitzgerald, *The Pentagonists: An Insider's View of Waste, Mismanagement, and Fraud in Defense Spending* (Boston: Houghton Mifflin, 1989): 1–73; and Walt, "Science of Strategy": 153n.
139. John P. Holdren and F. Bailey Green, "Military Spending, the SDI, and Government Support of Research and Development," *F.A.S. Public Interest Report,* Vol. 39, No. 7 (September 1986): 15.
140. Morgenthau, "The Purpose of Political Science": 73.
141. Morgenthau, "The Purpose of Political Science": 73.
142. Morgenthau, "The Purpose of Political Science": 73–4; and Hans J. Morgenthau, *Truth and Power: Essays of a Decade, 1960–70* (New York: Praeger, 1970): 246, 261.
143. Jacoby, *The Last Intellectuals*.
144. Jacoby, *The Last Intellectuals*: 141.
145. Jacoby, *The Last Intellectuals*: 126.

146 Robert A. McCaughey, *International Studies and Academic Enterprise: A Chapter in the Enclosure of American Learning* (New York: Columbia University Press, 1984): 232.
147. David M. Ricci, *The Tragedy of Political Science: Politics, Scholarship, and Democracy* (New Haven: Yale University Press, 1984): 197, reporting a study by Lewis Lipsitz.
148. Patricia Wilner, "The Main Drift of Sociology Between 1936 and 1982," *History of Sociology*, Vol. 2 (Spring 1985): 1–20. Instead the dynamics of mate selection were the favorite topic of contributors.
149. Richard Bernstein, "Age of Golden Clarity Bows to Hegemonicists," *New York Times*, August 27, 1988: 7.
150. David D. Newsom, "Foreign Policy and Academia," *Foreign Policy*, No. 101 (Winter 1995–1996): 52–57 at 62, 64. Parallel criticisms are made of economists. Thus Thomas Vogel writes of the many academic economists who "churn out papers strewn with Greek-letter formulas understood by few and interesting to even fewer." Vogel quotes a Norwest Bank official complaining that "I have tried several times to hire Ph.D. students [in economics]. They knew everything about rational expectations but not about economic forecasting or how the financial system works." Thomas T. Vogel, "Berkeley's Economists Attack Policy Issues With Unusual Gusto," *Wall Street Journal*, December 1, 1995: 1. Princeton economist Alan Blinder likewise complains that much scholarship by young economists is "theoretical drivel, mathematically elegant but not about anything real." Michael Weinstein, "Students Seek Some Reality Amid the Math of Economics," *New York Times*, September 18, 1999: A19.
151. Martin Anderson, *Imposters in the Temple* (New York: Simon & Schuster, 1992): 92. See also ibid.: 79–91, 93–102.
152. Richard J. Samuels, "Japanese Political Studies and the Myth of the Independent Intellectual," in Richard J. Samuels and Myron Weiner, eds., *The Political Culture of Foreign Area and International Studies: Essays in Honor of Lucian W. Pye* (Washington, D.C.: Brassey's, 1991): 17–56 at 42.
153. Kenneth Waltz is a striking exception to this dismal tendency. His writing has always dealt with questions relevant to policy and has directly addressed many important policy issues, including the U.S. war in Vietnam, U.S. policy in Europe and the Persian Gulf, U.S. nuclear strategy, and methods of war prevention. His example rubbed off on his students, many of whom have written prominently on a range of important policy matters.
154. Robert McCaughey notes "the deprecation of popularization [of international relations] as an appropriate activity" by the international studies community, and reports a survey of Asian studies scholars that found they put "public information and public educational activities" as the lowest priority for their professional association. McCaughey, *International Studies*: 224, 227.
155. Irving L. Janis, *Groupthink: Psychological Studies of Policy Decisions and Fiascoes* 2nd ed. (Boston: Houghton Mifflin, 1982): 2–13.

156. Quoted in Lebow, *Between Peace and War*: 153–54.
157. Three-cornered tests that compared the power of these explanations would be useful. On three-cornered tests see Imre Lakatos, "Falsification and the Methodology of Scientific Research Programmes," in Imre Lakatos and Alan Musgrave, eds., *Criticism and the Growth of Knowledge* (Cambridge: Cambridge University Press, 1970): 91–196 at 115.
158. These organizations include the Whistleblower Assistance Fund, the Government Accountability Project, and the Project on Military Procurement.

CHAPTER 10

Structural Realism and Interconnectivity

Andrew K. Hanami

As a theory, now decades old, it has been said that structural realism has run its course in explanations of international relations in the post–Cold War era. Presumably this is because since the end of the Cold War, there is now as expected the long-term absence of a major war between the major states. For some, it was the high-conflict era of bipolarity in which structural realism had its greatest explanatory power. But the occurrence of war was never the sole reason why structural realism explained international behavior. It was only its most dramatic, and in some ways, its most important. Structural realism today can be expected to endure as long as state preeminence endures and states remain the most important actors in the international system, even in peace, for in peace one finds the rudiments of war. In recent years, non-state and near-state actors have been put forth as decisive new units in a world now focused on economics, limited campaigns or on terrorism. The state therefore is said to have declined in relative importance. But one needs to identify the impact of such non-state actors in the world before we can make an assessment about the significance of the new relations they create, and the theory that explains them.

Interconnectivity is the relationship between states as conditioned by structure and state motive. Interconnectivity, as a feature of the prevailing international structure, allows that significant internal or even multilateral actors can forge relations across borders. The inside-out and outside-in perspectives can be seen to combine when individual personalities of key leaders, for example, may be pushed by internal, historical or group dynamics to act outwardly. An international organization may decide on an agenda simply from the internal inertia of its members. But personalities and organizations are important, in part, because they represent a state's power, and to be effective they must push with that state and act with one eye on their external environment. Personalities and organizations may initiate foreign policy, but foreign policy action that stems from internal drives but which goes against the grain of structure is risking failure, and over time, successful leadership will see that.[1]

The disappearance of the Soviet Union from the center stage for some seems to mean that suddenly unit-level explanations have replaced structure. But in reality the unipolarity that was created when the Soviet Union slid away merely gives unit-level actors like personalities the appearance of a greater relative profile because they stand on a narrower stage. They were there before. Systemic dynamics that operated then continue to persist. A change in history does not necessarily require a change in the general theory that explains history. We should not be repulsed by the continuation of the familiar just because it did not explain all actions in the past.

As the simplest structure, unipolarity may not seem as threatening to all states as bipolarity had been. If, however implausible, under bipolarity there was a direct U.S.–Soviet conflict of any proportion, the results would have significant systemic effects. But since the onset of unipolarity if the U.S. and any other power engaged in a conflict, there would be much less systemic impact. Thus all states feel the release of dread that accompanied the prospect of superpower confrontation in which they as smaller states could only watch, wait and weather as best they can. The change from bipolarity to unipolarity is forcing most states to learn more about themselves, and their world. Structure still instructs.

With a lone superpower, the challenge today is not only what the U.S. might do to second states, and they may feel the U.S. has less urgency to shape some of them as formerly was the case, but what other second states could do to them, directly or indirectly. Whether it was true or not, states believed that strong bipolar confrontations would have negative consequences sooner or later. Unipolarity, whether it is a moment or a few decades in length, has ushered in a more variegated and self-help environment and has thus caused states to focus on their most likely or immediate problems. Neither Asia nor a united Europe, as David Rieff believes, is likely to successfully challenge U.S. hegemony in the twenty-first century. In part, this is because European armies are shrinking both in "size and in capability." The only threats to U.S. leadership—terrorism, failed states, Saddam

Hussein, Slobodan Milosivic or even the heirs to Osama bin Laden are limited.[2]

In bipolarity, major confrontations being rare and their prevention by the action of lesser states was not possible, the international system below the level of the superpowers was, in a sense, frozen in time. Their maneuvers mattered less because it was the potential top tier movement that held the greatest leverage. Thus the orbit of state actions took place within a relatively immobile, stable and patterned bipolar world, as structuralists have predicted.

With the erosion to unipolarity, the calculus has changed considerably. Now more states must watch more states. There are not just two sides, therefore there is no "protection," sociology or structure of belonging to East or West. There is a sense of greater anarchy, or at least, greater uncertainty as to both the movement and consequences of the actions of states in an unbalanced world. This is worrisome particularly to smaller states because the prospect of rescue in unipolarity is reduced as the U.S. has greater choices of how and if to prop up second states in proportion to their value in a less bifurcated world. Both Africa and Latin America have received less attention and aid from the U.S. since 1990. This has caused Kenneth Jowitt to remark that large parts of the world today are now "disconnected" from the main states of the world.[3]

Therefore, many things suddenly become or appear to become important to smaller states: their economies, militaries, allies, rivals, relations with the U.S. and even their relations with bigger states like Russia, China or other regional powers. Everything matters more because the importance of margins has increased in a unipolar world as small gains or losses tilt states no longer buoyed by a superpower sponsorship. Indeed, the fact that the U.S. remains the only important superpower may have led Osama bin Laden to target the World Trade Center and Pentagon on September 11, 2001, as he and his al Qaida group tried to "balance" or, in their minds, punish or alter U.S. behavior in the Middle East.

Of course, even the lone preeminent international power, the U.S. cannot necessarily coerce all states to do its bidding directly or efficiently. It never could. It was rather the fear of bipolarity's combined superpower motion or clash that might unleash power in places that small states could not comfortably absorb that nudged them, reducing states unevenly and jostling them in an unmanaged way. That prospect helped discipline the system.

But without a comparable collision, the U.S. alone is not able to deliver a global event on that scale, nor does it need it to. The hegemon can feel relatively secure in a world without an equivalent threat. Unipolarity does tempt and require that the U.S. dampen down challenges even to its interests, and not just to its capabilities. Thus there is dynamism introduced into the system. The U.S. must take on challenges from allied, ad hoc or other groupings, and sometimes preemptively take action to keep even smaller and medium size challenges from adding up, which could embolden larger watchers, or groups of watchers. Using a microeconomic analog of the firm, Paul R. Viotti, Jr. says that under collusion, over time, states are likely to see that cooperation rather than competition is better for all concerned.[4]

The Persian Gulf War may have been as much an effort to halt the foundation of an opposition alliance cluster as it was to stop Saddam Hussein. Only an alliance of more capable states than those that currently exist in the Middle East could balance the U.S. and cause trouble to American foreign policy. Particularly worrisome to the U.S. would be if modern Japan aligned with Germany, forging together the next two most powerful states, especially if Japan and Germany acquired nuclear capability. As an alliance, or axis, they may not challenge the U.S. directly or by intention, at least not initially, but third states with grievances against the U.S. may rally over to Japan and Germany to champion their case, giving greater weight, or polarity, to the Japan–German axis. That structural change would take away much leverage from the U.S. and shift it toward a second center of global power, causing the U.S. to expend greater resources, compromise or retreat.

By keeping Japan and Germany locked in separate spheres, Japan in rough balance or contention with an emerging China in Asia, Germany within a uniting Europe, the U.S. can hold off such an alignment while housing both states within two overall U.S.-led condominiums. This results in a type of double containment: Japan and Germany are contained within their separate regions, and contained within the overall U.S. alliance system.

Yet the U.S. today, though it is the leading military and economic power, is in at least two important ways less imposing than what its status might connote. First, the U.S. must concern itself with the possible self-decline of imperial overstretch. Since all states calculate to maintain their power and sovereignty, this is always going to be a concern. Imperial overstretch, rather than defeat on the battlefield or in the global economy, is a reigning superpower's only serious Achilles heel in the days of unipolarity. Even a major terrorist event from a non-state actor cannot do more than cause limited and temporary damage to a state like the U.S.

Second, it is clear the U.S. can destroy the world many times over with its nuclear and conventional weapons, but it cannot remake that same world over many times. Though the U.S. remains the greatest single economy, it is still basically a two-state nation. If one were to combine the GDP of America's next two competitors, Japan and Germany, together they would nearly equal the GDP figure of the U.S. More would outweigh it. This fact does not mean the U.S. could not still blunt, stymie or cause such powerful secondary states to go into decline, to cooperate or to step aside. This is because the force of a great economic power is leveraged through a single state mechanism, not an economic alliance of states, which historically has not worked over protracted time or over a variety of issues.

But a two-state nation possesses the finite resources and economic capabilities of a single actor, and faces a world nearing 200 states. Of course multistates rarely, if ever successfully, perform the reverse—pool their economic capabilities in successful concert against a hegemon. But in an uncooperative world, even in the absence of a determined or allied economic state action, the U.S. may not over time have the vision, offices, skill or inclination to sequentially bend the economic arms of groups of unwilling states without risking its own assets, goodwill or self-depletion. The independent goals of other states can pull in different directions. States can lag, reduce their profile, or form regional blocs, insulating themselves as best they can from U.S. manipulation. States may be attempting this now. Most trade today is intra-regional, 52 percent in East Asia, 61 percent in the European Union (EU).[5] This suggests that a certain pattern of insularity vis-a-vis the U.S. has set in. The U.S. must aim realistically on what it can do, or on voluntary or induced behavior to efficiently manage the problems of the emerging bloc tendencies around the world; and the U.S. may not be able to tempt others into its camp via nation-building promises that are likely to fall short of their mark.

Therefore, the unipolar structure today exhibits the following characteristic: states are searching for their range of actions and relative ranking, which is more problematic today than in the past, when military power seemed to be the most important determinant of state power. In today's environment, economic power, technological innovation, financial growth and resilience, even regime stability affects judgments of state power because they foretell a state's probable national objectives in an era absent of large war threat for the time being. The time being is what most smaller states calculate, worry about and react to in unipolarity because any number of factors can quickly and perniciously reduce them. In the case of a state-like terrorist group like al Qaida, believing they enjoyed the security of a strategic defensive homeland in Afghanistan under the Taliban, Osama bin Laden made the error that the U.S. would not have the will to pursue him through his caves in that mountainous country. That mistake cost him his entire organization, and the demise of the Taliban, as well. Therefore, a state's choice of connections with another state or states will determine much of how well off it can be.[6]

Thus an unsettling nervousness has emerged among lesser states because more can go right or wrong for them in this less shepherded world. Since lesser states cannot bracket one superpower with another as successfully in unipolarity as some did in bipolarity, they exist somewhat more in isolation. First, smaller states are not assured of alternate support in exchange for their allegiance. Second, small states may not be able to stand up in significant or consistent ways to the U.S., and they regret that. Third, as lesser states, they are more vulnerable to even medium-size threats because they know they may either have to face those challenges alone, or broker a deal with others or the U.S., and that could damage their long-term interests.

In the unipolar era so far we have observed that the U.S. has not intervened regularly nor aggressively. From that observation, some might wonder why states did not feel more free to engage in more adventurist foreign policies. But the difference is if the U.S. unexpectedly chooses to act against an adventurist state, the penalties might be greater than such a state may be willing to pay, with little prospect of effective, multilateral redress from allies. This introduces some general caution in international politics and keeps the foreign policies of second states piecemeal, and within a predictable and incremental orbit. They must often react, rather than act, and smaller states cannot conduct grand strategy. Behavior of this level will not threaten the U.S., at least not in the short run.

Interconnectivity and Interdependence

Therefore, under unipolarity the relations of states has become characterized by intermittent interconnectivity, whereby states exhibit relational creation, extension and optional retreat with the recognition of constant amendment with others, as each gauges the results of others. The relations among states can be best described in terms of interconnectiveness. Since unipolarity, many states have increased their relations with other states. The "bloc" phenomena is one manifestation of this. Linking up with others is one strategy second states use to balance a hegemon. But there are others. Increased linkages suggest a more active structure released from a prior one. While the degree of interconnectivity has increased for many, the world is not thereby more interdependent. This is important because state relations have become more flexible. Significant consequences will flow from an individual state's choice of relations today. Interconnectivity suggests the lack of permanent alliance that states are willing to form because states are seeking to discover their optimal mix of connections with others. Interdependence, by contrast, commits states more deeply, and under unipolarity, that puts the assets of lesser states at greater risk as the U.S. twists its tentacles in unanticipated ways.

In other words, the unipolar structure remains a dominant system-wide attribute while interdependence is not. Interdependence is more limited, relevant perhaps most times to selected bilateral relations or small clusters of states, and varies by strength for each. Interdependence by definition must be at a low level generally throughout the system because of both the wide and growing disparities between the most powerful and the least.

Bilateral interdependence is vastly ephemeral and without assured staying power. In the late 1980s, the U.S. and Japan appeared to be at the apex of their interdependence with a still intact Soviet challenge, a surging Japanese economy and an America in modest but temporary economic recession. The Gulf War, which triggered the bursting of the Japanese economic bubble within a year of the Soviet decline, completely changed how we view that relationship, and put in further recess the implied near equality of interdependence between Japan and the U.S. Rather than catching up and overtaking the U.S., Japan was seen as surprisingly dependent on it, symbolized by Clinton's $2 billion bailout to Japan in 1997. Interdependencies, though some states approach that condition, are fleeting. Their impermanence suggests that they do not compose the "structure" of the international system. Instead, interdependencies comprise only temporary, substructural relations, or what I call perceived or niche interdependence, of the general global structure. Therefore, the level of interdependency among most states should not be mistaken for structure, but rather seen only as a manifestation and result of structure. What has been considered as the recent rise in interdependency around the world is actually the rise in worldwide interactions, which frequently lead to interconnectivity. Increased interconnectivity can result from such increased levels of international interactions, but this is not interdependence. This was true not only of the Bush coalition during the Persian Gulf War in 1991, but also George W. Bush's coalition built around the pursuit of global terrorism after September 11.

The reason for this is that interdependence demands sustained state commitment and contradicts the state's primary dictum of self-help and self-survival. Depending on the cooperation of others because of the pull of economic assets located abroad, risks more than states can afford in a competitive and suspicious world. It is, however, often said that civilian politicians, eager to form alliances for their own purposes, are apt to cooperate with others across borders. This is undoubtedly true. But if some politicians behave as if they are not suspicious toward others outside their state, and in time they should, certainly the militaries within their state are because they fear the other state's military assets, war-making or war alliance potential. States will remain independent as long as militaries remain independent, regardless of what one politician may do. No one can calm the military and make them interdependent with other militaries. Militaries remain fiercely independent and dedicated to the existence of the state because they created the state. They remain the core ingredient of a state's self-help make-up, and they know it. Military organizations sit at the very origin and center of states, and have a prime role in maintaining it, defending it and adjusting it. They form the circle of last resort.

Moreover, militaries are not as versatile as economic assets, their functions within the state are not easily adapted to other new purposes, even in the twenty-first century. Militaries young and old continue to stand as sentinels of the state. Militaries are relatively changeless, stand-alone defenders of states and are an independent force whose main mission is to preserve the political integrity of the state, regardless of who the civilian leaders are, say or do. Successful states do not have long or deep disputes between their civilian leaders and their militaries. A workable agreement must come into being, and civilian leaders must give as good as they get if they hope to be effective, long-tenure leaders. Militaries, on the other hand, have great staying power, and generals know that political leaders more frequently come and go and must often depend on them in crisis. Military leaders, as a class, are relatively autonomous because they are not easily co-opted by office holders or economic incentives. Down through history, militaries have not much evolved in their basic function. Because they hold the gun, militaries can acquire the necessary economic, social or material assets they require. Military leaders are the most patriotic, mission-driven, disciplined group who both stand for their society, but in a sense, outside of civil society. This dualism gives militaries much of their self-reliant qualities.[7]

In addition, the lethal and perhaps unknowable command structure to the adversary of a nation's military is such that even if civilian leaders, held in check by interdependent ties, hold back their generals, some weapons may be positioned, launched, or appear to be so, triggering a military response or crisis from others. Thus militaries are not easy to hold down with unpopular policies because even a single shot or maneuver may be taken as the start of aggression. Knowing this, a large and diffuse military organization holds a powerful, autonomous escalation capacity that is risky for civilian leaders, or scholars, to discount.

Dependence, of course, is to be avoided most of all, if possible. Interdependence is a desired step above that and is preferred because it allows relative "wiggle room." Lesser states may accrue positive gains through it. The emerging and apparent interdependence-inclined states of the EU are coalescing because they are attempting to resist dependence on the U.S., or the U.S.–Japan or U.S.–Asia bloc. It should not be understood that Europe is more interdependent through its own inertia but that it is adjusting to structural realities. Interdependence is a state-level strategy, not a broader condition of international relations. Needing others is not necessarily dependence but rather a subset of strategy or alliance politics. Bloc-forming is a reaction to unipolarity. All states protect their interests, and cooperation is often necessary to advance it, but it is a policy and not a natural feature of structure. If it were, interdependence would have occurred long ago in history, and we would think differently of both individual and political behavior than in fact we do today.

Susan Strange has remarked that in the modern day, the power of the state has slipped into decline, and private multinational corporations (MNCs) have replaced them. She deplores the replacement of the state by the corporation because the capitalist-inspired enterprise provides no social welfare to the society's population. Moreover, by inventing nuclear power, she implies the state has, in a sense, legislated war out of existence, and thereby itself. For her, the only value of armies now is to quell internal disorder.[8]

But James Rosenau has noted, despite the rise of MNCs, the state remains. In an increasingly globalized world, he says, people will tear away from their adherence to a single, local loyalty or "highest loyalty," and "give way to the development of multiple loyalties." This is likely to be true for substate actors like corporations who are as happy to operate in foreign cities as in American cities. But at the strategic level, highest loyalty is likely to remain among national-level elites toward the state. It is inconceivable to imagine, Rosenau concludes, U.S. generals, presidents or even important senators developing multistate loyalties, except as temporary alliance arrangements.[9] I agree with this.

Even at the economic level, MNCs exist and have the power, as William Keller and Louis Pauly imply, to globalize because they reside in a state. They say that states "foster the operating environments in which they flourish." States tax, regulate and shape MNCs. The MNCs, on the other hand, are not producing fundamental global norms and integration of national systems. The U.S., Germany and Japan alone are the "home states for the majority of the world's leading multinational firms." This is not mere coincidence. States continue to shape their future financing operations, R&D investment and trading strategies. German MNCs still link to German banks. Japanese MNCs still cling to their keiretsu, and the banks within. MNC growth requires more than technical innovation. It also requires state investments in "education, human resources (and) infrastructure." MNCs are state-confined structures. The proof is that other countries' MNCs do not enter successfully and displace them. Microsoft and IBM in the U.S. have not been displaced by Fujitsu, and vice versa. Instead, there come into existence "sanctuary markets—where leading export industries enjoy an unassailable position in their home base...." Foreign direct investment (FDI) inward is "effectively restricted or channeled, and local markets are protected in opaque ways." When basic corporate capital or technology is at stake, states do not "stand idly by." Though they are slow, states bring considerable weight when they do act. States protect their MNCs by their policies, laws and their marshall forces. In the end, big states determine their own grand strategy, not MNCs—how much trade, what type, FDI, who is to open up, stay closed or boycotted. States remain the basic unit of the international system.[10]

Interconnectivity Under Unipolarity

The relations of states under unipolarity I call unistructuralism, though unipolarity may connote too strong a level of capability for the U.S. today. Unimodality, with less followership potential, may be a more appropriate term. But the extent to which states now are more interconnected with other states than ever before is a reflection of the presence of a single hegemon. Whether states today are more interconnected than three or four decades ago is a good question. Certainly societies are increasingly interconnected due to travel, media, migration, education and the reestablishment of old divisions, as with East and West Germany, and the new railroad that is to link two North and South Korean cities after 2002.

But interconnectivity for states is more complex. Certainly nuclear weapons, and their potential spread, in a sense has interconnected a larger number of states because the concerned states must be wary of, respond to and balance or bandwagon with other states. Such allies or clustered states are connected in that each must take others into account when formulating their foreign policies. The globalization of Western-style markets has further connected national economies, and logically some aspects of each state's foreign economic policy becomes further linked with others. Even at the conventional military level, a number of joint exercises or blended militaries, including the United Nations' PKO, and some modest EU operations, show increases in the incidence of interconnected military policies and interests. These interconnections, however, do not necessarily lead to a more permanent interdependency, but rather, are a sign of each state's diplomatic or political policy to show cooperation, build confidence, reduce costs, achieve limited regional goals or balance another power.

Such interconnectivities can reverse themselves without damaging the central structure of the international system. Interconnectivity is the policy attempt of states that test which foreign behaviors achieve their national goals within the limits of structure. Those found wanting, or which are rebuked, are discontinued. Interconnectivities that profit or maintain a state without causing balancing action from others are continued. Interconnectivity is on the increase generally, but is variable, depending on shifting state goals, capabilities, resistance and will.

Under unipolarity, smaller states are testing, realigning, trying to balance or achieve increments of assets to maximize their independent strategies. But some aspects of the long-term, traditional alliances of the Cold War era persist. A kind of fatalistic interdependence exists among at least some of them. Interconnectivity can be a long-term relationship, intermittent, medium or short-term, is reversible and can be abruptly broken off. Interconnectivity does not connote ties that bind or divide, but encompasses both. Interconnectivity represents the lines that tie, and may be thin or thick between states. Duration of the relationship is separate from the magnitude or value of the relationship because duration is determined by more than economic criteria. In this way, interconnectivity is a more neutral term that does not bring with it the baggage of interdependence, which implies the mixing of national sovereignty with deep foreign tentacles.

Bipolarity caused a form of long-term interconnectivity because of the entrenched and enduring nature of the relationship between the two superpowers. That relationship tended to trap their respective camps into semi-permanent relations that were indeed very costly to break. States that broke away would face at a minimum, a myriad of tasks that might put at risk what their societies had been trying to accomplish to that point. Such breakaway states would lose the benefits of their original sponsor and face the prospect of converting their militaries, economies, ideologies and sympathies to fit in with, and hope to be taken in by, the other side. Egypt in the 1960s and 1970s may be among the few such cases, but needing greater weapons Egypt knew it had little choice other than Soviet arms, and was later able to proceed through the transition to U.S. arms with relative confidence because of its potential value to U.S. interests in the Middle East.

Under unipolarity, the interconnectivity of states is more varied and more performance-based, not ideological. State-to-state relations can be enduring in bipolarity, as with Japan, Britain and other frontline U.S. allies. But the relationship between these allied states, not simply between the U.S. and the one state, is what also becomes important, and problematic. Allies to the U.S., for example, need not be allies with each other. Had China succeeded in becoming America's economic partner, as the Clinton administration had once called for, that would have only further complicated and raised the negative factors between China and Japan, and others. Both Asian states would compete for U.S. benefits and each may perceive the other as profiting more, or unfairly, or out of proportion to their value—and that alone could tilt local balances or cause local threats to grow. The same logic applies to all other linkages be they dedicated or episodic because the nature of interconnectivity is sensitive to the changes in both strategic and regional balances.

Consistent with structural realism, under changed conditions of unipolarity, states continue to seek as much autonomy as they can achieve because they are concerned with relative ranking and the sustainability of their governments in this more active world. Iraq's continuing attempt to develop strategic weapons suggests that even medium-size states pursue independent strategies in the face of UN sanctions and world condemnation, even when it means depriving the Iraqi society of basic necessities for life. Ten years after the Gulf War, the U.S. is still not showing success in stopping Saddam's dogged movement toward acquiring NBC capabilities. U.S. weapons inspector Scott Ritter stated that inside Iraq today there are undiscovered "capabilities" that he believes exist, and that Clinton "tired" of pursuing the inspection ordeal.[11] The George W. Bush administration may be forced to revisit that problem.

Moreover, despite its inability to provide consistent electricity to its people on a daily basis, even in its capital city New Delhi, India is purchasing more than $2 billion worth of arms from Russia. India is acquiring antimissile systems, up to 50 Sukhoi fighter planes, 3 frigates and 2 submarines. It is India's "biggest defense deal signed this century." India is balancing China, but also fears the growing Islamic threat headed by Pakistan, made seemingly more antagonistic by its nuclear testing and military leadership takeover in 2000.[12]

Anupam Srivastava says India's growing missile ambitions are designed to offset both Pakistan and an evolving Chinese capability, and include larger missions, like "attack, deterrence or active defense," as well as for increased multilateral influence. India believes that China's long-range missile capability, aimed to deter the U.S. from interfering with its aims in East China Sea, can easily be redirected to threaten India. For its tactical missile needs against both Pakistan and China, Indian strategists have concluded they need 350 nuclear missiles. New Delhi also hints of a future need to balance Russia, as well. Currently, India possesses the most advanced nuclear missile capability among developing states, with ICBMs capable of ranges around 7,000 miles, and include sea-launchable cruise missiles. Submarine capability is expected in November 2007.[13] This purchase underlines the fact that the state will provide for its security needs first, its population second.

Lawrence Freedman provides an illustration that shows how unipolarity strongly influences the way lesser states maneuver or form strategies even in warfare. Since they cannot directly fight with the U.S., lesser states wish to either keep the U.S. out of the wars they think they can win, or bring the U.S. into a war they may lose. This explains why Saddam tried, albeit poorly, to "internalize" the Iran–Iraq War in his favor and to the disadvantage of Iran, while three years later Saddam attempted to keep the U.S. out of his invasion of Kuwait by threatening to widen it, or cause environmental destruction if the U.S. entered.[14]

Interconnectivity and the Asian Financial Crisis

Interconnective dynamics, and even a heightened degree of interdependence, has gained greater importance at the financial level of clustered smaller states under unipolarity. The consequences can be quite significant. Interconnectivity heavily contributed to the Asian financial crisis, which accelerated after the fall of property and stock market prices in Thailand in July, 1997. The essence of globalization, writes Blanca Heredia, is not the widespread emergence of goods and capabilities but rather the increased mobility of capital. International transactions of equities and bonds among leading economies in 1980 expanded from 10 percent of GDP to "well over 100% in 1995." The growth rate of FDI doubled relative to world GDP in the same period, and now daily foreign exchange market turnover "surged from about $200 billion in the mid-1980s to around $1.2 trillion in 1995—approximately 85% of total world reserves."[15]

Because Southeast Asia's trade was largely intra-regional, as one country went down it pulled the others down, too. "Had they been less integrated," writes Robert Wade, "the regional multiplier effects would have been much smaller." By 1997 the U.S. economy looked very attractive and investors flowed there and this added to the fall. To pinpoint the cause, the "sharp pullout of funds by investors across the region triggered the slump (which was) panicky." The net private investment into the five most damaged economies—Thailand, South Korea, Malaysia, Indonesia and the Philippines was a plus $93 billion in 1996, a minus $12 billion the following year, amounting to 11 percent of their combined GDP. International capital flows are today 70 times international trade. These capital flows are "mostly short term: 80% have a maturity date of 7 days or less."[16] Interconnected capital flight can rapidly devastate even the growing, previously strong regional economies of Asia's tigers.

The currencies of five Southeast Asian states diminished 35–80 percent, and put those economies under extreme pressure, where 40 million people live on less than $1 per day. Karl Jackson specifies that excessive foreign borrowing was the prime culprit in the crisis, "exceeding 50% of GDP in Thailand, Indonesia and the Philippines." Short-term loans due within a year added further burden, amounting to 13, 14 and 22 percent of the GDP of Korea, Indonesia and Thailand. Nonperforming loans were estimated to be higher than 20 percent.

China also contributed to the crisis. By 1996, most of China's economic construction boom centering around Shanghai and Beijing had been completed, resulting in a drop of an estimated 50 percent in production levels in 1997 involving 900 major industrial products, dropping employment and resulting in nonperforming loans in major Chinese banks. Even China's auto production fell to half its levels by late 1996. As China's economy leveled off, it could neither absorb Southeast Asian exports nor assist them. Also, China's cheaper exports after 1994 "undercut Southeast Asia's" economy. China produced a 100 percent increase in its exports between 1993–1996. The lack of a strong economic center in Europe or Japan provided no escape and also contributed to the crisis. International capital flight quickly depressed Asian domestic elite confidence, and they moved their assets to safer Western accounts.[17]

As Ethan Kapstein explains it, "contagion" is a phenomenon in which assets from states residing close to a failing economic state will also experience a similar economic drain. This is because international investors in an otherwise healthy state will observe financial failings in the neighboring states and "fear that it will spread" to them next door. Fleeing the healthy state thus causes that state's economic decline, precipitated not by its internal weakness but by its geographic location.[18]

In that period of time, Japan could not rescue the crisis because it was experiencing its own economic decline. Japanese consumer confidence dropped as the U.S. entered war in the Persian Gulf, threatening oil deliveries. Japan's "high rent society" and "inefficient second economy" kept subsequent urges toward growth down to near zero. Japan's excess savings contributed to the crisis at its early stages because of the excess savings that flooded Japanese banks and then were rerouted into available but risky Southeast Asian projects. The much ballyhooed solution of exporting out of trouble did not materialize because Asian firms had no money to buy raw materials, components or acquire local banking support to produce and export at higher levels.[19]

A possible solution to the crisis was proposed by the Japanese in 1997 to create a regional Asia Fund managed in Tokyo that would inject monies into failing states right away. The proposed fund was to have fewer conditions on its clients and quicker delivery of monies than the IMF, which required internal economic restructuring. But the U.S. immediately insisted the IMF was to remain in charge. This shows that the U.S. wished to maintain control in the region. Some have even suggested that the U.S. is the "root cause" of the Asian financial problem because America's "dollarization" required Asian companies to meet U.S. corporate performance "set in the U.S." If they did not, Asia's companies would not attract sufficient returns to investors and negatively affect growth.

On the other end, U.S. firms were the first to profit from the decline. U.S.-based Merrill Lynch hired the "best ex-employees" from the defunct Yamaichi Securities firm, formerly Japan's fourth largest broker. Travellers, which merged with Citicorp, has also just formed links with "Nikko Securities, one of the remaining big three brokerage houses." Firms of the hegemon are getting richer, further extending economic unipolarity.[20]

The U.S. Over Japan

Under unipolarity, the U.S. is making good use of its position in the international system over Japan in the security field, as well. The U.S. maintains 235 bases and facilities in Japan. The U.S. economic interest is $400 billion per year in its Asia Pacific trade, with 3 million U.S. jobs tied to that trade. U.S. presence in Japanese bases provides a sense of security for the more than 1,500 U.S. companies in Japan, as well as a deterrent to war and maintains sustainability in the region, especially after the loss of the Philippine bases. Yokosuka, a naval city two hours from Tokyo, remains America's only deep water port in Asia. The U.S. encampments in South Korea, by comparison, are no substitute for those in Japan, which feature simple A-frame outposts lacking equivalent facilities for U.S. troops, and the Korean population is unfriendly to U.S. troop presence. If the Japanese bases were abandoned, the U.S. would have to pull back to Alaska and Hawaii to maintain current capabilities, and the distance would make rapid application of force more difficult. U.S. troops require first-class repair services, and a large, willing civilian population skilled in the widest range of manufacturing, engineering and high-tech resources.[21]

After the Okinawa rape case involving U.S. military personnel, it was speculated that the U.S. presence in Japan might be considerably scaled down. But that did not happen. U.S. forces have agreed to some reductions, but have otherwise not conceded much. U.S. forces occupy about one-third of the land of Japanese defense forces, or 314 sq. km., but it is interesting to note that the U.S. Air Force occupies the same quantity of airfield as Japanese air forces do. Further, U.S. carriers continue to practice takeoffs and landings in Iwojima, and use other islands as firing ranges. Additional Japanese islands off the coast are also being considered for U.S. defense relocation as a result of the modest Okinawa reductions. The U.S. wishes to maintain its stronghold in Okinawa. That location is important to U.S. interests because it is physically closer to East Asia as a whole, where the U.S. can project its all East Asian presence.[22]

Japanese bases also served as a take off point for the Persian Gulf War in 1991. Because of war shortages, the U.S. government even asked Japan to grant it "priority." One report suggested that the U.S. "directly approached NEC" for electronics, and the Japanese government used civilian ships to transport military electronics to the Gulf on behalf of the Americans. Even the more recent 1996 air strikes on Iraq "involved" Japanese bases, though the Japanese government refused to confirm it. Since that time, a noted security authority has said that the 47,000 U.S. troops stationed in Japan are "designed to play a leading military role as far away as the Middle East."[23] After September 11, the Japanese Prime Minister even promised to dispatch some of its naval assets to support U.S. operations around Afghanistan, overturning Japan's constitution that forbids dispatching troops overseas.

In further exchange for base reductions, and because of Japan's poor military support during and since 1991, the U.S. military has extracted more from Japan. The new 1997 U.S.–Japan Defense "framework" agreement obligates Japanese forces to step up from local defense to general cooperation with U.S. forces. The U.S. demanded that Japan acquire 75 missile destroyers, 25 offensive submarines (16 hunter-killer), 125 P3Cs, 14 interceptor squadrons and 8 support and early warning aircraft. U.S. forces are inducing Japan to widen its sea-lane patrols and prepare to offer positive support in the "initial stages of war." However, during any real conflict,

U.S. forces have said they would retain "command and control over operations" of joint forces.[24]

Japan's Efforts to be Independent

At least some Japanese leaders continue to press for an optimal, realistic status of independence for themselves even while under the American umbrella. They know in the present unipolar moment they cannot resist U.S. influence directly with much hope of success. So they make do by preparing incrementally for the two possibilities of continuing under U.S. leadership, or striking out on their own, simultaneously. But the shift from bipolarity to unipolarity itself has caused the Japanese much new ambivalence. Will Japan balance or continue to bandwagon with the U.S.? Do the Japanese view the Americans as still reliable under unipolarity?

No longer pressed by as great a Soviet threat, some Japanese are beginning to worry about the reliability of continued U.S. protection, and at the same time, about their own capabilities against their greatest likely threats.

With an apparent inability to reverse course in a timely way, Russia experienced nine straight years of economic decline since its breakup, and the civilian Japanese government downgraded the Kremlin's short-term threat level. But Japan's military continues to maintain a wary posture. They report that while greatly reducing its force presence, Russia continues to introduce new military weapons into the region, including its Akula-class nuclear attack submarine. Even today, the Russian Pacific Fleet "still maintains limited operation of both strategic and attack submarines" in at least coastal patrols. There are also still 3,500 Russian troops on the northern territories, four islands in dispute between the two countries, after it was thought that the troops would leave. For its part, the Japanese know that Russia sees the U.S.–Japan security agreement as a "threat to Soviet sea lanes" and also as a threat to its subbase in the Sea of Okhotsk, as well as its "diplomatic leverage in the region." Russian vessels routinely scout Japan's trade and oil routes. The Japanese are concerned because even if a small military operation were to occur, or even if dummy mines were planted through the Malaccan Strait, Japanese sources believe the Yen would tumble and oil prices would double overnight.[25]

But despite a seemingly modest Russian threat, Japan is looking with more concern toward China, who has been purchasing power projection weapons in the last few years. Beijing's post–Persian Gulf War policy represents a sharp and potentially menacing problem. China has turned away from its traditional "People's War" doctrine emphasizing manpower for defense to being able to fight "local wars under high-technology conditions," which grants it more "offensive than defensive scenarios." For this new doctrine, China has imported new weapons. The U.S. has "maintained stringent restrictions on arms sales" to China, though "Russia, Israel, European and even some Asian suppliers have eagerly sought to fill the vacuum." From the Kremlin, China has purchased four submarines "which have potential cruise missile launch capacity, and is understood to be considering the purchase of more." Such platforms, if equipped with nuclear warheads, would give China credible second-strike capability, effectively balancing the U.S. at the nuclear level. Waltz has said that he believes China has already achieved that. Currently China has one submarine that carries 12 missiles, and is reported to have 17–20 ICBMs capable of reaching the U.S. At the moment, China lacks the warhead miniaturization technology to produce warheads small enough to fit onto submarines or other advanced delivery platforms. But China has reportedly made efforts to obtain those and related secrets from Los Alamos via espionage.

Besides the new subs, China has purchased 50 Sukhoi attack jets. But China's immediate short-term goals seem to be strengthening its claims on Taiwan and the Spratly Islands. The lack of a full array of integrated weapons systems still prevent China from projecting and sustaining power. China's amphibious-warfare ships can place up to three infantry divisions; but without air defense, better interservice coordination or an improved centralized command control capabilities, China may attack but not stay long enough to see victory, yet. Concentrating on its economic development, Deng Xiaoping said, "we should not fight a war for 50 years." Thus at this moment China does not seem to be a primary security threat to the U.S.[26]

But there are derivative problems. In the post–Cold War era, China's continuing sensitivity to possible encroachments stems from its "unique" sense that in its past history it was "dismembered" by foreign powers. Hong Kong was taken from it, Taiwan escaped from it. This has made China more vigilant to questions of political independence concerning the Senkaku (Daioyu) and Spratly Islands. Moreover, after having been forced to back down by U.S. naval forces in July 1996 in the Taiwan Straits, the Chinese military has "for the first time since the 1950s" begun to "think seriously about how to use force to bring Taiwan under its sway." China is developing a hovercraft fleet to "speed across the Taiwan Strait," and to "contest sea control of a significant defense perimeter in the Western Pacific itself." In its military budget, China has prioritized its naval and air capabilities. In recent patrols, China has "repeatedly entered Japanese waters around the Senkaku Islands in utter disregard of warnings voiced by Japanese authorities."[27]

Wu Xinbo writes that since 1992, after decades of stable diplomatic friendship based on expanding trade, Sino-Japanese relations have "entered a period of competitive co-existence," in which each has become suspicious of each other's security aims. China fears perhaps a U.S.–Japan agenda that may attempt to incorporate Taiwan, which China believes is Japan's top priority. The new 1997 U.S.–Japan defense guidelines have propelled Japan to assist the U.S. in policing East Asia, not just modest local defense, making the Asia Pacific a "U.S.–Japan condominium." The Chinese are worried that with the acquisition of Theatre Missile Defense, Japan will acquire "a kind of strategic balance with respect to the PRC by using a TMD system to nullify the threat from China's limited strategic forces." China has even speculated that TMD could lead to the development of "offensive weapons" by Japan.[28]

China intends to build a "green water" navy within a few years across the eastern Pacific to the "first island chain" that includes the Kuriles and Philippines. Peter Jensen clarifies, "blue water" begins after that, encompassing the U.S. bases at Guam and the Marianas, which China plans to extend by 2050, and to branch out toward the Indian Ocean, as well. China has covertly formed alliances with seafaring pirates who attack ships from countries China wishes to pressure. Beijing has formed a relationship with the military regime in Myanmar to build and rent naval facilities in Burma's extended ports. David Shambaugh adds that by 2005–2007, China is thought to have a credible capability to block and attack Taiwan to establish domination in the area, and this would invite direct U.S. military reaction.[29]

How does Japan view its security situation in the region, does it plan to rely on the U.S. umbrella? The answer may be, Tokyo still remembers when JFK said, "Ich bin ein Berliner" (I am a Berliner), but recall that he did not also say, "But I am a Tokyo-ite, as well." Younger Japanese are skeptical about the reliability of the U.S. umbrella, and believe Japan needs to directly play a larger role in world affairs. Japanese increasingly feel that dependence on U.S. defense is "unsustainable."[30]

The Japanese military also does not feel that the U.S. is so inextricably committed to Japan. In recent years, a Japanese source reports that many generals have little faith in the U.S.–Japan security treaty, though their beliefs improved after greater joint exercises.[31]

Observing regional developments, the Japanese military have said they want offense, not just the "defensive capabilities" they developed over the past five decades. In the 1980s, there was a "general rebellion" within the military establishment itself over the Soviet action in Afghanistan, and other regional wars because Japan was unprepared with merely defensive systems.

The military advocated a new policy called "forward defense" against possible bases of attack aimed at Japan, and advocated a 2 percent military budget, not the present 1 percent ceiling set by an earlier decision. One general even remarked that under surprise attack, the Japanese reaction from its own civilian authorities would likely be too slow. Consequently, local military commanders would probably act "extralegally." In a famous incident, the Joint Chief of Staff Hiroomi Kurisu, Japan's highest military officer, even denied the validity of civilian control.[32]

Since 1897, the Japanese have been students of Alfred Thayer Mahan who taught that a dominating navy was essential for a nation's greatness. A small navy today is not capable of patrolling sea-lanes as distant as between Vladivostok and the Indian Ocean, and the Japanese navy knows it. The U.S. Navy cannot patrol the entire region, at least not on its own, and is increasingly relying on the expansion of Japan's navy. Further, recalling the island-by-island World War II strategy of the American Armada, which destroyed Japan's seapower before attacking the main island, Tokyo today is keenly aware of the value of its adjacent seas. Japan's sealane protection of its petroleum imports calls for an effective convoy escort, especially for oil tankers, and that requires helicopter carriers and offensive power projection in "all directions." Ninety-nine percent of Japan's oil passes from the Persian Gulf to the Indian Ocean to the Malaccan and Taiwan Straits. Japan is forced by its trade-oriented economy to no longer simply worry about protecting narrow sealanes, but whole areas, and that requires a blue water navy.[33]

British defense experts say that the upgradation of the 1997 U.S.–Japan Defense Guidelines "gives Japan its highest military profile in East Asia since the end of the Second World War." Suddenly, Japan has become a "significant regional force." Japan's newest tank-landing carrier craft, revealed in 1998, features a thorough flight deck that can serve as a "small aircraft carrier," and may be Harrier capable now.[34] This is the beginning of power projection.

Because of its new 1997 agreement, Japan has been called upon to join U.S. forces in military operations "surrounding" Japan that are "situational . . . not geographical." "Rear area" support used to mean the Sea of Japan but now is omnidirectional. This means "air and sealane defense." In a protracted Korean peninsula, conflict Japanese forces may be brought into "front-line combat defense," possibly requiring "air cover" as well as ASW, and at the tactical level defense can quickly turn to offense. Japan's four AWACS already monitor beyond Japan's territories, and since its embarrassment over its non-detection of a North Korean missile test last fall, the military will no doubt press for greater independent monitoring capability.[35]

What are Japan's Nuclear Options?

Since 1966 an official Japanese study concluded that it was "highly unthinkable" that the U.S. would risk a nuclear exchange with its leading adversaries Russia or China "for the sake of Japan." A former director of Japan's Nuclear Energy Division states that the U.S. is only likely to defend Japan in a conventional way. Even as prominent a civilian leader as former prime minister Keiichi Miyazawa warned in 1971 that Japan could go nuclear if the U.S. "push(ed) Japan around too much." It is understood among Tokyo leadership circles that Japan would go nuclear if the current five nuclear powers fail to eliminate their nuclear weapons, if Russia, China or North Korea further threaten Japan or if the U.S. umbrella loses its credibility.[36] The nuclear line is looking thinner.

Japanese prime ministers have set the stage by saying that nuclear forces are not prohibited by Japan's constitution and that nuclear warheads can be deployed for defensive purposes. They have also stated that the "3 nuclear principles" are a "policy" decision, not a constitutional prohibition. An already well established civilian nuclear power program gives Japan a "built-in weapons option". Even by the 1970s, Japanese studies acknowledged that if they direct nuclear reactors to military purposes Japan could produce 20–30 warheads per year. It is interesting that the U.S. is assisting the Japanese in perfecting techniques to "separate supergrade plutonium" at its Tokai plant, as revealed by Greenpeace.

An important phrase in a 1969 study states that Japan should be ready "should tactical nuclear weapons be introduced in a future emergency." At present, Japan's F-16s are nuclear-capable and can reach eastern Russia, and some East Asia targets. But Japan is also developing a potential strategic delivery system. Japan has tested solid-fuel rockets that could be "directly converted to intercontinental-range missiles . . . comparable to that of the U.S. ICBMs." They would have a range of 7,000–8,000 miles. The Japanese blended their H-2 rocket with a solid-propellant motor with the upper stages of a more advanced vehicle. The new vehicle may possibly carry between 5 and 10 warheads. One American space scientist estimated that Japan could deploy a counter-value technology "in a matter of months."[37]

The U.S. is not opposed to Japan's acquisition of nuclear capabilities. This was true as far back as three decades ago. Beginning with the Nixon administration, the U.S. thought it had to further induce Japan to stay under U.S. influence, given its opening toward China, and "might even agree, in time, to a two-key nuclear arrangement under partial U.S. control." This is important given that the U.S. concept of "theatre deterrence" was seen as no longer a case of ICBM exchange to protect Japan or other allies but allowing allies to "have their own tactical nuclear capabilities," minimizing damage to U.S. territory. The White House announced in November 1971 that the "U.S. is prepared to provide Japan nuclear warheads or the know-how to manufacture nuclear warheads."[38] This would balance out the European nuclear forces already possessed by Britain and France, giving the U.S. a two-ocean nuclear ally partnership.

At the tactical interoperability level, the U.S. and Japan may have gone farther in their joint nuclear patrols than has been previously known. Because U.S. subs or other vessels may sink in conflict or by accident, and only Japanese subs are likely to be nearby, an intriguing scenario has emerged. A source close to the Japanese navy has said that Japanese submarines may have been given the responsibility to offload, recover and possibly be able to utilize or make operational the weapons systems, including Tomahawk and nuclear weapons, onto Japanese vessels. In principle, if true, it would be only a small step for the Japanese to receive training and operational capability in recovering, loading, carrying, and potentially deploying tactical nuclear weapons from disabled U.S. platforms.[39] But given the politics of the region, this kind of arrangement is a big step. It should also be understood as an effect of close-in, joint security realities and is a logical, if quite significant, extension of Japan's military capability as it closes out, perhaps in a way that approaches full circle, so much of its history in the twentieth century. Japan, under unipolarity, may be extending its connection with the U.S. but may also be slowly wobbling out of orbit.

Notes

1. Kenneth N. Waltz, *Foreign Policy and Democratic Politics* (Boston: Little, Brown & Company, 1967), p. 15.
2. David Rieff, "A Second American Century?," *World Policy Journal* (Winter 1999/2000): 7–8, 10.
3. Kenneth Jowitt, media interview, "Uncommon Knowledge," Stanford University T.V., Hoover Institute, April 2000.
4. Paul R. Viotti, Jr., "Extending Structural Realism," unpublished panal paper, American Political Science Association National Meeting, San Francisco, CA, August 31, 2001.
5. Katsuhiro Nakagawa, "The Impact of the Asian Economic Crisis on Trade," *Journal of Japanese Trade and Industry* (January/February 1999): 34.

6. John Kifner, "U.S., Afghan Troops Corner al Qaeda," *New York Times*, as reported in the *San Francisco Chronicle*, December 12, 2001, pp. A1, A18.
7. Andrew K. Hanami, *War, Peace and Power in the Post Cold War Era* (Dubuque, IA: Kendall/Hunt, 1997), ch. 43.
8. Susan Strange, "The Erosion of the State," *Current History* (November 1997): 367–68.
9. James Rosenau, "The Complexities and Contradictions of Globalization," *Current History* (November 1997): 364.
10. William Keller and Louis Pauly, "Globalization at Bay," *Current History* (November 1997): 370–71, 374–75.
11. Scott Ritter's comments made on ABC's "Nightline," November 5, 1998.
12. Uli Schmetzer, "Russia to Arm India Despite Pleas by U.S.," *Chicago Tribune*, as reported in the *San Francisco Examiner*, September 6, 1998, p. A-17.
13. Anupam Srivastava, "India's Growing Missile Ambitions," *Asian Survey* (March/April 2000): 311–12, 315, 318, 320 and 322–23.
14. Lawrence Freedman, "The Changing Forms of Military Conflict," *Survival* (Winter 1998–1999): 50–53.
15. Blanca Heredia, "Prosper or Perish? Development in the Age of Global Capital," *Current History* (November 1997): 384–85.
16. Robert Wade, "The Asian Crisis and the Global Economy: Causes, Consequences and Cure," *Current History* (November 1998): 362–65.
17. Karl D. Jackson, *Asian Contagion* (Boulder, CO: Westview Press, 1999), pp. 1–4, 7–9, 15 and 17–18.
18. Ethan Kapstein, "Global Rules for Global Finance," *Current History* (November 1998): 359.
19. Tomio Tsutsumi, "Japan's Economy—Analysis of the Recent Situation and Future Perspectives," *Journal of Japanese Trade and Industry* (November/December 1998); and, Wade, op. cit., p. 363; also, Katsuhiro Nakagawa, "The Impact of the Asian Economic Crisis on Trade," *Journal of Japanese Trade and Industry* (January/February 1999): 34.
20. Jim Rohwer, "Asia's Meltdown: The Risks Are Rising," *Fortune* (February 1998): 16; and, Wade, op. cit., p. 371; also, "Far-Sighted Vultures," *Financial Times*, June 13, 1998, p. 18.
21. Michael Green and Mike Mochizuki, *The U.S.–Japan Security Alliance in the 21st Century* (New York: Council on Foreign Relations, 1998), pp. 4–6.
22. *Defense of Japan* (Tokyo: Japan Times Press, 1997), pp. 226–27, 231–39.
23. Selig Harrison, *Japan's Nuclear Future* (Washington, D.C.: Carnegie Endowment for International Peace, 1996), pp. 36–37; and, Peter Katzenstein, *Cultural Norms and National Security* (Ithaca and London: Cornell University Press, 1996), p. 140; also, Green and Mochizuki, op. cit., p. 9.
24. Tetsuo Maeda, *The Hidden Army* (Chicago: edition 9, inc., 1995): pp. 134, 234, 238 and 289; also, Andrew K. Hanami, *The Military Might of Modern Japan* (Dubuque, IO: Kendall/Hunt Publishers, 1995), ch. 3.
25. Green and Mochizuki, op. cit., p. 82; also, Maeda, op. cit., p. 171.

26. James Harding, "Rivals Act as U.S. Keeps China Arms Curb," Financial Times, February 19, 1999, p. 4; and, James Kynge and James Harding, "Decades Before Beijing Can Challenge Washington in Asia," Financial Times, February 19, 1999, p. 4; also, James Risen and Jeff Gerth, "Chinese Spy Scandal in U.S. Nuclear Lab," New York Times, as reported in the S. F. Chronicle, March 6, 1999, p. A13.
27. Charles Freeman, "Trends in Military Technology and the Asia-Pacific Region," *Asia-Pacific Review* (Fall/Winter 1997): 26–29; also, Tomoyuki Kojima, "China's Present Condition and Future Outlook," *Asia-Pacific Review* (Fall/Winter 1997): 104.
28. Wu Xinbo, "The Security Dimension of Sino-Japanese Relations," *Asian Survey* (March/April 2000): 296, 298–30 and 303.
29. Peter Jensen, "Chinese Sea Power and American Strategy," *Strategic Review* (Summer 2000): 18–19 and 23; also, David Shambaugh, "Sino-American Strategic Relations: From Partners to Competition," *Survival* (Spring 2000): 102.
30. Michiyo Nakamoto, "Japan's Tentative Military Advance," *Financial Times*, January 21, 2000, p. 11.
31. Maeda, ibid., pp. xvi, 267.
32. Ibid., pp. 218, 225–6.
33. Ibid., pp. 224, 231–3.
34. Damon Bristow, "Osumi Unlocks Japan's Maritime Potential," *Janes International Defense Review* (February 1998): 53.
35. Green and Mochizuki, op. cit., pp. 13, 68–69, 72; also, Katzenstein, op. cit., p. 135.
36. Harrison, op. cit., pp. 24, 26, 33–34.
37. Ibid., pp. 8–9; and, Maeda, op. cit., p. 270; also, Katzenstein, op. cit., p. 135.
38. Harrison, op. cit., pp. 14–15, 20–22.
39. Personal interview, name withheld, April 23, 1998.

Notes on Contributors

Robert L. Gallucci is Dean of the School of Foreign Service at Georgetown, and served as U.S. State Department Spokesman for the Bush administration during the Gulf War. He has authored *Neither Peace Nor Honor: The Politics of American Military Policy in Vietnam* (Johns Hopkins Press, 1975).

Avery Goldstein is Professor of Political Science at the University of Pennsylvania. He has written *From Bandwagon to Balance-of-Power Politics: Structural Constraints and Politics in China*, 1949–1978 (Stanford University Press, 1991), and "China in 1996: Achievement, Assertiveness, Anxiety," *Asian Survey* (January 1997).

Andrew K. Hanami is Associate Professor of International Relations at San Francisco State University. He has published *War, Peace and Power in the Post Cold War Era* (Kendall/Hunt, 1997) and *The Military Might of Modern Japan* (Kendall/Hunt, 1995), as well as numerous articles, including "The Emerging Military-Industrial Relationship in Japan and the U.S. Connection," *Asian Survey* (June 1993).

Susan B. Martin held a postdoctorate position at the University of Pennsylvania, and is currently a Visiting Scholar at Florida Atlantic University. Her dissertation is entitled, *Economic Power and International Conflict: Do States Balance in the Economic Realm?*

Benjamin Miller teaches in the Department of International Relations at the Hebrew University of Jerusalem. In 2001, he was Visiting Professor at Duke University. He has written, *When Opponents Cooperate: Great Power Conflict and Collaboration in World Politics* (University of Michigan Press, 1995).

Barry Posen is Professor of Political Science at MIT. He has authored *Inadvertent Escalation: Conventional War and Nuclear Risks* (Cornell University Press, 1991), and *The Sources of Military Doctrine: France, Britain and Germany Between the World Wars* (Cornell University Press, 1984), as well as numerous articles, including, "Nationalism, the Mass Army, and Military Power," *International Security* (Fall 1993).

Robert Powell is Professor of Political Science, University of California, Berkeley. He has written *Nuclear Deterrence Theory: The Search for Credibility* (Cambridge University Press, 1990). He has also written many articles, including, "Uncertainty, Shifting Power, and Appeasement," *American Political Science Review* (December 1996).

Shibley Telhami is Anwar Sadat Chair of Population, Development, and Peace at the University of Maryland. He authored *Power and Leadership in International Bargaining: The Path to the Camp David Accords* (Columbia University Press, 1990). He also coedited *International Organizations and Ethnic Conflict* (Cornell University Press, 1995). Dr. Telhami is a frequent commentator in the national media.

Stephen Van Evera is Professor of Political Science at MIT, and presently serves as its Dean. He has published *Causes of War* (Cornell University Press, 1999), as well as a *Guide to Methods for Students of Political Science* (Cornell University Press, 1997). He has also written a number of articles, including "Hypotheses on Nationalism and War," *International Security* (Spring 1994).

Stephen M. Walt is Professor of Politics at the Kennedy School of Government, Harvard University. He has published, *Revolution and War* (Cornell University Press, 1996), and *The Origins of Alliances* (Cornell University Press, 1987). He has also written a number of articles, including, "Why Alliances Endure or Collapse," *Survival* (Spring 1997).

Index